INTELLECTUAL
APPETITE

Paul J. Griffiths

INTELLECTUAL APPETITE

A THEOLOGICAL GRAMMAR

The Catholic University of America Press
Washington, D.C.

Library of Congress Cataloging-in-Publication Data
Griffiths, Paul J.
Intellectual appetite : a theological grammar / Paul J. Griffiths.
   p. cm.
Includes bibliographical references (p.   ) and index.
ISBN 978-0-8132-1686-7 (pbk. : alk. paper)   1. Augustine, Saint,
Bishop of Hippo.   2. Learning and scholarship—Religious aspects—
Christianity.   3. Curiosity—Religious aspects—Christianity.
4. Education (Christian theology).   I. Title.
BR65.A9G765 2009
230—dc22   2009011854

This book is for Reinhard Hütter and Bruce Marshall,

whose erudition instructs me, whose faith inspires me,

and whose friendship supports me

CONTENTS

INTELLECTUAL
APPETITE

1

INTRODUCTION

This book is about intellectual appetite. This appetite, Aristotle claimed at the beginning of the *Metaphysics,* is natural to us, a proper constituent of human nature like (he did not say this) the capacity to torture or to laugh. It is, he seems to have thought, an appetite other creatures lack. They seek food or sex or safety or sensual pleasure, and finding these involves seeking and getting knowledge of a sort—the whereabouts of the food or the mate, for instance. But dogs and cats, and even (probably) dolphins and nonhuman primates, are never primarily interested in knowing where the food or the mate is. No, what they want is to eat the food or copulate with the mate, and they seek knowledge as a means to that end. We often seek knowledge in this way, too, as a necessary means for getting something else—power, security, self-congratulation, adulation, money. But sometimes we do something different: we cosset and indulge an appetite for knowledge quite independent of any other end. Sometimes, it seems, we just want to know: how to prove Fermat's Last Theorem, whether there is life on planets in other solar systems, if that thing over there is an elm tree, what Dickens's plans were for bringing *Edwin Drood* to a conclusion, how best to explain the slaughter of

1

the innocents and the inevitability of betrayal. And it is this appetite, an appetite for knowledge *simpliciter,* for nothing other, that Aristotle seems to have thought of as properly and uniquely human.

I am not especially interested in whether Aristotle is right about the restriction of this appetite to human beings. Most of us—we human beings, that is—think that some living beings other than ourselves (angels, demons, pretas, djinns, sprites) have intellectual appetite, as well, and therefore judge the Aristotelean restriction wrong. Christians, certainly, think, unless they have misconstrued Christianity, that there are angels and that they have intellectual appetites. But these topics, interesting though they are, are not the topic of this book. I am interested only in the question of human intellectual appetite: what it is and how it should be catechized, disciplined, and configured.

What I offer in this book is a depiction or display of the grammar of a Christian understanding of what a catechized and disciplined appetite for knowledge ought to look like. Any such display involves depicting not only the lexicon and grammar of a particular account of what it is to want to know, but also, inevitably, some among the assumptions about the way the world is, the way human knowers are, and the point of seeking and finding knowledge, which inform any such account. It is not possible to think about intellectual appetite without also thinking about these difficult and controversial topics, and certainly, Christians make no attempt to avoid them. My display of the grammar of their account of intellectual appetite will therefore include the relevant ontological and teleological lexicon. And not only this. Thinking about intellectual appetite rapidly shows that this appetite always demands and receives formation by culture, and that this formation can be and is very varied, sometimes in the direction of deepening damage and sometimes in that of remedying it. Even if you think, as Aristotle did and as most Christians do, that intellectual appetite is natural to us, this does not mean that a human being in a state of nature—without the company of other human beings, for example—would be any more likely to develop a distinctively human form of appetite for knowledge than to become a language-user. And that means not likely at all. An account of intellectual appetite therefore requires attention to catechesis, curriculum, and pedagogy.

The Christian account of intellectual appetite—by calling it "the" Christian account I do not mean to suggest that all Christians would assent to it; I mean only to say, descriptively, that the vast majority of self-described Christians who have thought and written about the topic have given an account in essentials like this one; and, normatively, that this is in fact the account of the matter orthodox Christians should give (though I will not argue for that last claim)—has of course its competitors, and every chapter of the book will have contrasts and occasional debates with one or another among these competitors woven through it. This interweaving is meant to serve one of the book's subsidiary purposes, which is to show that no account of as complex and interesting a matter as the ordering of intellectual appetite can be free of commitment to controversial positions on ontological and anthropological questions, and that, therefore, the extent to which any particular account of this sort seems obviously or uncontroversially true to you is exactly the extent to which you have not thought about it. I will not, however, attempt to depict these competitors to the Christian view of intellectual appetite in anything like their fullness. That is a task for those who find them attractive or convincing. Their presence in my account is as foils to the Christian account, as examples of Egyptian gold, to use an ancient Christian figure for the good things to be learned from the pagans, good things that need always to be transfigured by baptism if they are to serve their proper purposes.

Neither will I be offering systematic arguments in favor of the Christian account and against its competitors. This is because I share with John Henry Newman the conviction, expressed most trenchantly in a sermon on faith and reason delivered in 1839 (while still Anglican) that, "When men understand what each other mean, they see, for the most part, that controversy is either superfluous or hopeless." Carefully descriptive juxtaposition of opposed or otherwise contrasting views, coupled with the making and offering of precise and perspicuous distinctions, is almost always more productive than argument, whether aimed at refutation of an opposed position or defence of one's own.

This lack of interest in argument does not indicate a lack of interest in truth. It seems to me that the understandings of world and person interwoven with the Christian view of intellectual appetite are perspicuously and seductively beautiful, while those belonging to its competitors are, in comparison, impoverished, parched, and opaquely inadequate to their task. If I do my job of display well, it is possible that some readers who do not already inhabit this account of things may be seduced into paying it a visit, and since the account I offer is very hospitable, indeed maximally hospitable (not because I am offering it, but because God has; all I am doing is transmitting it), the visit may turn out to be long, long enough that the visitor effectively takes up permanent residence. But that is a scenario for pagan readers. For Christians, I offer a reminder. The account of intellectual appetite in these pages has been forgotten rather than rejected by Christians, and this is because they are in unreflective thrall to one among its competitors without being aware that there is an alternative.

I have used the word "pagan" a couple of times already, and since it is a word with many connotations, it may be as well to say what I mean by it. It is not, in my usage, a term of insult but rather a descriptor for everyone who is neither Jew nor Christian. There may be functional pagans who are in fact Jewish (by birth) or Christian (by baptism); this is true of many, probably most, of the early-, high-, and postmodern thinkers whose thought has provoked me in these pages. But these are not the real thing; they need to recover themselves, not find themselves. The real pagans are those, increasing in number now in the United States and Europe, who are innocent of Jewish or Christian catechesis as well as lacking the ineradicable ontological marks of such identity. They include, outside the Europeanized world, Buddhists, Hindus, Confucians, and so on. Muslims provide a special categorial problem, and it remains an unfinished Christian task to think through how best to categorize them. My own tentative judgment is that since they are to some degree Jewish and Christian progeny, they cannot, properly speaking, be called pagans; they are, perhaps, quasi-Christian heretics (and certainly the vast majority of premodern Christian thinkers who wrote about Islam understood it to be a kind of Christian heresy), but they may also have something to teach that Christians badly need to learn. They certainly ought to be thought of by Christians as intimate allies against the deadening and violent weight of pagan, late modernity.

There is also another interest, present in the order of discovery if not in that of exposition, which prompted this book. It is an interest in showing what the conceptual conditions of the possibility of reform in our institutions of higher education really are, and what changes in thought and practice would have to occur were any genuine reforms to be possible. I do not think that significant reform is likely, though, like all prognostications, that is a very tentative judgment, and so my first interest is in encouraging Christians with an intellectual vocation to be wary: to think about how their intellectual appetites are being formed, about what they are being trained to seek and value in undergraduate and graduate programs in our now largely pagan (even when they retain the Christian title, as many in the United States do) institutions of higher education, and about whether there is more the church might do about the intellectual formation of those who belong to it, which is to say, of Christ's members. But since almost everything I write in this book remains at a very high level of abstraction—it is an essay in theological grammar, after all—I do not address the practical applications of the picture I paint. Doing so would require descending several rungs down the ladder of abstraction; and it would mean writing a very different book.

~

The book consists of fourteen short chapters. Other than the first (chapter 1, this introduction) and the last (chapter 14, in which I express gratitude), each begins with a short quotation from an authority (eleven from Augustine and one from Pascal, which show the lineage I claim clearly enough to those who care about such things), followed by a brief interpretive paragraph in which I say what I take the quotation to suggest and use it to point forward to the topic of the chapter. Other than that introductory moment, each of the twelve central chapters is without quotation or discussion of any authority's work or words. This introduction differs, lacking both the introductory quotation-plus-gloss, and making some (no doubt incautious) historical and exegetical claims. And the final chapter differs as well, also lacking the quotation-plus-gloss, and containing only my thanks to those, living and dead, whose work has been valuable to me in performing mine.

This lack of appeal to an exegesis of authorities in the body of the book does not mean I have no authorities: every Christian thinker does and must write under authoritative guidance, scriptural, magisterial, and so on; and no Christian thinker should prize originality or the significance of his own contribution to thought. One of the marks of a well-catechized intellectual appetite is that it has learned not to be interested in originality. But this does not mean that all Christian thought and writing needs to proceed, principally or at all, by way of explicit conversation with and gloss upon the authoritative sources that inevitably inform it. Sometimes there is virtue in the high-wire act of depicting and analyzing your topic straight, unveiled by the apparatus of humanistic scientific scholarship. One such advantage is that the analysis does not get derailed by debates about strictly exegetical questions. Sometimes it is worth trying to depict a phenomenon—in this case intellectual appetite—without at the same time trying to establish and comment upon what others have said about the matter. Doing that has its place, of course, for pagan and Christian thinkers both; but it is not the only thing to do, and attention to it easily displaces attention to the question at hand, which in this case is: how should intellectual appetite, the desire to know, be understood and catechized? Another advantage is that writing in this way checks the desire to display erudition at the expense of constructive thought, a desire to which I am subject. And a third is that writing in this way strips thought naked. Among the hardest things in the world to do is thinking and writing with clarity about a difficult topic. It is easier (for me) to avert my gaze from that task by turning it toward the question of what Augustine thinks or whether Pascal is right, and in refusing explicit address to those questions, I have tried to check this temptation.

Yet there are disadvantages to eschewing acknowledgment, quotation, and exegesis. First among them is the appearance of ingratitude. Others have thought more about my topic than I have, and have expressed their thought better than I can. I know this because I have read and talked with many of them. Shouldn't I then acknowledge my debts? This is an especially pressing demand upon Christians, who think (or should) that everything they have and can do is gift, received from outside themselves. Not to acknowledge the particulars of the gifts I have received from the thought and writing of others would be bad manners at least, and perhaps worse. This is true, but it does not require such acknowledgment to be woven into the fabric of what I write. I meet this demand, then, as best I can, in the last chapter of the book (chapter 14), in which are listed and discussed the principal gifts I've received and used, well or badly, in writing this book. This chapter also serves the purpose of suggesting avenues for further reading about the topics treated in this book.

A second disadvantage to the method and plan of this book is that it might suggest arrogance on my part. Perhaps I think my own thought more interesting, profound, or elegant than the thought of my predecessors. Perhaps that is why I do not quote or discuss them. Nothing, so far as I can tell (though I may not be the best guide: none of us has much by way of accurate self-awareness on these matters), is further from the truth. I write this book with an attitude of humility before those who understand my topic better than I do, as a means of clarifying my own thought to myself, and as an offering to the church and to the world. And I do, so far as I can, acknowledge with gratitude the gifts of an intellectual sort I have received from others, gifts without which this book could not have been written.

A third disadvantage is that a text unadorned with notes and ex-egetical engagements is a standing invitation to readers to find places in which the writer repeats what others have said without adding to or developing it, and thus indicates either his culpable ignorance or his knowing but veiled expropriation of what others have said. But that what I write may provide such an invitation I do not think a disadvantage. For reasons that will become apparent in the course of the book, I do not recognize originality as a virtue, and so do not think its lack a problem. If I have repeated what others have said, and what they have said is true and beautiful, then I am pleased to have done so. If I am ignorant of what others have said about my topic, then I am pleased to be instructed; but encyclopedism—complete mastery of an academic field—is without interest for me, and, when pressed as a desirable goal for all intellectuals, suggests a set of ideas about what the intellectual life is and how it should be practised that I will offer reasons for rejecting in what follows. And as to knowing but veiled expropriation of what others have said, the dread act of the *plagiarius* or kidnapper: that too will come up for discussion in the course of the book, and here I will only say that I do not recognize property in ideas or their expression, and think that no Christian should. And since the thought that there is such property is the principal one that informs criticisms of plagiarism, I am not much moved by that difficulty, either.

There is a fourth and final disadvantage to eschewing quotation and discussion of what others have written, this one perhaps the most serious. It is that unless a book written in this way is itself a thing of literary beauty, which this one is not in spite of my best efforts, the reader will lose the many benefits, aesthetic and conceptual, of direct exposure to the words and thoughts of the greatest among those who have given attention to the book's topic. This disadvantage I acknowledge with regret and with the hope that the advantages I have mentioned outweigh or at least counterbalance it.

~

Every project is undertaken in response to some stimulus and out of a construal of some situation, and I should clarify the stimuli and the construal that have given rise to this one. In doing this I will make claims about some authorities and offer some generalizations of a broadly historical sort. The sources I have used for these claims and generalizations will be found in chapter 14, and what is said about them here serves only the purpose of orientation to the book that follows.

My interest in intellectual appetite is prompted and stimulated by premodern Christian thought about it, and most especially by that of late-antique Christians writing and thinking in Latin. Among the terms they used to describe intellectual appetite was *curiositas,* which comes into English, inevitably but misleadingly, as "curiosity." It was a commonplace for all Latin-using Christian intellectuals from Tertullian at the end of the second century through at least to Bossuet in the seventeenth to say that *curiositas* is a vice, and that it needs to be distinguished from virtuous forms of the desire to know, which, beginning in the third century, began to be called *studiositas.* This Latin word, I suppose, has to be rendered "studiousness," though that is, if anything still more misleading than calquing *curiositas* with "curiosity." This Christian distinction shows at once that there are different ways to construe intellectual appetite descriptively, and to judge it normatively—or at least that Christians thought such distinctions necessary, and put a good deal of effort into making them.

The premodern Christian commonplace that curiosity is a vice is for us surprising and puzzling. This is because, beginning in the fifteenth century, curiosity was transferred rapidly and almost without remainder from the table of the vices to that of the virtues, so that by the eighteenth century David Hume, in *A Treatise of Human Nature* (2.3.10) could treat the topic as though the term unproblematically labelled a disinterested desire to know the truth—and could do so in apparent ignorance that there had been a two-millennia-long enterprise of trying to discriminate acceptable or virtuous forms of the desire to know from unacceptable or vicious forms of that same appetite, and of using "curiosity" to label the latter. For Hume, and, mostly, for us, Christian or not, appetite for knowledge is an undifferentiated good. The result of curiosity's transformation from a darkly destructive vice into a shining virtue for which we pat children on the head and compliment students is that, for us, the idea that there are vicious forms of intellectual appetite sounds at first puzzling and then, usually, obscurantist. For us there are only proverbial remnants of the idea that curiosity is a vice (we recall that it killed the cat). But for the most part, the enterprise of distinguishing good appetites for knowledge from bad ones is mysterious, and the long Christian tradition of attempting to do that largely forgotten, or, when remembered, excoriated.

Why did Christians make such distinctions in the first place? First, there are elements internal to the Christian tradition that suggest appetite for knowledge is not an undifferentiated good. Some among these are scriptural. The story of the fall of the first human beings in the opening chapters of Genesis appears on the surface of the text to have something to do with seeking knowledge that should have been shunned, or perhaps with knowledge wrongly sought. The compressed but suggestive account of the two banquets in the book of

Proverbs (9:1–18) suggests a distinction between understanding rightly offered and received, and understanding's simulacrum, deceptively offered and disastrously grasped. St. Paul, in the First Letter to the Corinthians (3:18–23), and in the Letter to the Colossians (2:4–8), inveighs against the wisdom of the world, and against empty, seductive philosophy; and St. John uses a phrase in his first letter, *hē epithumía tōn ophthalmōn* (1 John 2:16), which was early rendered into Latin as *concupiscentia oculorum* (sometimes, in the Old Latin versions, *desiderium oculorum,* but *concupiscentia* eventually became standard) and almost unanimously understood by premodern Christians to refer to a disordered appetite for knowledge. The seventeenth-century translators of Scripture into English appointed by King James rendered John's phrase with decided vigor as "the lust of the eyes," and a high proportion of Christian thinking about the question of intellectual appetite took place by way of gloss and commentary upon this phrase. If the eyes can lust, desire inappropriately to see, then surely they can also seek vision (knowledge) chastely and rightly. But what, exactly, is the difference between these two modes of knowledge seeking, these two kinds of intellectual appetite?

As the canon of Scripture approached closure in the third century, the texts just mentioned, along with many others, became interwoven with other urgent needs facing Christian thinkers to bring into being a fabric of thought and practice that encouraged them to write extensively and with energy about how to distinguish a rightly ordered appetite for knowledge from a wrongly ordered one, and to attempt to institute programs of catechesis that would order the intellectual appetites of Christians in the right way. Among these exigencies was the need for distance from what later came to be called Gnosticism. Gnosticism is a portmanteau term for a variety of movements of thought in the Mediterranean world of late antiquity that agreed on making human flourishing dependent upon possession of a kind of specialized knowledge available only to an elite. Some of these movements were pagan, some Jewish, and some Christian or quasi-Christian; orthodox Christians found it necessary to keep them at a distance. They did this by, first, rejecting the idea that salvation is dependent upon ratiocination, or upon the capacity to benefit from specialized intellectual training; and then, second, by thinking through what it is that all Christians do need to know and be able to do, and what, therefore, are the appropriate means of catechetical training to make it possible for them to know and do these things. All this required Christian thinkers to work at distinguishing their catechesis from that of the Gnostics.

Another circumstance that required Christian attention to formation of the appetite for knowledge was that they found themselves forced into awareness of and engagement with pagan catechetical regimes from the beginning. This was inevitable for a tribe occupying a subordinate place in a pagan world whose pedagogy was well established and unavoidable for all who sought literacy and a rhetorical and literary education that would permit them to interact as equals with the elite among their pagan rivals. Christians therefore had, for many centuries, catechetical regimes that depended upon and assumed those of the pagans: if you wanted to learn how to read and write Latin, or to master the pagan classics (Homer, Vergil, Cicero, Seneca), for instance, you could do so only in pagan schools. This resulted in anxiety: how to differentiate the goals of pagan catechesis from those of Christian catechesis? What, in the pagan catechetical regimes, could safely be accepted and used, and what had to be transformed or rejected? As Christians began to occupy a more prominent place in the still largely pagan culture of the late Roman Empire, pagans began to feel a reciprocal anxiety about their own catechetical practices, and to address it by entering the same theoretical territory, sometimes with heavy rhetorical and conceptual artillery. But that was a later development: the peculiar situation of western Christians in the first five centuries forced them to give sustained theoretical attention to what they wanted the members of the tribe to know and be able to do, and, therefore, to the catechetical disciplines likely to be most effective in bringing the desired results about.

In partial response to this theoretical pressure, Christian theorists developed the technical vocabulary I have mentioned, to which the term *studiositas* was central. This was a label used by Christians for their own preferred form of the catechized and disciplined appetite for knowledge, and in contrast to the disciplined form of the same appetite they thought preferred by their elite pagan rivals, for which they preferred the label *curiositas*. For pagans, too, *curiositas* could be a crass, vulgar, and dangerous appetite for knowledge no one should want, knowledge that would damage anyone who might be unfortunate enough to get it. Seneca and Apuleius both use the word in this fashion. But it could also sometimes be an appropriately passionate response to and redress of ignorance. For Christians, however, the word almost always labelled an appetite always potentially vicious and usually actively so; and their discussions of it were polemical, aimed at separating their catechetically-formed identity from that of their pagan interlocutors by offering a critique of the disciplinary regimes that produced *curiositas* by contrasting them with those that produced *studiositas*.

Christian thinkers had a balancing act to perform here. On the one hand, it was clear to them that the intellectual appetite could be malformed, and that some bodies of knowledge were of no interest to Christians and might be damaging to them: astrological knowledge and skill in various forms of magical technique were the standard examples. On the other hand, they wanted to affirm that the cosmos and everything in it must of necessity be good because it has been spoken into being by a good God, which suggests that knowledge about the workings of the cosmos and its inhabitants must also be desirable: why would God give human beings the capacity to seek and find such knowledge if it not to understand more fully the depths of goodness and beauty in the created order? Then there was the pressing question of whether, and to what extent, Christians should study pagan literature, and, if they did, what they should expect to get out of it. A gamut of responses is evident among late-antique Christians. Tertullian fulminates about Athens as a symbol of pagan learning; Jerome swears that he will stop reading pagan literature and then rapidly breaks his oath; and Augustine, among the most thoroughly imbued with pagan learning of late-antique Christians, lays out a careful program of study for Christians, in which literacy, pagan literature, history, and (what we would call) the natural sciences are given a place, but a carefully circumscribed and guarded one.

This gamut of response to the question of how Christians should have their intellectual appetites formed, and the extent to which they should study pagan materials has always been evident in Christian thought; versions of it remain with us today. But at every point on this gamut there was (and, largely, still is) agreement that some methods of disciplining the appetite for knowledge malform it, while some form it as it should be formed. "Curiosity" was the Christian term of art for the former, and "studiousness" for the latter.

Yet some care is necessary here. The pagan catechesis of the intellectual appetite criticized by western Christians in late antiquity as productive of curiosity was not in every respect dissimilar from the catechesis that produced the studiousness they commended. Both worked on the same appetite with the purpose of giving it form and making it active. Both, too, were concerned to emphasize that not every member of the tribe, pagan or Christian, needed advanced formation of the appetite for knowledge. Most did not, having neither aptitude nor need for such formation. They needed to have their appetite for knowledge formed only to the extent that permitted meeting material needs (usually, then, by training in some craft: farming, butchery, soldiering, building, navigation, and so on), and fulfilling whatever functions the tribe took to be incumbent upon all its members. These latter, for the Roman Empire, were few because the social order was highly stratified, which meant many stratum-specific essentials and few universal ones: the essential skills for slaves and citizens, for example, had little overlap. For the late-antique Christian church, less fundamentally and deeply stratified, there were some strongly marked functions—principally liturgical—required for every member of the tribe, and therefore a universal catechesis aimed at providing the knowledge and skill needed for these. But for late-antique pagans and Christians both, long and deep exposure to a regime of disciplined catechetical formation of the appetite for knowledge was for the few—as it also is for us, in early postmodernity.

This long-lived body of Christian theorizing about what it is to want to know and how that appetite ought to be disciplined is one of the principal theoretical resources for anyone who wants to think about this topic today. But it is not the only one. There is also a body of theoretical thought on the proper formation of the appetite for knowledge that is self-consciously not Christian and sometimes polemically anti-Christian. This tradition began in the fifteenth century (there are earlier anticipations), and had reached its classical form by the seventeenth. It is evident in the work of, among others, Descartes, Bacon, Spinoza, Leibniz, and Locke, for each of whom the provision of rules for directing the understanding—and, thus, the elaboration of a regime of disciplining the intellectual appetite—was a matter of great interest. Its high-modern form can be seen in Kant, and then, soon after, in Wilhelm von Humboldt, most especially in their works on the ordering and proper relation of the disciplines taught in the then-new research university. This concern was developed by Max Weber at the beginning of the twentieth century, and is most especially evident in his concern to separate fact from value and to limit academic work to the sphere of the former. All this implies a particular understanding—or, more accurately, a family of understandings—of forming and ordering the intellectual appetite.

Yet even in von Humboldt at the beginning of the nineteenth century, and much more dramatically in Heidegger's reaction in the 1920s and 1930s to Weber's advocacy of a pure, disinterested *scientia,* there is something else. The Germans call it *Bildung,* often rendered "education," but really implying not only the intellectual formation of those subject to it, but also their moral and spiritual formation. The interwar German advocacy of *Bildung*-plus-*Wissenschaft* as the twin poles around which the university should be ordered was largely discredited by its embroilment with Nazism, or if not explicitly with Nazism then with equally murky pagan views about the nature and meaning of the German spirit and the catechetical methods appropriate to its formation. There is a very approximate analogue to this concern with *Bildung* in American (and to some extent also French) resistance to the Weberian justification of the research university, evident most clearly in emphasis, evident in the literature of the last century or so, upon the importance of offering moral formation at least to undergraduates—and in the occasional clear and strident rejection of any such idea.

Cartesian and Baconian rules for directing the intellect (not identical with one another by any means, but similar in the matters raised here) are in many ways different from a Weberian pedagogy in pure science; in spite of these differences, however, there is a direct genealogical link between the seventeenth-century aspiration toward a *mathesis universalis*—of, that is, mapping all knowledge onto a manipulable grid and providing clear principles of method that would permit the attainment of certainty about any topic—and the late-nineteenth and early-twentieth century hope for institutions of higher education free of commitments to value. Both the link and the differences have been made clear by the explosion of work since the 1960s on the history and meaning of pedagogical practice in the West, prompted in considerable part by Michel Foucault's work in the topic, which is still in many ways definitive of the field.

The complex historical story can, in its American form, be summarized in the following way, at least with regard to elite institutions and their epigones (the story would be much more complex were I to say anything about self-consciously Christian or Jewish institutions of higher education): For a short while, from the late nineteenth century until the 1960s, European and American intellectuals, relying, usually unreflectively, upon this body of early- and high-modern theory about the proper formation of the intellectual appetite, had confidence in the regimes of intellectual discipline by which they had been formed and in the desirability of forming new generations in accord with them. They shared, in broad outline at least, a vision of what it meant to seek understanding and of how budding intellectuals should be trained to seek it, and this vision was given institutional form in the institutions of higher education we now inhabit. But once the Weberian orthodoxy about the vocation of the academic as an intellectual devoted to value-free analysis of what is found in the empirical sphere had crumbled, which it had by the 1960s in both Europe and North America, it became apparent that there were other possibilities, other ways in which the intellectual appetite could be formed, other regimes of discipline (again, Foucault's language, unavoidable and very useful: it's Christian language *manqué*); and the anxiety this produced led to worried depictions and explanations of the decay of the university, enthusiastic advocacy of committed scholarship in which the scholar is understood principally as an agent of social change, and so on. Most institutions of higher education in North America and Europe are now explicitly, and often publicly, aware that there is no unanimity within their walls about what intellectual appetite is and how it should be formed. They are also aware that the catechetical regimes they have in place are, by and large, not doing a job that makes anyone happy. Hence the flood of worried literature, which shows an anxiety interestingly analogous to that evident in late-antique Christian theorizing about catechesis. Both bodies of work show a distinctively academic form of anxiety about what it is to want to know and how that appetite ought best be catechized, an anxiety produced by the challenging awareness of a multiplicity of competing understandings of and recommendations about these topics.

This study is written out of this context: forgetfulness on the part of Christians of our heritage of serious thought about the proper formation of the desire to know; and confusion and anxiety on the part of pagan thinkers about the same topic.

2

CURIOSITAS

Quamobrem omnis amor studentis animi, hoc est volentis scire quod nescit, non est amor eius rei quam nescit, sed eius quam scit, propter quam vult scire quod nescit. Aut si tam curiosus est, ut non propter aliquam notam causam, sed solo amore rapiatur incognita sciendi; discernendus quidem est ab studiosi nomine iste curiosus, sed nec ipse amat incognita, immo congruentius dicitur: odit incognita, quae nulla esse vult, dum vult omnia cognita.

And so, every love that belongs to a studious soul which wants to know what it does not know is not a love of what it does not know but rather of what it does know. It is because of what it does know that it wants to know what it does not know. But someone so curious as to be carried away by nothing other than a love of knowing the unknown, and not because of something already known, should be distinguished from the studious and called curious. But even the curious do not love the unknown. It is more accurate to say that they hate the unknown because they want everything to become known and thus nothing to remain unknown.

~~~

Augustine writes here, in the tenth book of his work on the Holy Trinity (10.1.3), that the love which belongs to the studious is prompted always by a love for something already known, not by a love for what is not yet known. He then notes that the curious might be carried away or dragged off by force (all implications to be found in *rapiatur,* a word that lies behind the English verb "to rape") solely by love directed at knowing what they do not yet know, and might in that way be distinguished from the studious. But even the curious, so understood, do not really love what they do not know. It would be better to say that they hate what they do not know, because they would like that set to be null, an ambition to be realised only by coming to know everything. Therefore, they wish to extinguish all unknowns. The studious, by contrast (it is not said in this passage, but implied), have a more limited desire, which is to come to love what they know more fully by seeking knowledge toward which its love (both subjective and objective genitive intended here) points them. The studious are directed, then, by love; the curious, knowledge seekers though they are, by anxious hatred of what they know not.

⇌

Premodern western Christians used the word *studiositas* for what they thought of as well-formed intellectual appetite, and *curiositas* for its deformed kissing cousin. It will be useful to begin with a formal definition of each. The definitions that follow are concordant with those found in the Christian tradition, but are not identical with any of them. I give them not in an exegetical spirit, but rather as a contributor to a tradition of thought whose authority I accept, and that I consider it a privilege to speak out of and thereby to extend.

Curiosity is a particular appetite, which is to say a particular ordering of the affections, or, more succinctly, a particular intentional love. Its object, what it wants, is new knowledge, a previously unexperienced reflexive intimacy with some creature. And what it seeks to do with that knowledge is control, dominate, or make a private possession of it. Curiosity is, then, in brief, *appetite for the ownership of new knowledge,* and its principal method is enclosure by sequestration of particular creatures or ensembles of such. The curious want to know what they do not yet know, and they often want to know it *ardentissimo appetitu,* with supremely ardent appetite. But the appetite for new knowledge that belongs to them ravishes them: they are violated and dragged away, with full consent and eager cooperation, by what is likely to seem to them a noble desire for *nihil aliud quam scire,* nothing other than to know the *incognita.* The appetite of the curious is in that way closed, seeking a sequestered intimacy: the knowledge they seek is wanted as though it were the only thing to be had, and this means that the curious inevitably come to think that the only way in which they can be related to what they seek to know is by sequestration, enclosing a part of the intellectual commons for their own exclusive use, and thus mastering it

Studiousness, like curiosity, is a particular love, a specific ordering of the affections. And like curiosity it has knowledge as its object, which it seeks. But the studious do not seek to sequester, own, possess, or dominate what they hope to know; they want, instead, to participate lovingly in it, to respond to it knowingly as gift rather than as potential possession, to treat it as icon rather than as spectacle. A preliminary definition of studiousness, then, is: *appetite for closer reflexive intimacy with the gift.* The appetite of the studious may rival that of the curious in ardor; but the former, unlike the latter, treat what they seek to know as iconic gift and thereby as open to and participatory in the giver. Objects of knowledge so understood can be loved and contemplated, but they cannot be dominated by sequestration. The studious therefore seek a peculiar reflexive intimacy with what they want to know, and they seek it with the understanding that they, as knowers, have creaturely participation in the giver in common with what they want to come to know. This understanding carries with it another, which is that this commonality makes cognitive intimacy possible. And the studious are committed to treating the intellectual commons as indeed common, and not as a field of conquest, a set of objects to be sequestered.

Both intellectual appetites seek knowledge: that is what makes them forms of intellectual appetite. But they do so with different purposes: where curiosity wants possession, studiousness seeks participation. They also differ in the kinds of knowledge they seek. Curiosity is concerned with novelty: curious people want to know what they do not yet know, ideally, what no one yet knows. Studious people seek knowledge with the awareness that novelty is not what counts, and is indeed finally impossible because anything that can be known by any one of us is already known to God and has been given to us as unmerited gift. When, therefore, one of us comes to know something we had not known before, something new to us—and of course this is frequent—we do no more than participate in what is given and we delight in that fact. Local novelty—coming to know something new to you or me or new to a particular place and time—may occur for the studious, but it is not of central importance to them and is certainly not the reason for which they seek knowledge. But the deepest contrast between curiosity and studiousness has to do with the kind of world that the seeker for and professor of each inhabits. The curious inhabit a world of objects, which can be sequestered and possessed; the studious inhabit a world of gifts, given things, which can be known by participation, but which, because of their very natures can never be possessed.

These formal contrasts between two highly catechized forms of intellectual appetite need to be given sense by closer analysis of the constituent terms of the definitions. I begin that analysis with attention to the grammar of the world, first in its universal form, and then in its specifically Christian construal. I pass then from world to appetite—for both curiosity and studiousness are forms of appetite thoroughly formed by catechesis into inhabiting a particular world—and thence to knowledge as a kind of intimacy, which is what both appetites seek. I then turn to a series of contrasts between curiosity and studiousness, and conclude with a meditation upon the homologies between the stammeringly responsive seeking of intimacy with God evident in the liturgy, and the mode of seeking of intimacy with creatures evident among the studious.

3

WORLD

*Mundus enim appellatur non solum ista fabrica quam fecit Deus, coelum
et terra, mare, visibilia et invisibilia: sed habitatores mundi mundus vo-
cantur, quomodo domus vocatur et parietes et inhabitantes. Et aliquando
laudamus domum, et vituperamus inhabitantes.*

What is called "world" is not only the fabric made by God—heaven
and earth, sea, visibles and invisibles; those who live in the world are
also called "world," just as the term "house" includes both walls and
those who live inside them. And sometimes we praise the house and
criticize its inhabitants.

∼

Augustine here (*In Epistolam Ioannis* 2.12) comments on 1
John 2:16, in which (in the Latin version he knew) the posses-
sive desire of the eyes *(concupiscentia oculorum)* is said to belong to the *mundus,* the world, and therefore to be shunned.
What, he asks, does this word "world" mean? Isn't it the ordered beauty of the fabric woven by God, things visible and
invisible, the heavens and the earth? Why then should saying that something belongs to it imply that it should be
shunned? Wouldn't calling something "world" or "worldly"
rather suggest that it is to be loved and embraced? He then
says, to check this move, that "world" can be used to refer

not only to that created fabric, but also to those who live in it, just as "house" can refer not only to the walls but also to those who live within them. "And sometimes," he says rather baldly," we praise the house and criticize its inhabitants." If, then, "world" means all there is, what it refers to is both dark and light, presence and absence, damage and healing; and what is to be shunned is the darkness, the damage, and the absence.

∾

"World" is an item of central importance to the lexicon of intellectual appetite. Its extension—the range of things it embraces—is all that is, seen and unseen, heard and unheard, touched and untouched, tasted and untasted, smelled and unsmelled, thought and unthought. This covers everything of which knowledge might be sought, which explains its centrality to the grammar of intellectual appetite. Intellectual appetite is appetite for knowledge of something, or some ensemble of things, or some set of relations connecting a thing or things, or (even) for all things and all relations. That is to say, it is a transitive appetite that may also be reflexive (one may seek knowledge of oneself, as well as knowledge of the appetite that one has for knowledge: that latter is what I seek in this book), and so "world" is a term proper to the universal grammar of intellectual appetite.

This is not to say that the English word "world" belongs to that universal grammar. It is what that word means that so belongs, in both its sense (all that may be known) and its reference (all that is . . .). Even in English, other words are possible: "cosmos," the beautifully ordered whole, has strong credentials, for example; and "world" has come to have other senses (planet, for example). But still, "world" seems best for users of English: short, fully Anglo-Saxon etymologically speaking, and, for most native speakers, easily comprehensible in the meaning given.

Defining the extension of the term "world" as "all that is" is not intended to suggest any commitment as to what it means for any particular or ensemble of particulars to exist, or as to what kinds and particulars there are. There are many incompatible views about these matters, including at least those held and sometimes defended by idealists, solipsists, and materialists (and, as we shall see, Christians); but holders of all such views must, in stating and defending or assuming them, accept and use the sense and reference of the term "world" just given. Differences about the being of the world, of any particular in it, and of what particulars there are in the world belong to particular construals of the world, not to its universal grammar.

The world is given to us without our request or consent. It is a place where we have found ourselves as far as our memories can reach, and which we cannot leave without dying. We have no control over either state of affairs. The world in which we find ourselves gives itself as an array of particulars related one to another. These particulars—this dog, that tree, my mother, the United States of America, the opening notes of the C-Major prelude in Bach's *Wohltemperierte Klavier,* azalea blooms in May, Mary Theotokos, the humidity of a summer's afternoon in the American Midwest, the sudden setting of the sun in the West African tropics—appear at first to us in an unbroken flood. We receive them as particulars only by learning to sort the flood into kinds, and to catalog instances of those kinds as they come before us. Absent that learned capacity, the world's particulars (whatever exactly their kinds) still give themselves, as does the world; but they cannot be accepted as given because they cannot be recognized.

Fortunately, sorting and cataloging are learned early and quickly, if at first crudely. The mother's touch and smell, and especially her breast, are rapidly recognized as importantly different from other touches and smells; the caress of light on the eye is soon distinguished from darkness, and is sought as pleasurable and desirable, as are warmth on the skin and sweetness on the tongue. And then, with an unfortunate inevitability but equal ease and rapidity, pain is recognized for what it is and its occasions avoided whenever possible.

These early sortings, which have mostly to do with the feel of things to the infant, become quickly more complex, exponentially so as language is acquired, for every natural language is a treasure-house of sortals, a thesaurus of terms for kinds and for the ordering of those kinds into hierarchies of value. And these later more complex sortings of the particulars of the world cease to have to do mainly with the feel of things, with the physical and emotional valence of things as they appear in consciousness. They begin now to have to do also with local wisdom, the wisdom of the tribe about the kinds of things there are in the world. This wisdom always uses criteria additional to those deployed by the infant, criteria that often have little to do with the phenomenal feel of things.

Among these criteria are appeals to value: kinds are always ordered hierarchically by their value, whether value directly to those doing the sorting, or value according to some hierarchy more or less distant from the sorter. Although there is much disagreement about the kinds of kind there are, and about the place each bears in a hierarchy, and about the boundaries between, and therefore the individuation of, particulars, there is universal agreement in practice that there are particulars, that they must be sorted into kinds, and that these kinds are not all of the same value. All of us do and must behave as if we thought this, and all who think about such matters at all (a small portion of humanity, fortunately) do and must agree that such hierarchical sorting of apparent particulars is unavoidable.

This is not to say that all agree on the account to be given of what we do when we individuate particulars one from another and sort those individuated particulars into kinds. Some think that in so acting we conform our language and thought to a mind- and language-independent order of things. Others think that we construct useful fictions. And yet, others think that we sometimes do the one and sometimes the other. It is another and still more difficult question whether we should have much confidence in the degree to which our particular sortings and individuations conform to a mind- and language-independent order of things, even if we think that there is such an order. Disagreements about these matters belong to construals of the world's universal grammar, not to that grammar itself.

There is universal agreement about much more than the inevitability of sorting particulars into kinds and ordering those kinds hierarchically. There is universal agreement in practice about the claim that the semantic content of anything said or written in one natural language can be rendered with no more than partial semantic loss into something said or written in some other natural language. And this agreement, which requires no agreement about how sentences (or words) mean, or about just what is done when translation occurs, has important implications. Since you are reading these words, you can read English, the language in which I am writing. Even if that is not your first language, and even if as you read it you are translating it mentally into some other, you have some understanding of what I have written. And if it is your first language, an easy habitation for you, then you will have understood me with ease. These facts mean that the sorted, ordered, hierarchically categorized world which has been given to me, that, with more or less ease, I inhabit as natural, overlaps to a very considerable extent with the one that has been given to you. You, unlike me, may not distinguish wasps from bees, working instead with a single undifferentiated sortal such as 'yellow-striped flying stinging insects'; you may doubt the existence of some particulars (the parrots that live wild in Chicago—perhaps you think, wrongly, that parrots live wild only in tropical and subtropical regions), which I take to have been presented to me; we may disagree about the properties that some particular has (I think that the Chicago White Sox has the property of being the baseball team that all rational people should support, and you, while perhaps acknowledging the existence of such a team, doubt that it bears any such property); and so on. But these differences do not go deep, as their easy comprehensibility itself shows. We—you and I, that is, and all other humans—assume that we inhabit a world sorted and ordered in very much the same fashion. Our assumption that we can communicate with one another shows this; and that what I have written can be translated into other languages, with, we all think, nothing worse than mild betrayal and moderate loss, and thereby be made understandable to those who inhabit those languages, establishes it. All natural languages, we all assume, are intertranslatable; it is a criterion of languagehood that this be so; languages are engines for sorting, hierarchizing, and cataloging particulars; and so, linguistically particular orderings of the things in the world are intertranslatable. The differences between my sortings and yours are, then, I assume (and so do you), no serious or unremovable bar to my understanding of what yours are, even if there are things about your sortings I neither like nor agree with.

The world becomes habitable as a world when its flood of appearances is sorted and cataloged. Any such sorting and cataloging amounts to a construal of the world, which is to say a specification and precision of its universal grammar. There are many, perhaps infinitely many, possible construals of the world; but only a few are of deep and lasting importance for the history of human thought. Most of those are what we would now (not very usefully) call religious: Buddhist, Christian, Jewish, Islamic, Confucian, and so on. The construals of the world offered by these traditions of thought and practice differ very significantly one from another, but they share some formal features, most notable among which is that they are articulated with an understanding of what human life is for, which is to say of its proper goal. Each of them is thus also committed to an understanding of what constitutes a well ordered or a disordered life. The religious construals of the world are not alone in that; they share it, for example, with Marxism, and with late-capitalist liberalism. But these secular construals, as their name suggests, are the more-or-less malformed and corrupted bastard offspring of their religious parents.

4

DAMAGE

Factus est oculus tuus particeps lucis huius et vides; clausus est? Hanc lucem non minuisti; apertus est? Hanc lucem non auxisti.

Your eyes participate in the light and so you see. Do they close? You have not diminished the light. Do they open? You have not increased the light.

This elegant and pithy passage, from Augustine's commentary on John (*In Ioannis Evangelium* 39.8), occurs as part of an exposition of the various senses in which God is triune, as an element of which Augustine discusses the idea of participation—participation, that is, of the three divine persons in God, and, for the purposes of illustration, participation of all that is good in humans in God's goodness. The aphorism here (perhaps not original to Augustine) shows what it means for something imperfect to participate in something perfect. The example is the sighted's participation in light. Those who can see can shut out the light by closing their eyes. They thereby become (temporarily) blind. But in becoming so, they do not alter the omnipresence of the light in which they stand. If they open their eyes again, the light is

29

the same, and with it their vision. They did not decrease the light by closing their eyes, and neither can they increase it by opening them. This stands as an illustration of the locus and cause of damage, lack, and absence: these have nothing whatever to do with God.

∾

The world's universal grammar, depicted briefly in chapter 3, is construed in a particular way by Christians. What follows is a display of that construal. The display builds upon and assumes the depiction of the world's universal grammar, for the Christian construal is a specification or precision of that universal grammar.

In calling what follows "the" Christian construal of the world I do not mean to suggest that all those who call themselves Christians would assent to it or even recognise it. Christians have a long history of dispute and disagreement about many things, some of which have led to deep ecclesial and political division; and some of the disputes have been about topics I am about to take a position on. My purpose here, therefore, is not simply descriptive; I am not offering a display of what all self-described Christians hold in common about the world in which we find ourselves (that would be rather a short list), but rather a display of what I take to be the intellectual tradition's fundamental and central commitments on these matters. What follows is, in my judgment, a depiction of the way in which you ought to see the world if you are a Christian.

The world, the array of particulars with which we are faced whether we like it or not, is bathed in light. Everything in it, from the inanimate to the rational, is in its own characteristic way translucent, shone through by omnipresent light like a piece of clear glass in the sun receiving and reflecting light according to its nature. Light is a figure for God, a figure meant to prompt the mind to some dreamwork: light as changeless and omnipresent; light as itself beautiful and the condition for the possibility of seeing beauty; light as identically available for all, incapable of privatization and individual ownership; light as warmly caressing, grateful to the skin; light as medium of vision in which all knowledge occurs; light as painful to the dark-adapted eye; light as giver of life to which all healthy living things turn and to which they respond with movement and growth; light as medium in which there is no obscurity, no shadow, no hidden place, no lack, no absence.

The light-saturated beauty of the world can also be described, though more abstractly and less vividly, in the technicalities of Christian theology. In these terms, the world, a shorthand term for everything, corporeal and incorporeal, that is not God—which is the Christian construal of all that is, seen and unseen—has been brought into being out of nothing by God's free and gracious act. Because the world is, without remainder, the gift of the supremely beautiful one, it is itself beautiful, reflective in its harmony and order of the changeless harmony of its creator. That the world as a whole exists at all is (to us) a suprising and delightful good; we, as inhabitants of the world, are (or ought to be) equally suprising delights to ourselves. The surprise and delight in both cases is, when fully itself, responsive not only to the world and its constituents, including ourselves and other people, but also to the world's giver and to the world as gift. The gift is given freely and without expectation of return; indeed, it is and must be such that no obligation-discharging return is or could be made, for the gift comes before any return and itself constitutes the possibility of return; and so what is returned—piety, laughter, adoration, joy— must itself be what has been given.

Human existence, yours and mine and all of ours, is lived first datively, as people addressed, called, and gifted; and only secondarily nominatively, as subjects looking out over a world displayed for our delectation and consumption. The truth of this priority of the dative over the nominative ought to be obvious enough to anyone who thinks about it for long. To live nominatively is to live as a grammatical and psychological subject, an "I" looking out at and manipulating the world. In this mode, the world is the field of your gaze: it assumes the status of something looked at, something spread passively before you for your delectation and manipulation. You, the looker, the gazing subject, are the active one, the one who initiates, undertakes, performs, and controls. By contrast, to live datively is to live confronted and addressed by a world that questions, forms, and challenges you, the one addressed. It is to live in a world prior to and independent of yourself, a given world, presented unasked, whose overwhelming presence presses you into a responsive mold whether you like it or not. Agency, on this model, belongs as much to the given world as to the perceiving subject responding to it. And this is a more adequate and accurate way of describing the relation between world and person than an exclusive emphasis on the nominative life. You are constantly confronted and addressed by a world not of your making and largely beyond your comprehension and control. The sensory arrays that appear before you, the fabric of time that enmeshes you, the manifold of language in which you have your *habitus,* the social order in which your roles are given to you, the sea of faces of human others, constantly addressing you, calling you into being—all these make of you an indirect object and give you a dative, which is to say a called and donated, life.

Christians have an explanation for this fact of givenness, this phenomenal priority of the dative over the nominative. In giving it, I leave behind, for the moment, the realm of appearances with which phenomenology deals, and move toward that of concept and judgment, in this case specifically Christian theological judgment. The explanation of the world's givenness, and of the interweaving of darkness and light with which the world presents itself to us, begins with the fact that the world need not have been, which is to say that God was not constrained or compelled to create it: it was given without demand or bargain, presented to itself without desert or merit. Some among the world's beings were gifted with the possibility of receiving this gift knowingly, which is to say recognizing it as gift; but even they (we, but not only we; also the angels and whatever other beings are capable of such knowingness) were given both themselves and the world gratis. The world was offered as a gift of love by the God whose nature it is to love, and like all gifts of love made to those who can know them for what they are, it came with the entreaty that its beloved recipients would receive it as the gift it is and not attempt to make it theirs by expropriation or by other responses that would corrupt it.

And the world was given as a cosmos, a vast and ordered beauty, whose knowing members contribute to that beauty by appreciative and responsive contemplation, which is their mode of offering participatory gratitude to the giver, and whose unknowing members contribute to it just by being what they are. This gift, the beautiful gift that is the cosmos, was not made as artifacts are; rather—and this is a distinctive and puzzling feature of Christian thought about the world as gift and God as giver—it was created, brought into being *ex nihilo,* out of the nothing to which, without its creator's sustaining presence, it would inevitably and rapidly return. The gift of the cosmos and all its components is the archetype and paradigm of all gifts because, strangely, it brings into being the gift it gives and those to whom the gift is given: it is a gift without preconditions because it was preceded by nothing other than the act of giving. All other gifts therefore depend upon this one, and all, to the extent that they are gifts, image this one. Creation is, then, prevenient gift. And since creation includes both us as knowers and almost all we can know (the "almost" is needed because we can, with severe limitations, know God, who is by definition not part of the created order, not part of what is given but rather its giver), so to understand it must have effects on how knowledge and the appetite for it are understood.

"Creation" labels, in English, both act (what God did in order to give being to beings) and result (the ensemble of beings). Every being, then, every particular in the world, which is the ensemble of beings, is a creature, just as every being is a gift given. "Creature" and "gift" are the basic terms in a Christian ontology (perhaps, too, in a Jewish or Islamic one): there is no going behind or beneath them to find a more fundamental explanation or construal of what it is to be a being. But arriving at this understanding does not tell us anything about the kinds of creatures there are in the world, nor about how those kinds are related one to another. It indicates only what creatures have in common, which is essential to but insufficient for a depiction of the world as it appears to catechized Christian eyes. For that, another fundamental distinction is needed, and it is that between sensibilia and intelligibilia, a division into kinds that is exhaustive in the sense that there is no *tertium quid,* no third kind that cannot be embraced by and included in these two. (Some creatures, as will become evident, are neither exclusively sensible nor exclusively intelligible; but there is nothing about any creature that is neither sensible nor intelligible, and no creature that is anything other than sensible, intelligible, or some combination of the two.)

Fundamental to the world's hierarchies is the relation between sensibilia and intelligibilia, which are ordered to one another as lower to higher. Sensibilia are things sensed, or capable of being sensed, by corporeal beings with bodily senses. When you read a sonnet, hear a harmony, stroke silk, smell sassafras, or taste truffles you are engaging with sensibilia, all of which are extended in space and through time and are therefore themselves physical and changing. The vast majority of these physical and temporal things come into and pass out of being unaffected causally by human work. This is true of all sensibilia that existed before we were (galaxies, planets), and of all those that, though they share a cosmos with us, are beyond our reach in principle or in practice (everything, for example, on the surface of the sun). Some, although independent of our work for their coming-to-be, have been destroyed or significantly changed by us (the dodo, the reservoirs of oil beneath the surface of our planet, the weather, and the genetic structure of some cereals). And others have our work as necessary condition for their existence (novels, music, buildings, machines). Some are beyond the reach of our senses while accessible to those of beings constituted differently (bats hear what we cannot, dogs smell what we cannot); and some neither have been nor could be sensed by any being currently living. But all, because they are extended in space and time, could in principle be sensed by a being with a body of the right kind.

All sensibilia are beautiful. To say this is merely another way of saying they exist and are ordered. But this is not to say that all sensibilia will seem beautiful to all those who sense them. It seems reasonable to think that the cat's claws do not seem beautiful to the rat as they rake its eyeballs; and most of us shudder with revulsion when faced with the maggots that infest rotting flesh. All these are sensibilia, however. Why do they not seem beautiful? Their failure to do so is among the evidences for the world's fallen and disordered condition. It is an instance of darkness rather than light, causally produced by whatever exactly it was that disordered the world in the first place—a matter that need not detain us here. Were the world as it should be, what is beautiful would also seem beautiful, and particular creatures would lack none of the qualities they ought to have in order to be as beautiful as they could be. But the world is not as it should be, and so particular sensible objects can (and do) lack some of the goods they should have, and some are misperceived as ugly when they are not. These unpleasantnesses are instances of damage, and the fact of such damage is sufficient to establish its possibility. But this establishes an important fact about sensibilia, a fact that shows why things of this sort are lower in the hierarchy of being than intelligibilia: it is that they are subject to change, and not only to change but to change for the worse, which is to say to corruption and decay. The apple can rot; the human being—you, me—can become corrupted by misplaced love into someone capable of the violence of hatred and domination;

and everything organic dies. Peonies grow fast in the spring, blossoming riotously and excessively into blowsy flowers whose overblown beauty falls fast into the chaos of petals rotting on the ground.

Intelligibilia, by contrast, are not subject to change of any sort, and hence also not to decay or corruption. This is because they are extended neither in space nor in time: they are nowhere, which is the same as to say they are everywhere, because the categories of spatial location have no application to them. For the same reason they are nowhen, which is to say everywhen. Such things can be known, but not by the bodily senses. They are knowable by the intellect, the faculty of understanding, which, although for us it may have certain physical states among the necessary conditions for its exercise (perhaps we need bodies, and more specifically brains, in order to understand anything), is not reducible to or definable in terms of the operations of anything physical. Consider, for example, understanding that two and two make four; or that Goldbach's conjecture—that every even number greater than two is expressible as the sum of two primes—is very likely true; or that good people should be admired and emulated by the less good; or that the part is greater than the whole; or that you are a knowing agent. These acts of understanding, and many others like them, have a phenomenology, which is to say that (usually) it seems like something to those who arrive at them to do so, and the something it seems like is misrepresented, misdescribed, if it is accounted for exhaustively in terms of states of the brain. When you are watching a game of chess played by those with better skills than yours you may have the experience of not understanding the strategy of either for the first fifteen or so moves, and then suddenly seeing, intellectually speaking, what they are up to. This realization will seem like something to you, though it is beyond my skills to describe that seeming: perhaps it will include a sense of fitting together sensible data (you were watching the moves in the flesh with your eyes) with judgments about what white will likely do at move twenty-two, judgments that may (but certainly need not) be connected with sensory imagery, and that are likely also connected with intellectual (and perhaps also visceral) pleasure at coming to know something you did not know before. You will shift in your chair, and if the understood strategy is especially elegant and unexpected, the hair on the nape of your neck may stir with pleasure.

Therefore, the act of understanding is itself in part a participant in the realm of intelligibles, which is to say that it is itself in part nowhere and nowhen, even if it occurs, as for us it always does, to a particular person, in a particular place, at a particular time. That our acts of understanding belong in part to the realm of intelligibles is easier to see (and in seeing to exemplify this feature of them) if you consider the nature of some of the things we understand. Mathematical objects have no existence in space and time: if the number two exists in any way other than as an artifact of ours, it is not in such a way that it can be tripped over, picked up, or transported from here to there. Neither is it in such a way that it changes over time. It is, instead, an eternal, nonspatial knowable. The same is true of what it is you come to know when you judge something beautiful or someone just: in each case, you are judging the thing or the person to be conformed to and thus a participant in the eternal order of beauty or justice. On this view, truths of beauty and justice are like truths of mathematics: eternal, nonconventional, nonartifactual, incapable of being sensed but capable, when conditions are right, of being known by rational creatures like us.

Saying only this much about sensibilia and intelligibilia should suffice to show why intelligibilia are hierarchically above sensibilia, and why sensibilia are ordered to them. Beings in both categories are alike in being beautiful in their kinds, that is, in being receptacles for the illimitable light in which the world is bathed, and in refracting that light in their own inimitable way. Their goodness and their beauty are coextensive, and it is as beautiful and good things that they are knowable and known. This is the only way in which anything can be known. But the important difference between the two is that sensory objects can change, lose goodness, become ugly, decrease by way of damage, while such alterations are impossible for intelligibilia. Eternal objects of the understanding do not come into being and cannot go out of being; neither can they sustain damage; and this is because they participate in the being of God—in what God essentially is—in a way that makes these things impossible. They are intimate with God in a way that sensibilia are not, which is what makes them incapable of decay. We, to the extent that we share this intimacy, are similarly incapable. We do not share it in every respect, however: although we are in part like numbers and harmonic intervals and proportions and justice and beauty in being participants in the eternal realm (what you come to know when you come to know yourself as a knower is exactly your participation in the intelligible realm), this is not all that we are. We are also bodies in time and space; and, more importantly, we are free creatures who can will what is good for us or refuse to do so, and to the extent that we refuse to do so we damage ourselves and in so damaging remove ourselves us from the kind of participation in God for which we were made. This movement from greater to lesser is not possible for other intelligibilia because they lack the capacity to will and therefore also the capacity for self-damage or any other kind of change.

The world of sensibilia is also ordered hierarchically, most fundamentally into those creatures that have life and those that lack it. Inanimate corporeal creatures, those without life, include some to whose existence human action is irrelevant: this is true (probably) of all those not on our planet, and of most of the very large and very small features of our planet (mountains, oceans, clouds, subatomic particles). But other inanimate corporeal beings are brought into being by our work (tables, computers), usually by combining, shaping, and ordering those we have not brought into being. Whatever our contribution to the existence and character of particular, inanimate corporeal things, they are alike in lacking the good of life. And what is this good? It is, like all goods, a certain kind of participation in God; but in this it does not differ from the good of being extended in space, which is one that characterizes all inanimate sensibilia. The good of life adds to that good a kind of internal order that permits (and sometimes requires) growth, development, reproduction, and death. An animate corporeal thing, then, possesses all the goods that inanimate corporeal things have and adds to them a good of a higher order. We, as animate creatures, respond very differently to other animate creatures than we do to inanimate ones. Scruples we feel about chipping rock from a cliff face are different in kind from scruples we feel about hacking branches from a tree, and each of these differs from scruples about amputating limbs from a human being. We do all these things; but we do them in profoundly different ways, and with a sense that those who treat each of these actions identically are damaged in deep and troubling ways just because they do not perceive a hierarchical distinction—a distinction of value, that is,—between the inanimate and the animate. As usual, a hierarchy in the order of being has an accompanying difference in the order of knowing.

The animate order is itself arranged hierarchically. The principal distinction here is between living things with rationality or its possibility, and those without. Rationality, to oversimplify a complicated matter, is a capacity for a particular kind of knowing, of which the paradigm case is knowing yourself as a knower performing the act of knowing. Suppose you identify someone walking toward you as a friend or an enemy or a lover—as, that is, someone bearing a particular, well-marked relation to you. When the identification is clear, you behave appropriately: you greet, you embrace, you avoid or you attack, as the case may be. This is not rationality: your dog or cat does as much, and probably with more reliability and alacrity than you do. Rationality adds to this the sense you have of yourself as a being making and acting upon such identifications, a sense that you also attribute to those you identify in such ways. As your lover walks toward you, you identify her not only as your lover but also as someone identifying you as hers; and not only this, you also identify her as a being who is aware of herself as your lover, just as, or in much the same way as, you are aware of yourself as hers. The capacity for such knowledge is among the things that separates rational living creatures from nonrational ones. It provides a depth and complexity to the phenomenal properties of experience that nothing else can; and it is a criterion for being a fully functioning member of the human species. It is also the principal condition for the possibility of coming to know and to develop particularly human virtues, a condition typically, though not inevitably, supplemented by explicit and reliable testimony about those matters. If we take ourselves to be in the presence of a creature whose kind makes rationality impossible for it, we do and should treat such a creature differently than we do one like ourselves, one who is or may be rational. The capacity for rationality orders animate creatures hierarchically in much the same way that the possession of life orders creatures in general. To possess either is to possess a great good.

You may doubt that this hierarchy (inanimate-animate-rational) is one of value; about that there can be reasonable disagreement. But you cannot, without effort of a kind difficult to maintain and unattractive to undertake, behave as if you doubted it. You will—you do—behave as though the constraints upon what may properly be done to animate creatures run deeper and wider than those upon what may properly be done to inanimate creatures; and you will—you do—behave as though those that constrain what may be done to rational creatures run deeper and wider yet. If you were not to differentiate behaviorally in these ways—if, say, you were to treat rocks just as you treat people, crying over a shattered piece of slate as you do over a shattered human skull, this would be good prima facie evidence of your own status as a radically and atypically damaged human being. It is among the elements constitutive of proper function as a human being to behave as though these distinctions have purchase. Offering a theoretical account of them is a different matter: few do that, and fewer are confident in their offerings. Inhabiting the world of light, which is also the world of gift, requires that when you make a theoretical judgment about the nature of this hierarchy it is one that attributes value to it, that makes it a hierarchy of the good and the beautiful as well as a hierarchy of being. To be animate rather than inanimate is to be better at least in the sense of possessing rather than lacking a great good, as is also true of being rational rather than irrational. The value in question is that of participating more fully in the being of God, which is the light with which the mundane is saturated.

⁓

The world is radiantly translucent, but it is not only that. It is also shot through with darkness. The divine light does not shine everywhere, but the places of shade and shadow exist only as its absence, its lack, its privation. They can be described only by negation, sought only by aversion (the closing of the eyes), and entered only by embracing the loss in which they consist. Such an embrace damages: the eye accustomed to the dark loses, perhaps temporarily and perhaps permanently, its capacity to see; it sustains damage, more or less deep. And the places of darkness are also places of chaos and disorder in which the demons of disorder—Leviathan, Behemoth, Diabolos— prowl, making less what was more, expropriating the beauty and order of the place of light and in doing so removing it from its proper glory and turning it into desolation, the place of dissimilarity, anguish, famine, and destitution in which the praise-shout becomes the wail of anguish, trailing gradually off into the peevish murmur of the self-wounding seeker of darkness. The regions of darkness are visible only by courtesy, as rents and tears in the seamless garment of light. They are the places in which knowledge becomes ignorance, vision becomes blindness, beauty ugliness, harmony discord, and, most fundamentally, life death. To seek them is to seek nothing; to live in them is to live nowhere; to offer them is to offer the empty gift; and so to seek to live and to offer is to diminish, to hack at the body of one's being with the sharp sword of a disordered will until that body is limbless, bleeding, incapable of motion, approaching the second death from which there is no rebirth.

That the world is like this, light shot through with darkness, is what gives it drama. In such a world, sanctification, the ordering of intellect and will so that they harmonize and resonate with divine music—to shift the figure from the visual to the aural—is always a beautiful possibility and always a real one, genuinely on offer. But so is sanctification's opposite, the downward trajectory that issues in damnation by means of the embrace of the nothing that brings will and intellect into discord with themselves and thereby with the condition of their own possibility. Things matter: they can be on the way to the final healing from damage that is salvation, or they can be tending toward the not-being from which they came. Human life, social and individual, shares in this drama, and so there are always two stories to be told, that of what tends toward damnation (final damage, damage beyond healing) and that of what tends toward salvation (final healing, healing beyond damage).

The drama in these two stories is one of darkness and light, and the abyss into which the self-pleasers, the lovers of pride and graspers of nothing, go down is that of nonbeing, light's absence. They go down into it because of the ponderous weight of their habituated desires, desires, which drag them toward nothing. By contrast, those who submissively and lovingly seek wisdom, which harmonizes the minds and wills of those who have it with the world of light, confirm and enhance what they are, receiving thereby a radiant lightness of being which does not have to be borne but need only be delighted in. Membership in either group, that of the damned as well as that of the saved, is a matter of the will: what is wanted and sought is what is received, and the drama of the world of darkness and light is that the tragedy of human existence is neither getting nor not getting what you want, but rather the real possibility that you will guarantee yourself success at failure by seeking the darkness of absence that you can in fact obtain. This drama is heightened and intensified by the fact that each of us is opaque to ourselves, and as a result cannot easily tell—and certainly cannot tell with certitude—which of our actions and habits grasps nothing, and which conforms us to wisdom.

The beautifully ordered world is brought into being out of nothing, which is another way of saying that God's gift is complete and unparalleled in its generosity. Nothing comes before or underlies the gift and nothing extraneous to itself was used in giving. The gift includes not only the particularity of every thing, but also the sheer, factical givenness of that thing. And the gift of creation out of nothing has another implication, which is that no particular thing, no creature, whether animate or inanimate, rational or irrational, is self-given or self-sustaining. Rather, each creature is from nothing by gift, and without the gift of being, given as the first grace of creation and constantly regiven as God's sustaining grace, it returns toward nothing, slipping and sliding deeper into the abyss of nonbeing. The extent to which particular created things make this move from being to nonbeing is also the extent to which the cosmos of light is shot through with darkness: light figures being and darkness figures being's absence. The darkness and danger of the world is what it is because of the nature of that world as created out of nothing and tending to return to nothing. The lacks to which the world is subject, the vitiation of its created goodness, are evident most clearly in death, violence, and pain, which are not part of the divine gift but are instead clear signs of its corruption. And those signs are everywhere. The nonhuman animate world is an ocean of blood flowing from violent death; and the human world differs from it in this only in the scale of the violence and the ingenuity of its performance, in both of which our world far exceeds the nonhuman one. There are lesser signs, too: the decay of love, the grasp of ownership, the bitterness of envy, the uneasy exaltation of pride, the desire for dominance, and, at the root of all these, the self-caused and eagerly sought diminution of the capacity to respond to the gift of being and all the beauties that accompany it by expropriation of the gift, by treating it as if it were not gift but one's own creation and one's own property.

The seriousness of the world as an arena for seeking and finding both salvation and damnation is rooted in what it is and what it has become: deep damage is already a fact, and it can be exacerbated by confusion and the disorder of desire. These are the portals through which the darkening of the radiant perfection of the world has entered, and they are not closed. For rational beings like us, damage is aready a fact: we do not know what we should and could know, and we do not want what we should and could want. The etiology of this damage is not fully available to us, though the third chapter of the book of Genesis contains a story about it, a story of Adam and Eve's disobedience to divine command and their consequent gaining of knowledge and condemnation to suffering and death. The story is indispensable but opaque, as the history, long and gorgeous, of its interpretation by Jews, and Christians, and Muslims, and latterly by those who would like to read it free of any such commitments as those, amply shows. It can be read negatively as a story about pride, greed, disobedience or lust for power—or about those ingredients combined and woven in various patterns; or it can be read as a story about an inevitable and even proper move from childhood's innocence to an adult understanding of human possibility; or it can be read as a dramatization of a genuinely damaging event which is nonetheless taken up and transformed by God into a final redemption—as, that is, a *felix culpa,* a happy fault. The enterprise of reading and interpreting Genesis will not soon cease, and the opacity of the text, its capacity for generating multiple and incompatible readings, is an important part of the reason why. Genesis in general, and its third chapter in particular, serves as an excellent example of the fecundity of Scripture's opacity, and as support for the claim that it is important that Scripture not always be transparently clear and, as a result, easily exhausted.

But even though the third chapter of Genesis is in many respects opaque, it comports well with the view that damage—the interweaving of the world of light with threads of darkness—is exhaustively explicable by appeal to human agency, which is to say by appeal to the actions of rational agents not determined to particular ends. The logic of this position is simple enough. If the beautifully ordered world has been brought into being out of nothing by the gracious gift of a God who has and can have no interests in and no causal connection with the removal of order, harmony, beauty, and being, but only in and with their sustaining; and if, manifestly, there is damage to the world; and if, axiomatically, everything other than God was created out of nothing and is sustained in being by God—then it follows at once that the only cause of damage to the world must be found among created things. And among those the obvious candidate is us, though perhaps not only us; there is also an angelic order, and there may be other rational beings capable of effecting such changes. Ontological damage, therefore, is explained anthropologically, and this underscores the seriousness of the world: we have damaged both ourselves and the cosmos we inhabit, and we are continuing to do so.

We are born damaged into a damaged world, and we then proceed to damage both it and ourselves further. The damage with which we are afflicted independently of the devices and desires of our own hearts has both corporeal and incorporeal elements. Corporeally, we decay toward death from the moment of conception; from birth to death we are subject to pain, ranging from the undignified and annoying to the consuming and destroying; and intense pain, whether from toothache or childbirth or torture, typically turns us into passive objects before its force, removing our sentience and thus also our freedom. We are always at the edge of bodily disruption and death. If anything, incorporeal damage is worse. At birth, we are greedy solipsists eager to use violence to remove obstacles to the satiation of our desires. Much then depends upon the catechesis we get from family and from the local social, political, and economic order, whatever that happens to be. This catechesis is indispensable and unavoidable, but it can go well or badly, be more or less violent, more or less loving, more or less opposed to the order intended and desired by God. Yet however well or badly it goes, it will always in part be an instrument for the further corruption of what has already been badly damaged.

Damage given to you by parental or cultural catechesis is not the whole story. There is also damage produced by your own free action. This is sin in action, sin willed, intended, and undertaken. When you intend and perform an action improper for you, one damaging to what you are, you add to the damage you have inherited in ways to which you are disposed by that inheritance. For the inheritance, you are no more responsible than you are for the color of your eyes or your largely genetically determined intellectual capacities. But to the extent that you remain free (and that extent is properly disputable), the particular sins you freely choose are your responsibility as the damage you have inherited is not. If, for example, you choose to indulge an appetite for dominating others so that you become habituated to the kinds of action that indulge such an appetite, you will be acting in a way unfitting for a human being, an image of God, and you will be responsible for having done so. You will be establishing ever more firmly your membership in the society of those the weight of whose desires is hurling them into the abyss.

The drama of human existence in this world of darkness and light is deepened and made more troubling by the fact that neither kind of damage, not inherited damage and not self-inflicted damage, can be finally and fully removed by your own efforts. You, like me, are a cripple who cannot heal yourself, a beggar who needs the gifts of God and of other human beings even to maintain yourself in existence and much more to be healed of the damage that afflicts you. The damage inherited is beyond your capacity to heal in much the same way that you cannot make yourself taller or shorter by wishing: in this respect, you are what you are, which is always and necessarily less than you could and should be. But the same is often true of the additional damage you have freely embraced. This may yield habits—of cruelty, of despair, of indulgence, of violence, of hatred, of timidity, of bitterness, of envy—that become so deeply entwined with your character that you can no longer imagine what it would be like to be without them and can certainly do nothing to remove them. Not to know this and to act as if it were not true is to subjugate yourself to the fantasy of independence and self-determination, to pretend that you are captain of your soul and master of your fate. And this is the most damaging of fantasies, for becoming habituated to it guarantees that you will not get the help freely to be had by asking for it, but which can only be had in that way. The fantasy of self-sufficiency, the determination to please yourself coupled with the illusion that you can, is the unforgivable sin against the Holy Spirit, for it, and it alone, guarantees that you will not beg, will not ask the forgiveness you need; and since the only condition placed upon the reception of the love of God is that you acknowledge that you need it and do not merit it, this is the worst of all possible habits. Better for you to be sadistic, miserly, gluttonous, racist—and you will end by being some or all of these, or something worse—than unable to beg.

The darkness that is damage serves, for Christians, to explain the evil that is good's absence in the world external to ourselves. The corporeal world is out of joint, not as it should be; that is why the ensemble of causal connections that constitutes its activity is so often destructive to beings like us, and indeed to the harmony of the whole. Earthquakes, and tsunamis, and plagues are, at least in part, the world not working as it should. We tend to call such things "natural disasters," but this is misleading. They are not natural if by that is meant that they belong to the world as it should be, the world as it was brought into being by its creator. Rather, they are anti-natural, instances of the chaos that disorder the world's nature rather than of the order that constitutes its beautiful harmony.

But we need to be careful here. Our intuitions and judgments about what is ordered and what is disordered are not always reliable because we are ourselves disordered and may therefore interpret a painful result of our own disorder as chaotic when it is nothing other than the inevitable pain of self-wounding. If you put your hand into the fire, your flesh will char and you will suffer. But the fact that fire burns your flesh is not itself (probably) an instance of disorder's damage; the disorder lies in your decision to put your hand there. By contrast, the violent death of multitudes brought about by events beyond the control and absent the initiation of human beings, such as the Lisbon earthquake of 1755 or the Indian Ocean tsunami of 2004, it seems more reasonable to think, is an instance of the world's disorder, and not just because such events bring suffering to us. Any such judgments about what is and what is not evidence of the external world's disorder are disputable, and should always be made with the deep epistemic modesty appropriate to our limited and damaged capacities for knowledge. We—we Christians at least—can, however, be sure of the basic principle, even though we must doubt our ability to discern its application to cases. The principle in question is threefold: there is damage and disorder in the nonhuman world; all such damage is causally traceable to human agency, though not necessarily to the agency of those who suffer from it; and such disorder may be terribly destructive to particular human beings who have, individually, done nothing to deserve it other than to be born into a damaged world. The book of Job serves, still, as the best literary depiction of how this works, and of what the proper response to it is.

This situation begins to seem not so much dramatic as desperate. For Christians, however, it is not, because healing, whether as justification, by which the burden of damage is lifted, or as sanctification, by which the residues of damage are gradually burned and smoothed away, is to be had through and in Christ, by means of the divine gift of the virtues of faith, hope, and love. That is the economy of grace, both prevenient to and supervenient upon the order of nature, which is, in turn, this world of darkness and light. We are beggars, but we are also glorious, made in God's image and capable of having the damage and distortion that image has suffered remade and transformed. But that story goes beyond the story of the world.

5

GIFT

Supererogatur tibi [sc. Deo] ut debeas, et quis habet quicquam non tuum?
Reddis debita nulli debens, donas debita nihil perdens.

We do more for you, O God, than is necessary, so that you might be
in our debt. But which of us has anything not already yours? You
pay debts while owing no one; you forgive debts without losing
anything.

➥

This passage is part of Augustine's extensive hymn of praise
to God with which the *Confessions* opens (I take it from 1.4.4).
Using paradox, Augustine tests what can be said about God
in the language of exchange and debt, and in so doing shows
the limits of that language. Suppose we humans pay back to
God more than we owe—suppose, that is, we do more than
we need do for God (*supererogatur Deo*). Then God would be in
our debt. But, since everything any of us has is already God's
(*quis habet quicquam non tuum?*, echoing, perhaps, 1 Corinthians 4:7, *quid autem habes quod non accepisti?*), this is absurd: if
you give back to someone what's already theirs, then no matter how much you give back you cannot place them in your
debt. What, then, about God's gifts to us? The language of

exchange breaks down here too: God repays debts when he does not owe any *(reddis debita nulli debens)*; and in the act of repayment he loses nothing *(donas debita nihil perdens)*. The rhetorical flourishes are meant to indicate the inadequacy of the language that belongs to an economy of obligation, an economy in which every gift establishes a debt, and every return presupposes a prior, obligation-producing gift. The negative way through that language is to turn it into laughable paradox, as Augustine does here; the positive way is to speak of the pure, nonobliging gift, which he does elsewhere.

∽

The world appears as gift. Or, more exactly, the world, being light shot through with darkness, appears in part as gift and in part as its opposite. To the extent that light is obscured, the world appears not as delightful gift, but as constrictingly repetitive burden whose days and nights pass with the rapidity and numbing sameness of the weaver's shuttle, a region of desolation and hunger composed in equal measure of pain and boredom. But the world of light, harmony, and liberating order, the real world, that is, rather than its negative image, its dark twin, appears as gift that delights when it is welcomed and embraced.

The world appears as gift because the divine economy is ordered by and to gift. That economy is active in the relations of the divine persons one to another; and it is active and partly evident in God's creative act of bringing the cosmos into being; and it is paradigmatically active and evident in his management and direction of the salvation of the damaged cosmos by incarnation as the divine-human person, Jesus the Christ. Depicting this economy principally in terms of gift is not without puzzles and difficulties. Economies are not all of one kind, and the most familiar sense of the term after Marx makes a noncompetitive economy of gift no economy at all, for the definition of economy has come to include the competitions of obligation, exchange, reciprocity, and contract. However, this is not a necessary move, and to show that it is not, and in so showing to elucidate what it means to say that the world is gift—something that must be both said and understood if a properly Christian account of what it is to want to know is to be offered—the distinction between an economy of obligation and an economy of gift must be made with all the precision possible. Both economies involve the managed transfer of goods, which is to say that goods circulate within both. This is why they are called economies; managed circulation of goods is what defines an economy. Most often, goods circulate by being handed over from one person or group to another. But the circulation of goods proper to an economy of obligation is different in most interesting respects from that proper to an economy of gift: in the purposes and motivations of the agents involved; in the relations established by the act of transfer; in the kinds of goods circulated; and in much else.

In transfers that belong to an economy of obligation, a giver hands over ownership or use, ordinarily of some exhaustible good, to a givee, if this barbaric term may be allowed—it has the advantage of preserving the semantic connection between the one who gives, the act of giving, and the recipient of gift, and it has begun to have some limited currency in English. A transfer like this creates a debt to be discharged by exchange or restitution, and so it is typically accompanied by calculations about the nature of the debt incurred, about whether the givee is willing and able to discharge the debt, and about whether and in what ways the contemplated transfer and the relation of obligation it brings into being serve the interests of giver and givee. Reason works calculatively in an economy of obligation, and where the goods involved in a transfer are necessary for survival or flourishing (food, shelter, clothing), it may be a matter of desperate importance that the calculations be made correctly. Even where this is not so, much in the way of status and security may hinge upon the correctness and adequacy of calculation.

Consider, as an ideal type of transfer under the sign of obligation, the exchange of labor for money. You might be a CEO who signs a contract of employment according to which you serve the company's shareholders with your time, expertise, and energy: these are the goods you transfer to the shareholders. In exchange, they transfer to you cash and other benefits. Your obligations to one another are spelled out in a contract, and there are legal sanctions upon both parties should these obligations be transgressed. Or, suppose you want to buy a used car from me: again, we enter into a contractual relation in terms of which I transfer the car to you and you transfer cash to me. Or, suppose I am a student in the university class you're teaching: the syllabus you hand out at the beginning of the semester serves as a contract between us (this is the language universities in the United States now use about the relation between student and teacher), and by its terms I am obligated to you to do certain things (come to class, read books, write papers, think), and you have obligations to me to do certain things (come to class, give lectures, grade papers, think). Goods, in this case incorporeal ones, are exchanged or transferred here too, and obligations are incurred by the transfer.

The transfers that take place within an economy of obligation need not be contractual in the strict sense, and most are not. Suppose that you and I both hold elected office in the same legislative body. We are of different parties and we usually support opposed and incompatible policies, but we both see the need for compromise in order to make progress toward the political goals each of us has, and so I offer you my support on an issue of deep concern to you but about which I am neutral or negative, on condition that you do the same for me when our positions are later reversed. In this example, I am giving or transferring my floor vote to you, and thereby obligating you to give yours to me later. There will be no formal contract, and the obligation may never be explicitly stated. Nevertheless it will be real, and there will be real results if you don't reciprocate by transferring to me a good of the same kind as the one I have already transferred to you. My transfer of political support to you places you in my debt, even if exactly what would count as discharge of the debt is not an explicit part of the initial transfer—even if, that is, there is no explicit contract.

Transfers of goods within the economy of obligation may be even less explicit than this about the kind of obligation they create. The local potentate throws a party for his subjects, let's say, transferring to them food, drink, and entertainment. But he does this without it occurring to him or to any of his givees to specify in what sense those who eat his food and drink his wine are thereby indebted to him, or just what they should do in order to reciprocate. Nevertheless, those who eat the food and drink the wine are obligated at least in the sense that their status as dependent recipients and the potentate's status as the lord of largesse have been displayed and affirmed by the giving and receiving of the party. To reject or transgress this relation later, by plotting revolution, transferring allegiance, or bad-mouthing the potentate, would be to offend against an obligation implicitly accepted when the potentate's hospitality was accepted. Among the most common purposes and results of transfers made within an economy of obligation is exactly this display of status and its accompanying affirmation and hardening of a hierarchical relation of dependence between giver and givee. Such gifts are the beneficence of the *dominus,* the lord who dominates. They may provoke counter-gifts intended to trump, question, or adjust the obligation of subservience brought into being by them, but their essential purpose is to represent and inculcate a relation of subservience and domination.

The governing motto of the transfer of goods within an economy of obligation is the Latin tag *do ut des,* "I give so that you might give back": protection for loyalty, labor for money, love for love, cash for kind, sex for shopping, courtesy for courtesy, and command for obedience. Almost all transfers are like this, sometimes condensed and formalized into contractual form, but more often not, more often part of the loosely woven fabric of political, social, professional, sexual, and family life. The idea enshrined in the tag is twofold: not only does my gift to you oblige you to give to me; it is also the condition of the possibility of your gifts to me. For those who think in these terms there is no free gift. But in fact not all transfer occurs within an economy of obligation. Some, radical and radiantly pure, occurs under the sign of gift.

These transfers, transfers of goods under the sign of the gift, are noncalculative and do not bring debt or any other obligation into being. Gift-givers in this economy do not concern themselves with the credit worthiness of those to whom they give; they do not consider whether those they gift are deserving; and they do not give with expectation of gratitude or any other return—though they hope that the gift given will be accepted as what it is, and as a result bring joy, and the flourishing that goes with joy, to its givees; they may also entreat their givees to accept what is given as it is given, just so long as they do not make the gift conditional upon such acceptance. Givers in this economy also often transfer inexhaustible goods, goods that when given and accepted are not lost to the giver. Those who accept a transfer within the economy of gift are, when they accept the gift as given, therefore obliged to nothing, and this makes the relation between giver and givee in the economy of gift simpler than that connecting those involved in the transfer of goods in the economy of obligation. In the latter, there is debt, discharge, and calculation as well as goods transferred; in the former, there are only giver, gift, and givee.

You may doubt (certainly some do) that there is an economy of gift. Perhaps you think that all transfers of goods bring obligations with them, and that there are therefore no noncalculative acts of giving, no gifts without debts—at least among us. This doubt is likely to be empirical. That is, you are likely to think in this way, if you do, not because you take the idea of a transfer of goods under the economy of gift to be incoherent; it is just that you think no such transfers occur in the human sphere. Among us, you may say, there are only gifts under the sign of obligation, debt-bringing gifts. But this is too quick: all that's needed for the refutation of this view is a counter-example, an instance, that is, of transfers of goods within the human sphere that bring no debts or other obligations into being, or at least that tend in such a direction. If there are such instances, and there are, then their analysis will require that they be distinguished from the usual obligation-creating transfers, and it will then follow that not all transfers can be fully accounted for by the economy of obligation.

A somewhat more subtle version of the objection to the idea of a nonobliging transfer of goods is the claim that all transfers, when recognized as such, require the acknowledgment of obligation. There clearly are transfers of this sort. If you transfer to me a large sum of cash together with the understanding that I should pay it back over three months at an interest rate of 50 percent on pain of having my kneecaps broken should I fail to do so, not only do I know at once (if I understand the transfer in these terms) that I have entered the economy of obligation-creating exchange, I would be contradicting my own understanding were I to deny this. But are all transfers like this? Not obviously. The definition I have given of a transfer under the sign of gift does not carry on its face the establishment of an obligation; and so the decision as to whether obligation must be thought always to accompany the understanding that a transfer of goods has been made to me will depend upon the possibility of displaying examples of recognizable and recognized transfers that do not bring obligation with them.

A preliminary distinction will be helpful here: Being obliged to reciprocate a transfer of goods is not the same as being assured (and sure) that you will undergo damage if you treat what is transferred in a particular way, but not if you do not. If your doctor prescribes medicine for you, with strong and clear warnings that if you take the medicine in any way other than that recommended by him your illness will get not better but worse, this does not suffice to place the transfer under the economy of obligation. You may or may not choose to take your medicine as directed and you may or may not believe what your doctor says. What she offers you is not an obligation but a warning, a prediction, and (if she is a compassionate doctor) an entreaty. The warning is about damage, the promise about healing, and the entreaty that you do what is necessary to avoid the damage and move toward health. None of this obliges you to anything: if you owe your doctor anything, it is not because she has promised, warned, and entreated you. This distinction, between obligation on the one hand and the complex of promise, warning, and entreaty, on the other, is not present in most rejections of the possibility of the gift's recognizability. The gift in the example just given brings healing if accepted, and consequent upon its rejection is the continuation, and perhaps the worsening, of damage. Gratitude is no more or less than acceptance and proper use, which is certainly a kind of reciprocity, but not one of debt or obligation.

It remains, then, logically, psychologically, and phenomenologically possible that goods may be transferred under the sign of gift. But what is meant by "goods"? I have said that goods transferred under the sign of gift are typically but not inevitably inexhaustible. But what does this mean? Some goods, once transferred, are no longer in the possession of the giver: they have been given away. These are exhaustible goods. They pass without remainder from the hands of the giver to those of the givee. Most corporeal objects are like this: if I give my kidney to you, I have one fewer than I had before; if I give you $100, that is $100 I no longer have; if I give you an hour of my time, that's an hour I no longer have and cannot get back—and that last is incorporeal, which shows that not all exhaustible gifts are corporeal (neither, as we shall see, are all corporeal gifts exhaustible). More generally, anything of which the giver has a finite supply is an exhaustible gift. But not everything giveable is of this sort. Some goods, when transferred, do not leave the possession of the giver: if I give you a pint of my blood, while it is true that I no longer have that particular pint, I soon replace it, and without deliberation or effort, whether I like it or not; if I give you an idea I have or a poem I've composed, I still have them, as, now, do you; if I give you a skill I've mastered—that of riding a bicycle, say, or of making a bed with tight, hospital corners—by showing you how to do the same, the skill remains with me as it is now also with you; and if I give you my love I do not thereby lose it. This last example differs from the others, perhaps, in that it is only by giving you my love that I can have it at all: it comes into being only when given, unlike blood, ideas, poems, and skills. But love is like these others in that any token of the type is inexhaustible: when given it does not give out and cannot be given away.

Consider the example of teaching. Teaching someone else what you know, whether by writing or speaking, does not mean that you know it any less than you did before you taught it. Its gift—the act of giving it away—does not reduce or corrupt it, and does not take it away from its original possessor. And not only this. Giving what you know to others by teaching them is necessary if you are to have the knowledge you have in the way you ought to have it. If you do not give that knowledge away by teaching it, hugging it instead to your bosom in the privacy of your bedchamber, turning it over in solitude, gloating over it inside your skull as the miser counts his money only when he is alone, then it will curdle, ceasing to be what it could and should be. This is because all knowables belong by definition to the public sphere, and to expropriate them from that sphere into an utterly private one is to perform a recursively incoherent act—an act like that of attempting marriage to no one in particular, or like making love to the beloved by masturbating while thinking about her. But these points cannot be pursued more fully at this stage of the depiction; I note them here as illustrations of the dual possibility that some things can be given away without being thereby lost to the giver, and that some things will be lost if they are not given away (your beloved will likely not long reciprocate your love if you give it to her only in the way mentioned).

But more needs to be said about what gifts of this kind might be like in the human sphere. The ideal-typical example is God's gift of the cosmos, which is not strictly speaking a transfer at all because the goods in question were brought into being out of nothing, not moved from one place or one ownership to another. But it is the gift of something: being-out-of-nothing, without which there are no other gifts, and at least in this sense, as also in the sense of being a gift unmerited and undeserved by its givees, a gift that binds them to nothing, and a gift of loving entreaty. Transferring goods within the human sphere can never be quite like this, for two fundamental reasons. The first is that human beings are not God: we lack the capacity for creation *ex nihilo,* and so the gift of being is beyond our abilities and means. The second is that both we and the cosmos we inhabit are already damaged, not, that is, as God created us and as God wishes us to be. The most we can hope for is that there may be human gifts that bear the vestigial trace of the divine gift, as indeed there are. Turning our gaze toward these will help to explain what it means to think of the cosmos as sheer gift, and will thereby support the enterprise of thinking through what it means to want to know that cosmos, in whole or in part.

∾

Consider first the gift of blood. The needle goes into your vein and the rich, red fluid moves from the warm haven of your body into a sterile, temperature-controlled container. It is tested for disease and for other imperfections, and if judged pure, potentially life giving, it may then move from the sterility of storage into the warm confines of someone else's body, replacing blood lost to accident, illness, or sugery. Perhaps your gift permits the givee to go on living when otherwise he would have died. Other scenarios are of course possible: your gift of blood may never leave storage because no suitable givee is found before your blood has lost its life-giving efficacy; your blood may be given to someone who dies anyway, in spite of your gift; or, rarely, your gift may bring death instead of life if it is the wrong type, or if it carries some undetected disease. But, ideally, your gift will pass into another's body and will give life to that other. And when this happens, your gift approaches quite closely to being a transfer under the sign of gift.

Why this proximity? Why is the transfer of blood from one body to another closer to the economy of gift than to the economy of obligation? First, the gift given does not diminish you, its giver, or at least does so only temporarily. Your blood is not an inexhaustible gift, though it does approach that condition. Most people can give a pint or two of blood a week without serious ill effects, and ordinarily the body replaces blood given away within a day or two. So while it is true that you no longer have the self-same pint of blood you gave—it, you hope, now circulates in another's veins—the one you've replaced it with is its replica, and you can go on performing the magic of blood replication until you die. But that this gift does not diminish the giver is not all that approximates it to a transfer within the economy of gift: you do not ordinarily give blood with any particular givee in mind, which means that you do not give by calculating the merits or worthiness of potential givees. You think little or nothing about that, and to the extent that you do you are likely to take need for blood as the only criterion for worthiness to receive, and this does not require any calculation by you: such calculations as are needed for it you give over to others, to intermediaries: doctors, nurses, technicians, and bureaucrats.

Even this is not all. The gift of blood binds or obligates the givee to nothing whatever: not to the offering of thanks to the giver (who will in any case almost always be unknown to the givee), and not even to the giving of the same gift to others. All the givee has to do is welcome the gift given gratis, and this can be done easily by permitting the free circulation of the gift in her veins. Opening your veins to expel the intruder would cancel the appropriate welcome, certainly; but it is hard to imagine what else would. In all these ways, the gift of blood bears the trace of the divine gift of the cosmos: just as damage results from refusing the gift in the case of the transfusion, so also it does from refusing the gift of the cosmos—though the latter refusal can occur in many more ways than the former; and just as the gift of the cosmos is given by God with entreaty that it be accepted and enjoyed by its gi-vees (it is not a stoical gift, not one given with the blank apathy of the bureaucrat or the calculating expediency of the consequentialist), so also—at least ideally—with the gift of blood.

There are potential dissimilarities, too. Unlike the divine gift, the gift of blood can be corrupted by the giver as well as by the givee. For example, the gift of blood can be transferred to the economy of obliga-tion by being commercialized, sold by the giver, and purchased by the givee, as is already the norm in some countries. And the giver of blood can do more than entreat the gift's welcome and the givee's resultant flourishing: she can hug to herself the thought of her own generosity, thanking God that, unlike others, she is generous, and thereby trans-muting herself from being a giver into being a feeder of her hungry ego, a self-pleaser like the Pharisee who congratulated himself on his own righteousness. But even these corruptions do not entirely remove the trace of the divine gift from the gift of blood.

Almsgiving, too, bears traces of the divine gift, though they are more easily effaced than in the case of the blood gift. To give alms is to give the materials of sustenance (food, shelter, clothing, money) in response to need. Often, need will be expressed by the givee and made known directly, without intermediary, to the giver: the needy one will have a face upon which the giver can look. This was the case with the Good Samaritan in Jesus' parable, as it is also the case for those who live and work in any city in the world at the beginning of the twenty-first century, for in every such city there are thousands of such face-to-face requests and responses every day. But the gift of alms can also be made facelessly, by writing a check to a tax-deductible charity or-ganization, or by putting cash in your church's poorbox. Almsgiv-ing, for us, approaches more closely to a transfer under the sign of gift when the giver and givee do not know one another. The anonymity of the faceless gift of alms checks the tendency on the part of givers to make the gift dependent upon the apparent worthiness of its givees, and (worse) to expect a reciprocal offering of submissive gratitude from the givee when she receives the gift. Face-to-face almsgiving is almost inevitably calculating in these ways, and to the extent that it is, it erases the trace of the divine gift and replaces it with an obligating transfer of goods. Anonymous almsgiving may avoid these corruptions, though it is unlike the divine gift (and unlike, too, the gift of blood) in giving away an exhaustible gift, a gift lost to the giver by being given away to the givee.

In addition to the gifts of blood and alms, though very differently, the gift of oneself to another in friendship and erotic passion bears the trace of the divine gift. To become and remain a friend is, in part, to make a gift of yourself. The gift is of time, attention, and love (at least), and it does not depend essentially on judgments about the friend's worthiness to receive these gifts. Likewise, but with the added gift of the body, in the case of a friendship that includes erotic love. These gifts, more than those of blood or alms, are creative in the sense that their givees are to some degree brought into being by them. We are so made that we cannot fully be ourselves unless we are given by others the gift of being their friends or lovers. When you give yourself to me as a friend or lover, what you give is not only yourself but also me to myself: your caress, whether fleshly or verbal, brings me to be more fully myself than I could have been without it. This is most obvious in the case of the caresses parents give to children: without these gifts, children cannot come to be what they should be, which is to say that they will remain undeveloped, persons *in nuce* but not persons full bloomed. But it is true, too, of the caresses of time spent with a friend, of lovemaking, and of washing, feeding, and caring for the bodies of the sick.

These gifts of oneself to another, however, are subject to corruption, and in extreme cases to the almost complete erasure of the trace of the divine gift. They may be corrupted much more easily than can the faceless gifts of blood and alms. This is exactly because they are not faceless. When a particular human other is face-to-face with you, the corruption of your gift of yourself to her is, since the fall, to some degree inevitable. You will treat her as a screen on which to project yourself, and to the extent that you do so you will erase her by absorbing her into yourself. Or, you will treat her as an object to be dominated and owned; or as a mere occasion for your own physical pleasure; or as a prop, support, and collaborator for your projects of self-damage. The possibilities are endless, and most of them are actual to some degree or another in every transfer of goods between self and other. Such transfers are much more easily poisoned than faceless gifts. But they are also, in one quite fundamental sense, closer to the divine gift, more fully its image, than faceless gifts can be. In their intimacy—the requirement that giver and givee be face-to-face and know one another's name—they provide the closest possible image of the divine call by which God brought each of us into being. The breath of the Spirit is in the nostrils of each of us, blown there with loving care for our particular face. Before God we are always named, and always face-to-face (unless we insist, as we may, on averting our gaze); and this is why each of us so eagerly seeks the life giving gift of the caress from human others. It is one of the most grievous results of the fall that the corruption of this gift we can give to one another makes it more potentially damaging than the corruption of anonymous and faceless gifts. We are most dangerous to one another when our faces are closest and our names most deeply known.

Corruption is never complete, however, even though it is always present. The principal evidence of its absence lies in the nexus that connects the giver's entreaty that the gift may be accepted as given with the givee's welcoming delight of the gift. The baby responds to the parent's caress with delight; the lover's kiss, given with entreaty, may be received with delight; and the suppportive arm given to the infirm may likewise be offered with entreaty and accepted with joy. The most fully Christian (but also Jewish and Islamic) form of this nexus between entreaty and welcoming delight is to be found in worship which, in its ideal type, precisely is our joyful acceptance as givees of God's self-giving.

～

All gifts share the formal features just described, but not all are equally intimate with their givers. Four degrees of intimacy are conveniently and fairly easily distinguishable so far as human givers are concerned, and distinguishing them will be of help in coming to a fuller understanding of the relation between God and his gifts.

The first degree, the gift most intimate with its giver, is the gift that until given was a constituent or product of its giver's body. Blood, internal organs, and body parts are like this. So are semen, eggs, hair, nail clippings, sweat, urine, and excrement. If I give you any of these things, I transfer to you something that could not have come into being without my body, something that was, until given, either a body part or a body product. Such gifts warrant special treatment, as we ordinarily recognize by our attitudes to them, positive and negative, when they are accidentally spilled or in some other way separated from their bodily home; or when they are stored and used independently of the body from which they came. There are medical versions of such storage and use, in organ, blood, and semen banks. And there are religious ones, in the use of corporeal relics. Martyrdom is the extreme case of a gift like this: martyrs give their bodies entirely, and with it their lives (the question of the givee of that gift is more complex); but there are many less dramatic gifts of the kind, such as donations of blood, organs, semen, or eggs; or, more prosaically, the gift from one lover to another of a lock of hair; or the infant's proud gift of excrement to his half-disgusted parent. Gifts of the first degree, profoundly intimate with their givers though they are, can be given without the giver's full and lively personal presence because body parts or

(margin handwriting: falls short of spiritual self-gifts)

body products are detachable from that presence, and once detached can be handled and passed on in such a way that their provenance is forgotten or deliberately obscured. Givees of such gifts often do not know who their giver was; and givers often do not know who their givees may be. The intimacy between gift and giver, real though it is in the order of being, may be absent in the orders of knowing and use.

Gifts of the second degree require the physical presence of the giver, or some closely derived product of that physical presence such as the voice over the telephone, the image on the screen, or even the photograph, before the face of the givee. These are gifts of time and presence, whose mark is that when you give them you are keeping company with their givees. Not all such company-keeping is a transfer under the sign of gift: your time with your colleagues at work is in part contractual, and therefore a transfer under the sign of obligation. But some approaches a nonobliging and nonobligatory transfer, as when you give your time with delight to your friends and family. These gifts are more intimate than gifts of the first degree because they can only be given when the giver is present; but they are less intimate because what is given does not belong to the very body of the giver.

Gifts of the third degree are transfers of goods that you, the giver, have made. These goods are the works of your hands or of your mind, and bringing them into being requires that you intentionally shape the things of the world. Most such works take corporeal form even when they are not exhaustively accountable in terms of matter. The architect's design for a house or the entrepreneur's business plan for a new corporation belong in part to the realm of thought and imagination, and are therefore incorporeal. But they will usually take physical form (the blueprint, the written plan), and in order to be transferred as gifts to others they must necessarily do so, even if only as spoken word or movement of the body. Gifts of your own making have a certain degree of intimacy with you, their maker. They bear the signature of your style, which in part identifies the kind of creature who made this, the kind of creature whose work shaped it from materials to hand or in mind: human makings are different in style and signature from those of birds or mice or ants, and any work of yours or mine will show this difference to those who know how to read it. But your style-signature may also identify not only the species to which you who made this gift belong, but also you yourself in your individuality and particularity. Sometimes the style-signature that identifies the kind of creature who made this will be important: what counts about your gift (the chair, the house, the garden, the poem) may be, from the viewpoint of the givee, that it was made and given by a human being, that giver and givee are of the same kind. It may be neither possible nor desirable to know more about the maker and giver than that. Monuments from the past are often like this. When I go to look at the stupa of Borobudur in Java, or at Durham Cathedral in England, the principal thing of importance about the givers of these gifts is not their names and genders and histories, but rather the fact that they, like you and I, were human, returning God's gifts to him in praise and thanksgiving. (I do not of course mean that this is what they thought they were doing—it may or may not have been—but only that it is what they were doing.) But sometimes, the identity of the maker is very important to the giving and receiving of gift. If your lover or spouse or child gives you a gift of their own making, this will be significant to you in large part because of the individual identity of the giver, not just because the giver shares a species with you.

The signature of style that belongs to the works of your hands and mind may sometimes serve to identify you as the maker. That literary style, that brushwork, that way of playing Bach—these may be enough, at least to the cognoscenti, to identify you and only you as the maker. But more often not. Your makings may be seamlessly combined with those of many others, as when a painting is worked on by many hands in a studio, when a committee issues a cowritten document, or when you contribute as a line worker to the making of a product to which dozens or hundreds of others have also contributed. In these cases, the signature of style that belongs to you may be evident only as much as is a drop of salt water in an ocean. Nonetheless, it will be present, and when a gift is given which is of your making, in part or in whole, the degree of intimacy it bears to you will be indexed to the extent to which your style-signature underwrites and informs it.

Gifts of the fourth degree, those least intimate with their givers, are all the rest, every other good that can be transferred. Most often, these will be corporeal objects, and they will be independent of the giver's body, they will not require the giver to keep company with the givee, and they will be neither the works of his hands or his mind. A gift of a box of chocolates from you to your employee is like this, as are the flowers given on Valentine's Day or the toys and trinkets exchanged at Christmas. These are, or may be, nonetheless gifts, but they are relatively distant from the giver, and ordinarily this distance will be reflected in the attitudes adopted toward such gifts by their givees.

Gifts, then, serve as signs of the kind to which their givers belong, and sometimes as signs of the individual identity of their giver. The degree to which a particular gift is a sign of either will depend largely upon the degree of intimacy the gift bears to its giver. Gifts of the fourth degree may communicate little or nothing of the individual identity of their giver, and perhaps not very much about the kind to which the giver belongs. This last claim may seem surprising, but remember that gifts can be given by corporate entities as well as individual ones. A company through which I make most of my travel reservations occasionally sends me small tokens of its esteem because I make quite a large number of such reservations. But clearly, whatever response is appropriate to such transfers of goods, it does not include the thought that I have been given anything by a human being. And even in cases where the gift given is intimate with the giver and does therefore reveal something of the giver's nature and identity, it

What about the widow's mite?

may nonetheless be the case that the givee is not in a position to know what the gift in fact shows about its giver. There is, in this case as often, a rift between the order of being and the order of knowing: the blood you receive in a transfusion identifies with perfect precision the identity of its giver through the genetic signature it bears, but you are unlikely to be in a position to identify the relevant information; the style-signature of a particular painting may identify it as a Zurbarán, but you may be too ignorant to know this; and the world may bear the style-signature of the one who spoke it into being out of nothing, but it does not follow that all who inhabit the world will recognize that it was made by its maker, even if it is the case that all should.

∾

These remarks about the relations that gifts may bear to their givers in the human sphere serve to prepare consideration of the relation that the cosmos as gift of God bears to its giver. It is not that the analysis I have provided of human givers and their gifts can be applied straightforwardly and without remainder or difference to a depiction of the relation that God as giver bears to the cosmos as gift. God is, in essential and fundamental ways, not like us, and this means that his givings and gifts are in essential and fundamental ways not like ours. Christians certainly must think of God as giver, the cosmos as God's gift, and we humans as recipients of that gift: this is language deeply woven into the fabric of both Scripture and tradition. But how best to think of God in these terms is not given by Scripture or authoritative, magisterial tradition: what Scripture delivers on this matter is largely poetry and figure, not concept and definition, for which we should be grateful; and although Christian thinkers have speculated a great deal about the best way of applying the term "giver" to God and of understanding the cosmos as his gift, there is no unanimity among them about this and no precise, magisterial formulations.

What we must do, in such a situation—when we are recipients of ways of speaking about God that we cannot abandon and remain

Christian, and recipients also of a variety of speculation about how best to understand and develop this language—is to deploy some ordinary rules of thought about the things of God. Most prominent among these is that when we want to develop the precision and abstraction of our understanding of one or another of God's attributes—his wisdom, say, or his goodness; or in this case his gifts and givings—then we must begin from what we know of gifts and givings among ourselves, this knowledge itself already informed by what we make of what the tradition has yielded us on these matters, and must ascend from that understanding by removing from it anything that on other grounds we judge inappropriate to say or think of God, and by maximizing within the limits of coherence those things we do think it appropriate to say and think of God. Even when we Christians do this we should do it with deep epistemic modesty: we are likely to be wrong, to arrive at concepts that appear more adequate than they are for an understanding of God's nature; and we are still more likely to obscure this likelihood of error from ourselves because we want so badly to have adequate concepts at our disposal. Thinking analogically about God's being is more difficult than any other intellectual enterprise: we grope, we fail, and our failures are magnified by our unwillingness to recognize the depth and scope of what we do not know and of the errors in whose truth we have confidence. The remarks that follow should be understood in this light.

A transfer of goods under the sign of gift is, ideal-typically, a nonobliging, noncalculative, entreaty-laden giving of inexhaustible goods from giver to givee. Transfers of goods among us can only approximate this, but God's gift of the world is the archetype from which and by partial participation in which our gifts of blood and alms and selves can arrive at such approximation as is possible for us. The various degrees of intimacy with which we are related to what we give are also approximations of and partial participations in God's intimacy with what he gives. Formally, this much at least can be said. The cosmos is something other than God. It is not a part or constituent of God (God is partless, without constituents), and therefore God's gift of the cosmos is in this fundamental respect not like our gifts of our body parts to one another. That kind of intimate relation to gift is possible for God only in the self-giving that constitutes God's triune life, and that is a topic beyond my scope here, other than to say that when we give ourselves to one another we are participating in God's self-gift as triune and as incarnate. But these analogies will mislead if they suggest to us that the cosmos is God's body and that its parts or constituents bear a relation to him formally similar to the relation that your body parts bear to you or mine to me.

This is not to say that the analogy to our gifts of blood or semen or eggs is in every way inappropriate for understanding God's gift of the cosmos. The fact that God was not limited or constrained by anything external to himself in bringing the cosmos into being is illuminated in some small degree by the peculiar intimacy of the relation between my body parts and me. There is no gap or external constraint between my intending to give blood and the nature of what I give. My blood is what it is because I am what I am, and in this limited sense, the analogy applies: the cosmos in whole and in its parts is what it is because God is what God is. There is nothing else, nothing external to God (with the caveats to be entered in a moment) capable of intervening between God and his gift of the cosmos; in something like the same way that there is nothing that does or can come between me and my making of blood. Your blood inevitably bears the style-signature of your DNA because of this unmediated intimacy between it and you, and similarly the cosmos bears the style-signature of God because of his unmediated intimacy with it.

The difference lies in freedom: you and I have nothing to say about whether our bodies make blood, while God was free to create or not to create the cosmos. This explains why God could and did judge his work of creation to be very good, a judgment given depth if framed by acknowledgment that what was done need not have been done. We do not ordinarily judge our making of blood to be a good work in this way (though we will lament, usually, if we sustain damage in such a way that we cease to be able to do it). But just as our bodily natures mean that when we make blood we must make the kind of blood we make (you would lose a property as essential to you as being human should you lose the property of making the blood you in fact make), so, also, God's nature means that when he makes the cosmos he must make the kind of cosmos he makes, a cosmos of great and radiant beauty, fully participatory according to its kind in the nature of its maker and giver.

It is consideration of our gifts of the third degree—the works of our hands and mind—that, if the account of them is appropriately purified and developed, helps us most to understand the sense in which the world as a whole and in its parts is God's gift. When we make things by reordering constituents of the world, we in part recapitulate God's work of creation. The qualification "in part" is necessary principally because our makings, unlike God's act of creation, require something we have not made that we can work on. This means that there will always be something about our makings independent of and prior to our work of shaping and forming, something that because of this priority and independence does not bear our style-signature. But in God's case, because everything made by him is made out of nothing, there is and can be nothing recalcitrant to or obstructive of his intentions as maker, nothing that does or can fail to bear his style-signature as its maker. Things made *ex nihilo* are transparent to the intentions of their maker. They can do nothing other than bear the style-signature of that maker to the degree proper to their kind: both what they are and that they are is accountable exhaustively by appeal to the intentions of their maker.

Our makings fail in other ways impossible for God and God's makings. We can fail to make what we intend to make, perhaps because our understanding of what can be made is flawed or because we lack the skill to make it. Were I to design and attempt to build a house the result would fail in both ways because of that lack. But we may also fail even when our understanding and skill is what it should be, as when a skilled architect is distracted or drunk or ill and fails thereby to notice a flaw in his blueprint that in an unimpaired state he would have noticed and corrected. You and I can also make malevolently, which is to say that we can attempt to reduce or bring to nothing a good the world contains, and in so doing make the world as a whole less than it would otherwise have been and less than it should be. Failings of this sort are impossible for God in his making: he makes just what he intends to make just as he intends to make it and does so always with maximal benevolence, with the result that the cosmos as a whole was, when God made it from nothing, a perfect witness to God's intentions as maker. Each of its particulars was fully transparent to his purposeful will, the bearer, to the extent possible for its kind, of his image.

Consideration of our gifts of the fourth degree is the least illuminating. Gifts such as this are in every significant way not possible for God. Gifts of this sort, recall, are those given by one who is not their maker; when you give a gift of this sort, you have not participated in its making, and its transfer to your givee does not require that you keep company with her. God cannot give like this. He participates in all makings—or, better put, all makings, whether ours or those of other creatures—participate in his and in him, and he can never be sufficiently distant from us that he ceases to keep company with us. God keeps company even with the damned, if there are any. They have withdrawn themselves from him, not he from them, and so long as they are capable of penitently asking that the distance between him and them be bridged, he will respond affirmatively. But none of this is true for us. Our givings of the fourth degree are so distant from God's, so remotely unlike his, that they scarcely participate in them and are scarcely worthy of the name 'gift' at all. They are, almost without exception, transfers under the sign of obligation rather than under the sign of gift.

In the order of being, then, the cosmos and its constituents are without remainder divine gift. Because they had no existence before God's calling of them into being—which is the first gift, the gift of creation—there is and can be nothing at all about them that is not gift. This in turn means that neither the cosmos nor its constituents explain themselves. They are not founded upon themselves, and no particular—no dog, no tree, no rock, no person, no galaxy, no number—is exhaustively explicable or comprehensible in terms of itself or in terms of its relations to any other set of particulars in the cosmos. I have, as I write these words, a five-year-old husky bitch named Anna lying at my feet. Her existence is not exhaustively explicable by the existence of her parents and their acts, or by the existence of all the huskies and all the dogs and all the mammals and all the particulars there have been in the cosmos prior to her conception in the womb of her mother early in 2001. Appeal to these things is relevant to understanding that and how Anna is, but it will not provide a complete account. Anna, too, is divine gift, which means at least that she participates according to her kind in the divine giver without whom she would not have come into being in the first place and without whom she could not now continue to be. The same is true, with appropriate changes, for every other particular in the world, as well as for the world itself.

But this is a negative thesis, claiming only that neither the cosmos nor its constituents are self-founding or self-sustaining. It must be supplemented by its positive correlate, which is that the cosmos and everything in it participates intimately with its giver: it is, from beginning to end, saturated with God's glory, radiant with God's light, made beautiful by God's caress, given to its givees with entreaty to see it and to rejoice in it for what it is.

The preceding paragraph describes the world of light. This is the real world, the world of particulars transparent to God as maker and giver, ordered to one another and to God in such a way as to ravish those like ourselves capable of seeing things as what they are, in such a way as to dazzle us with their beauty and to serve for us as saturatedly iconic images of God's presence. But the real world is, as we have seen, not without remainder the world of light. God's beautiful gift is deeply damaged, and the signs of that damage are everywhere. Death and violence are the two principal signs of this damage, though not the only ones. This fact of damage, and its depth, means that the image of God in the cosmos has been shattered. It is now the vestige, the trace, hard to discern, insubstantial: the fabric of being from which God wove the cosmos is now tattered, almost shredded, by the threads of nonbeing woven throughout it. Were the image's trace finally to be removed, there would be no cosmos to know and no knowers: the trace is what sustains things in being to the extent that they remain so. But the trace can become very tenuous. And this, while it is a claim in the order of being, a claim about how things are, has deep effects upon how knowledge of a world so damaged should be sought and how it may be found.

The world has been given as knowable and beautiful gift. Its shattering does not remove its character as gift. But we, its potential knowers, are also damaged, as is a child who consistently throws the gifts of its loving parents back in their faces or, worse, hugs their gifts to itself as though they were its right and it their owner. This damages what is given, but the child who does it denies its nature as well as the nature of what is given, and thus damages itself as well as the gifts it refuses. The seeking of knowledge, which involves the reformation of the appetite for knowledge away from its own characteristic forms of damage, thus becomes more difficult than it would be were damage to have occurred only to what is knowable and not also to its knowers.

6

PARTICIPATION

Nos quoque per eius gratiam facti sumus quod non eramus, id est filii Dei:
sed tamen aliquid eramus, et hoc ipsum aliquid multo inferius, hoc est filii
hominum. Descendit ergo ille ut nos ascenderemus, et manens in natura
sua factus est particeps naturae nostrae, ut nos manentes in natura nos-
tra efficeremur participes naturae ipsius. Non tamen sic: nam illum natu-
rae nostrae participatio non fecit deteriorem; nos autem facit naturae illius
participatio meliores.

For we too have been made by his grace something we were not: that
is, children of God. However, we were something previously, something very much inferior: that is, children of men. Therefore, he de-
scended that we might ascend: remaining in his nature he became a
participant in ours, so that we, remaining in our nature, might become participants in his. It was not, however, that participation in
our nature made him worse; but participation in his nature makes
us better.

⁓

Here Augustine, in a late letter (*Epistola* 140.4.10) to Honora-
tus on the subject of grace, provides a brief statement of the
grammar of participation. The graceful gift of God, he says
makes of us what without it we could not be, which is to say
filii Dei, God's children. Without the gift, we were only *filii*
hominum, children of men. God did this by becoming a *par-*

ticeps, a participator in or partaker of, our nature, which is to say of human nature, with the result that we then became participators in, partakers of, his nature, which is to say divine nature. The two-way nature of the participation-relation is thus established. Augustine then points out the asymmetry of the relation by saying that God's participation in the human *non fecit deteriorem,* brought about no deterioriation (and thus no alteration) in him; but our participation in God improves us, *nos facit meliores.*

～

To think of the world as damaged gift is an important first step in understanding how things are. It can be given more precision—and certainly more conceptual elegance—by specifying more exactly what it means for a creature to act as gift. Doing this will begin to move the discussion from being—how the world is—toward the rational creature's knowing response to the world, which is the principal topic of this book. The essential concept in building this bridge is that of participation: to exist as a creature is also, and more precisely, to exist as a participant in God. To exist as a knowing creature, as we do, is to participate in God in a peculiarly full and intimate way. It is to bear the divine image and likeness. And to perform the act of knowing is to attain a participatory intimacy in what is known.

But how is all this to be understood? First, as always, in terms of theology: participation is a concept meant in large part to elucidate the relation between God and world, which is to say, between God and all that is not God. The idea of participation belongs to and helps to elucidate the fundamental grammar of Christian thought about that relation. The first syntactical principle of this grammar is that God is not one being in the world over against other beings and is not one agent in the world over against other agents and is not one good in the world over against other goods. From these denials, and from others formally like them, it follows that God's being, agency, and goodness do not compete with the being, agency, and goodness of others. Only things of the same kind can compete with one another: corporeal beings for space (my body and yours can't occupy the same space at the same time), temporal beings for time (if you have my full attention now, someone else would have to compete with you to get some of it), and, most generally, finite beings for resources of which there is a finite quantity (nations for oil, plants for water in a dry climate, baseball players for the career homerun record, authors for having written the best book on Buddhist philosophy to have been published in 1986). But beings whose kind means that they do not and cannot have properties of a certain sort cannot compete for properties of that sort with creatures able to have them. Neither you nor I can compete with the number ninety-seven for anything, and certainly not for being the highest prime number under one hundred.

In similar fashion, where God is or acts, the existence and action of others is not thereby diminished or displaced. The relation is noncompetitive. Neither my agency nor yours is reduced by the fact that God is the one who made both of us as agents, who sustains each of us in being from moment to moment, and is thus implicated causally in every action we perform. This is because the correct category to use to describe the noncompetitive relation our agency (and our existence, and our goodness) bears to God's is that of participation; and this category, when rightly understood, shows that participants and what they participate in neither exclude one another nor compete with one another. Participation is therefore a peculiar relation: its virtue is to permit you to partake of (to share in) some quality or property not proper to your own nature—a quality you would not possess were you not to gain it by participation, and which therefore comes, ideal-typically at least, from what and where you are not, as gift. Your freedom to act as you choose is like this. It is a participated freedom, which means that it is yours but is not from you; you may and do exercise it, but when you do, it is, again, not as yours but as gift. That it is gift does not, however, mean that you are less free than you would have been were your freedom not participated, not given. It simply means this is the kind of freedom you have. Participation, then, is a concept developed to explain what it means to be a creature.

The account just given does not resolve, and is not intended to resolve, properly disputable questions about how best to describe human freedom. Neither does it commit me to any particular theoretical understanding of how best to describe the causal relations between human and divine action. What it does do is place some constraints upon accounts of either topic of they are to remain accounts of God's (rather than some particular being's) relations to human freedom and human action. If, for instance, an account of human freedom is couched in terms of an understanding of God's agency and ours as possibly or actually competitive—even if it is concerned to show how such competition can be construed in such a way as to avoid determinism, or in some other fashion to preserve the possibility of human freedom, which is essential to Christian orthodoxy—then it is on the wrong track to begin with. And since a very large proportion of contemporary discussions of these matters is couched in such terms, the constraint placed by beginning with the idea of participation is in fact quite strong.

More formally and precisely: participation names a relation between a participant and a participated. If x participates in y, then x receives or takes part (*partem accipere, partem capere*) of or in y. This means that y is participated in, which is to say gives part (*partem dare*) of itself to x—though "part" need not be interpreted here corporeally. The verbal adjective "participated" then marks what is taken from y by x, and, equivalently, what is given by y to x; it may also be used by extension to label y as participated in by x. The term "participation" therefore marks a two-way asymmetrical relation, which can be formulated in either direction depending on whether the emphasis lies on x's taking and receiving, or on y's giving and granting. It is, further, a noncompetitive relation: neither x nor y is diminished by entering into this relation, though x will be increased or added to by it.

The fundamental case of participation, to which all other instances analogically approximate and from which they are all derived, is the example of being, gifted to everything that is not God as participation in God. You (and I and all of us and everything there is) participate in God exactly to the extent that we exist at all. The bare fact of your existence—not yet the kind of thing you are, which is to say human, but just that you are at all—is given you by your participation in God. You swim in the ocean of God's being like a mackerel in the Atlantic; and just as the mackerel dies if taken from the Atlantic, so you cease to be if taken from the ocean of God's being. But your participation in God is radical in a way that the mackerel's in the Atlantic is not and cannot be: the Atlantic, or something like it, is necessary for the mackerel's continued life, certainly, but is not responsible for the mackerel's coming-to-be, nor for its being the kind of thing it is. God is responsible for all these, and you, as participant in God, therefore accept participated existence from God to the extent that you exist. Also, God is participated in by you in the sense that he gives (*partem dare,* recall) to you the gift of being, which is to say that he gives you to yourself by donating himself. There is much more to say about you than this, of course; but this will suffice to apply the logic of participation to the question of your existence.

For you to be at all, therefore, is for you to participate in God, as is true of all creatures. This idea specifies the fundamental Christian distinction, which is that between God and creatures, and it does so in a way that holds together a profound intimacy between God and creatures, an intimacy of which that between lovers is a distant, participated shadow, with an equally profound difference and distance between them. God is *interior intimo tuo,* interior to what is most intimate to you; but God is also vastly and immeasurably different, other, and superior to what is most exaltedly yours. When you know yourself to be confronted and addressed by God, then, it is proper to respond with an inseparable mixture of grateful rejoicing and agonized penitence.

You know yourself simultaneously to be a bearer of the image and likeness and therefore an intimate participant in God, and one who is distant from God both because of essential ontological difference and because of adventitious damage.

Thinking about these intimacies and distances provokes figures: we swim in the ocean of God's being, are translucent to his radiance, vibrate to his speech, are wrapped in his caress; but also we are shattered images, exiles from Eden, poor creatures, hungry ghosts ravenously wandering the desert, cloaked in the attempt to own and control ourselves, shrouded in the grave clothes of complacency. These are phrases that flow easily from fingers to keyboard, but they resist imaginative apprehension at least as much as do the prima facie paradoxes of set theory and the imbricated intricacies surrounding the idea of infinity. Nonetheless, using participation as the fundamental concept for specification of the ontological difference, the difference, that is, more significant than which there is none, between God and what is not God, between creator and creatures, means that those who wish to think as Christians can abandon neither the figures for intimacy nor those for difference.

Participation is not, however, the only figure that Christians have developed to illuminate the difference between God and creatures. Two (at least) kinds of objection to this figure have been mooted by Christians (many more by pagans, but with those I am not at the moment concerned), all of whom agree, as they must, that there is a difference and that it is essential to figure it, but who prefer other figures.

Some have jettisoned participation altogether, and have substituted for it the machinery of existential quantification and the modalities of necessity and possibility. According to this machinery, to say of any particular that it exists is to say that there is something such that it is an x—let's say you, or the oak tree in the quadrangle, or the number seven, or the unicorn laying its head in the maiden's lap (and thus figuring Christ), or the prodigal son's father, or . . . . It is then a further task to say in detail just what the particular in question is. In your case, this would be done by specifying the kind of thing you are (a human being), and then the particular properties that differentiate you from other members of your kind (having been born to particular parents at a particular time, having a particular DNA signature, and so on), and then, if appropriate, the mode or kind of being you have, which in your case is that of contingency, which is to say that you might not have been—had, for instance, your parents never met or made other choices, or had a cosmos with humans in it never been brought into existence.

The same account, formally, is given, by those who like this way of talking, of God's existence. God, too, is treated like a particular subjected to the existential quantifier (there is an x such that x is God), and then differentiated from other particulars by listing his particular properties (perhaps "creator of all that is," "the one who is maximally wise," "the one who is maximally good," and so on), and by specifying his mode of existence, which, it might be said, is necessary rather than merely possible, which is to say that it is not coherently conceivable that God might not have been. In these ways, the difference between God and creatures is established and spoken of by those who eschew talk of participation and think that all that needs to be said about the ontological difference can be said with the machinery of existential quantification and the distinction between necessity and possibility. And then, in order to specify the distinction between God, construed in this way, and creatures, it will be said that the difference has two aspects. The first is that God exists necessarily while creatures exist contingently; and the second is that creatures were created, brought into being, by God, which is to say that God's existence and action provides the necessary and sufficient conditions for the existence of any creature in particular, and for all of them together (though not, of course, for all the properties that individuate them one from another).

There are some difficulties here, difficulties that lead those who prefer this as a way of talking about God's existence and his relation to what is other than himself almost irresistibly to a kind of idolatry, that is, to a substitution for the thought of God the thought of something else, something lesser, something altogether too much like a creature. The first such difficulty is that existential quantification as a means of stating what it is for something (anything) to be provides an account of that matter which is applicable identically and indiscriminately to God and creatures. It is an account whose grammar (and it is primarily a grammatical account, a depiction of the syntax and semantics of existence-talk) suggests, even if it does not quite imply, an understanding of being, of what it is to be, arrived at independently of thinking about God, given form independently of reference to God, and then applied univocally to creatures and God. On such a view, your existence and mine, together with that of all creatures and God, their creator, is of the same sort: we each belong to a kind and are individuated from other members of that kind by a list of our unique properties. God, for Christians, will on this view be the only member of his kind, but he is not alone in that: there was once a first and only human, once a last and only dodo, and now a one and only cosmos. And if it is possible that there be other members of that kind, other gods, they are differentiated from the one who counts, YHWH, by a different set of particular properties. He is the God of Abraham, Isaac, Jacob, and Jesus; Krishna, by contrast, is the consort of Radha and the slayer of Hanuman; Zeus is the one who sends lightning-bolts from Olympus and, swan-like, deflowers Leda; Superman is the one who can leap tall buildings at a single bound and outrun speeding locomotives. Scripture often writes in this way—not of course about Krishna or Zeus or Superman, but as though YHWH, the Lord, might be a member of a kind. He is, after all the *deus magnus super omnes deos*; and it is beyond dispute that the Hebrew (plural) noun *elohim*, rendered *theos* in Greek, *deus* in Latin, and *god* in English, is a kind-term, a sortal that does or could indicate a set with more than one member. In this it is un-like the Hebrew term for the divine name, YHWH (*Kurios, Dominus, Lord*), which, being a name, does not place its bearer into a kind by suggesting that there might be other bearers of it.

None of this means that Scripture should be read to suggest that there are many gods, or that the machinery of existential quantification is the best way to talk and think about God's existence. It is meant to suggest that if you do think and talk about God's existence in this way, you will have an affinity for the confused task of trying to differentiate God from other beings in the world by listing and defining his particular properties. According to this view, what differentiates YHWH, the god, from Superman the (quasi)-god, is particular properties. Superman is vulnerable to kryptonite; YHWH is not. YHWH became incarnate as Jesus the Christ; Superman did not. Superman loved Lois Lane; YHWH chose the people of Israel. And so on. All this is both blasphemous and ridiculous, but it is what you will be drawn to if you think about God's existence in terms of existential quantification. Such thinking is unlikely to be about God. It will be about William Blake's Old Nobodaddy, about a being among beings in the world. It will be, in short, idolatrous rather than theological. Such thinking is also, probably, what most Christians (and, I suppose, most Jews and Muslims) engage in when they think about God. It is a deep and seductive temptation.

You may think that when existential quantification is combined with the idea that God exists not contingently but necessarily, and with the idea that he is the creator of all that is without whom there would be nothing other than himself, the criticisms of the preceding paragraph have less bite. Don't these claims, fundamental to Christian doctrine as they are, remove God from the status of one more being among beings, and give him a status neither possibly nor (therefore) actually possessed by any being other than God? Won't those moves ensure that we are talking and thinking about YHWH, and not some

Superman- or Zeus-like entity? And won't they do so without requiring the ontological mystifications of the doctrine of participation?

Well, they may. But if they do, it is because when pressed they tend exactly in the direction of participation. Creatures, if they have been brought into being out of nothing, certainly are profoundly contingent, which is in part to say that they hover always upon the edge of the nonbeing from which they came. To say that their creator's being is necessary while theirs is contingent is a step in the right direction, and is certainly not wrong. But so saying sets thought about God's being on a track whose end is the idea of participation, for if there is just one necessary being, YHWH, whose existence logically, definitionally, and actually precedes the being of every creature, severally and conjointly contingent as they are and must be, then it is certainly natural and perhaps inevitable to ask for a further specification of the relation between God and creatures, and to ask that any such specification should begin with God and not with creatures. And if this is done, participation is the unavoidable result because this idea, and this idea alone, succeeds in specifying what it means for you and me to be in terms of what it means for God to be. The distinction between contingency and necessity does not yet do this—it begs for it to be done.

Distinguishing God from creatures by appeal to the difference between necessary and contingent existence is, then, not wrong but incomplete. When taken with sufficient seriousness this distinction leads to the view that the being of creatures is best understood in terms of its relation to God's being, and that so understanding it is to arrive at the doctrine of participation, according to which the being of every creature is what it is because of the peculiar extent to which it takes part in the being of God. What it is to be is in this way specified and understood exhaustively in terms of God: ontology is subsumed into theology, and the appeal to the difference between contingency and necessity is completed by arrival at participation. This subsumption and completion is barred, however, by thinking about God's existence in terms of existential quantification, for this way of thinking is closely wedded to an understanding of what it is to be arrived at independently of God and applied univocally to God and creatures. If you think in this way about God, you will be an idolater. Everyone who thinks about God is to some extent an idolater; that is among the noetic effects of the fall. But when it is possible to identify a contaminant that is ingredient or sympathetic to idolatry, and to leach it out of our thought, this is a good thing for Christians to do, or at least to attempt.

There is another drawback to thinking about God in terms of existential quantification and necessity. It is that such thinking does not suggest, and tends to contradict, the intimacy between God and creatures intimated by talk of creaturely participation in God, and, along with it, an understanding of the intrinsic goodness of creatures. If all that you are participates in God's being, which is to say in the illimitable ocean of his goodness, then it follows at once and by entailment, that everything about you is profoundly intimate with God and therefore necessarily and intrinsically good. It is from clear perception of entailments like these that the vast majority of Christians who have given thought to the matter have concluded that evil is and must be an absence, a privation of good, and not some force independent of and opposed to God. Insofar, then, as you are evil, you are not— which is the same as to say that the extent to which you are evil is exactly the extent to which you have ceased to participate in God in the mode proper for your kind. "God" and "being" are exchangeable on this view, from which it follows that "evil" and "nonbeing" must also be. Intimacy with the all-good-one is harder to claim and harder to understand if you eschew the doctrine of participation than if you affirm it. Thinking about God's being under the rubric of necessity and existential quantification makes it all too easy to think of the act of creation as capricious, and certainly makes it opaque to us, an exercise of the divine will without comprehensible reason and perhaps even without any reason other than God's willing of it. If you think in this way, you will likely become blind to the indissoluble intimacy between goodness and being, and their linkage in a bond of beauty. Unseemly and finally incoherent speculations about God's creative responsibility for evil become possible, and may become attractive. And, above all, the relation between God and you tends, if you hold such views, to become externalized, a matter only of will and command from without, of heteronomy in the bad sense, the establishment of dominance and control by someone, some capricious super-fascist, extrinsic to you. This is not Christianity: it is another species of idolatry (a voluntarist species, theologians are likely to say), to which rejection or incomprehension of the idea of participation predisposes.

There is a second and almost opposite kind of Christian objection to the figure of participation. According to it, speaking of the relation between God and creatures in this way is unavoidably wedded to the categories of substance and cause, and since these categories, understood metaphysically as providing access to the order of things, and understood epistemically as providing categories comprehensible and convincing to all rational creatures, have been shown decisively (by Descartes, by Hume, by Kant) to yield aporias and therefore not to be rationally defensible, Christians should not figure God's relation to creatures in this way. This is a complex criticism. Suppose it is true that the post-sixteenth-century European critique of broadly Aristotelean ontology (a term itself not current until the seventeenth century) does yield the result that, the categories of substance and cause (at least) cannot any longer defensibly be used in a systematic ontology. It would then follow that Christians ought not to be using these categories in the service of any such system. But that is not how I use the category of "participation" here. I use it as a figure, one so deeply woven into the fabric of Christian thought about the relation between God and creatures—about, if you prefer, the ontological difference—that it can scarcely be avoided if Christian thought and talk are not to be abandoned. I do not use it as a category in an ontological system. Indeed, among the principal points of using it is to indicate that it is part of the grammar of the Christian account of things to say that no account of what it is for things to be can be given that does not begin and end with God. This is exactly to reject ontological system and to place ontology where it belongs, which is as a part—and always a derived and subsidiary part—of theology. Christians talk about how God is and how creatures are always together and always beginning with God. "Participation" as figure achieves that end, and it does so in considerable part by refusing substantive speculation about the nature and mode of God's being. The figure places a limit on such speculation by directing Christian thought toward the interwoven intimacy with and distance from the creator that characterizes all creaturely being, and most especially that of human beings. And by doing this, it does not fall victim to the elevation of a particular set of categories into an ontological system that captures God and makes an idol of him. It is a figure for God's being as related to ours which is at one and the same time indeterminate and open (when used to figure God's being as participated), and specifically circumscribed (when used to figure the being of creatures, whether as individuals or kinds). The importance of the figure is that it maintains the possibility of the created order disclosing its creator while at the same time banning circumscription of God by the categories of an ontological system. No other figure so effectively maintains these two ways of talking, and for that reason, as well as because speaking of participation does not commit the speaker to the Aristotelean categories as the first or the last Christian word, this second Christian criticism of participation-talk does not require its abandonment.

All participation, finally, is participation of creatures in God, and all creatures, so far as they exist, do so as, and only as, participants in God: without participation, no being. This is true of you and me, of dogs and cats, of lichens and viruses, and of stars and rocks: we all share this formal relation of participation. But, of course, not all these things participate identically in God: they participate to the extent appropriate to their kind, which is to say some more and some less. No creature participates fully in God in the sense that it imitates the exemplar without loss. This is possible only for the mode of participation in the godhead that characterizes the persons of the trinity, a subject that cannot be pursued in this study. Rather than this *imitatio perfecta exemplaris,* there is a diversity of modes of participation in God, and creatures are ordered hierarchically in terms of the degree to which they participate in God—which is the same as to say the degree to which the fullness of what they participate in is limited by their mode of participation. Every participant limits to some degree what it participates in: that fact belongs to the definition of the participation-relation. But not every participant circumscribes what is given to it in participation in the same way or to the same degree.

Consider, in order imaginatively to grasp this, the various modes in which different things participate in the radiant heat of a forge (a traditional example). Iron placed in a forge becomes itself radiantly hot, but its heat does not belong to the definition of what it is to be iron. The heat it has comes without remainder from outside itself— from the forge—which is to say that it is gift, received from without. While the iron is in the forge, the total amount of heat present in the forge does not increase nor decrease. What heat the iron has just is part of the heat the forge has: it generates none of its own. And, the heat the iron has varies only with the heat of the forge so long as it remains there. The forge's increase in heat does not come at the expense of the iron. As the forge gets hotter, so does the iron; as the iron gets hotter, so does the forge. If the iron is removed from the forge, its heat ceases to be participated heat (the donor is now absent) and becomes a rapidly-vanishing property, a property that must vanish because iron can only possess it by participation, and when it is no longer a participant it is no longer hot. But if a piece of glass is placed in the forge, things will be different. If the forge is hot enough, it will melt and disperse, eventually decomposing into its components and ceasing to exist as what it was. It, too, participates in the forge's heat, but does so differently, less fully than does the iron. Other things—wood, human flesh, granite, asbestos, potassium—will render the forge's heat differently by participating in it differently.

This example has its limits, but it may serve to show, imaginatively, how different kinds of thing, different kinds of creature, participate to different extents and in different ways in God, each according to kind and individuality, even though each is, to the extent that it exists as the kind of thing it is and the individual it is, a full participant in God. Creatures participate in God as likenesses (similitudines) of God, but they do so in different degrees and according to their kinds, which is the same as to say that each bears an analogous likeness to God, a likeness arrived at by a particular determinate circumscription of God's being. This circumscription is different in the case of dogs than in the case of azaleas, and different again in the case of one dog (my husky bitch, Anna) and another (the bulldog next door). These limitations of participation in God are according to kind and individual: the limitations of my husky bitch's participation in God are given by, first, the fact that she is a dog, and, second, the fact that she is the particular dog she is, with the particular genetic signature and particular history that make her who she is. These particular circumscriptions are themselves gifts, not problems: they are traceable finally to God's creative act. The fact that there is a harmoniously beautiful cosmos with particular creatures in it requires that there be creatures who participate differently in God, creatures, that is, who participate more or less fully in the ocean of God's being. Anna's limitations, like mine and yours, belong in significant part to the kind of creature she is, and the response of a properly ordered knower to them, so considered, is admiring delight.

But not all determinately limited modes of participation in God's being are intended by God. Some are the result of the fall, and are evidence of the damage to which the harmoniously beautiful cosmos has been subjected. That Anna is a dog is a determinately limited mode of participation of the first sort, to be savored by knowers like us with delight. That she is a killer, one who delights in crunching small living beings in her jaws and savoring their blood as it runs over her tongue (I assume; she does not get the chance to do this, but her behavior often suggests she would like to), is a determinately limited mode of participation of the second sort, an instance of damage. Or so I tentatively think. While it does clearly belong to the grammar of Christian thought to say that there is almost omnipresent damage, best construed as lack, the absence in particular creatures of goods they should have, there is considerable and reasonable dispute among Christians as to what belongs in the category of damage and what does not. I suggest that carnivorousness, together with the blood lust that inevitably acompanies it, is among the evidences of damage. Anna lacks a good she should have, which is harmonious coexistence with all other sentient creatures, a coexistence that ought to include a lack of desire to kill and eat them.

The cosmos, we may speculatively say, as constituted and intended by God, lacked death and thereby lacked a feature now evident almost everywhere in it, which is the dependence of some creatures for their life upon the killing of others. If this is right, then Anna's carnivorousness does not belong to her first, undamaged nature—which is why it is good to say that it is second nature, not first, to dogs to chase small animals with intent to kill. A formally similar account should be offered of the damage to which we humans are subject. Some of it, like Anna's carnivorousness, is handed to us independently of our wishes or actions, as though it were a genetic defect or an infection. Our pride, complacency, violence, fear, and so forth, are like this: we tend toward these by second nature, whether we like it or not; and there is no human being, with the exception of Jesus and his mother, who has not to one degree or another liked it. This is deep and inherited human damage. But for us—and here we are unlike Anna, and even more unlike azaleas and rocks and stars—it is also possible deliberately to twist the damaging knife more deeply into the wounds we have inherited. We do this by using our freedom improperly, as sinners. We can use the same freedom to salve wounds and nurse the damaged back toward wholeness.

But whatever the causes and remedies of damage, the result is always the same: damaged creatures participate in God less fully than they should, and this provides another cause of the differing degrees to which particular creatures participate in God. Not only do the differences in the first natures of particular kinds of creature produce a hierarchy of being, according to which different creatures participate in God differently in accord with their kinds; but this same hierarchy is altered for the worse by differences in the degree and kind of damage with which individuals and kinds have been afflicted. This damage is not restricted to sentient creatures, much less to rational ones. It afflicts the entire cosmos, as Christians should never forget: the cosmos in its entirety groans in anticipation of its salvation to come.

7

APPETITE

. . . quod diligenda sit etiam ipsa dilectio qua diligitur quod diligi oportet; sicut odio habenda est dilectio qua diligitur quod diligi non oportet. Odio quippe habemus concupiscentiam nostram qua caro concupiscit adversus spiritum: et quid est ista concupiscentia, nisi mala dilectio? Et diligimus concupiscentiam nostram qua spiritus concupiscit adversus carnem: et quid est ista concupiscentia, nisi bona dilectio? Cum autem dicitur: Diligenda est, quid aliud dicitur quam, concupiscenda est? Quocirca quoniam recte concupiscuntur iustificationes Dei, recte concupiscitur concupiscentia iustificationum Dei. Hoc enim alio modo sic potest dici: si recte diliguntur iustificationes Dei, recte diligitur dilectio iustificationum Dei. An aliud est concupiscere, aliud desiderare? Non quod non sit concupiscentia desiderium, sed quia non omnis concupiscentia desiderium est. Concupiscuntur enim et quae habentur, et quae non habentur: nam concupiscendo, fruitur homo rebus quas habet; desiderando autem, absentia concupiscit. Desiderium ergo quid est, nisi rerum absentium concupiscentia?

. . . we should love that very love by which we love what we ought love, just as we ought hate the love by which we love what we ought not love. For certainly we hate that yearning of ours by which we yearn for the flesh against the spirit—and what is such yearning if not bad love? And we love that yearning of ours by which the spirit yearns against the flesh—and what is that yearning but good love? For when it is said, "you should love that," what else is meant but that "you should yearn for that"? And because of this, when God's just ways are rightly yearned for, then yearning for God's just ways is rightly yearned for. This can be said otherwise: if God's just ways are rightly loved, then the love of God's just ways is rightly loved. Or is it one thing to yearn and another to desire? It is not that desire is not yearning, but that not all yearning is desire. It is possible to yearn for what you have and for what you do not have. For in yearning you enoy the things you have. But in desiring, you yearn for what is absent. What else is desire, then, than yearning for absent things?

⁓

Augustine, in this part (8.4) of his commentary on the very long Psalm 118 (119 according to the enumeration of most contemporary Bibles), begins by distinguishing between good *dilectio*, here translated "love," and bad: we may have *dilectio* for what we ought to have it for, in which case it is good; but we may also have *dilectio* for what we ought not to have it for, in which case it is bad. Even *concupiscentia*, here translated "yearning," can be good or bad, depending upon whether it seeks the flesh or the spirit. And so, in a striking formulation, *recte concupiscitur concupiscentia iustificationum Dei*—yearning for God's just ways is itself rightly yearned for. Is there, then, he goes on to ask, any distinction between *dilectio* and *concupiscentia*? He answers that question by introducing a third appetite-term: *desiderium,* here translated "desire." Some, but not all yearning is desire: desire is directed only toward what is absent, while yearning is directed both toward what is absent and what is present. Augustine is here playing with words which had not yet been given the degree of technical precision they were later to receive. The importance of this passage—and of many like it in his work—is that in it he depicts a part of the grammar of appetite: that the goodness or badness of appetites is given largely by what they seek rather than by consideration of their phenomenology apart from their objects; and that there is an important distinction between appetite for what is present and appetite for what is absent.

⁓

English has a large and subtle vocabulary for wanting. No doubt every language does: we humans do a lot of wanting and we are usually quite interested in this fact about ourselves. The range and depth of English's lexicon of desire is both cause and effect of this interest. A moment's thought about English gerunds yields: loving, yearning, wishing, ravening, desiring, hungering, thirsting, hoping, and craving. Latin does not do badly, either. Thinking infinitively for a moment yields *desiderare, appetere, amare, concupiscere,* and *velle.* There is no single and inevitable way of sorting this variety: it is possible, for instance, to arrange kinds of wanting according to intensity, duration, object, intimacy with observable action or many other variables. Different classifications and orderings of appetite will be appropriate to different purposes. The depiction here is only of appetite's universal grammar, which is to say of the lexicon and syntax that must be deployed if appetite is to be discussed.

Appetite is a kind of wanting. Wanting, and hence, appetite, belongs only to living things: rocks, galaxies, and oceans want nothing, even if we sometimes speak of them figuratively and anthropomorphically (the hungry sea, the murderous avalanche) as if they did. And while it is more reasonable to say, as we often do, that nonhuman living creatures (dolphins, dogs, angels, oak trees) have appetites, the analysis that follows is concerned only with the appetites we humans have.

Appetite's distinction from other kinds of wanting is given by the kind of thing it wants: common to all instances of appetite is wanting to make a particular absence present, and wanting to do so under a particular description. If all appetites seek the presence of an absence, then loathing and other negative forms of desire fill the bill. Loathing something (academic committee meetings, political stump speeches, cold winds) means wanting to maintain its absence when it is absent, and seeking its absence when it is present. The absence whose presence is sought by those in the grip of loathing or boredom is best characterized negatively: it is, for example, the end of the committee meeting, and, therefore, the blissful beginning of its absence. Loathing and lusting are in this way formally alike, which is to say that both participate in the universal grammar of appetite.

But not all wanting has this form, and so not all wanting is appetitive. It is possible, for instance, to want a particular presence to continue, without at the same time seeking the presence of some absence. This is not appetite: it is instead a form of delight. This means that delight has presences as its objects: those taking delight are enjoying (savoring, caressing, tasting) what is there at the moment of delight. To delight, is not, by definition, to be in the grip of an appetite, for the object of interested is not absent: it is present as an occasion of delight. Wanting to kiss the lips and caress the body of the absent lover is appetite. But when the lover is present, being caressed and kissed, there is delight rather than appetite. Or, the keen observer of a game of chess may be eager to understand the strategy informing white's rather odd opening. That is appetite: the absence whose presence is sought is a kind of understanding. But now, after the fifteenth move, the observer sees the strategy. The pieces of the puzzle fall into place and, with the hairs on the back of her neck rising, she delights in the understanding now present.

This conceptual distinction is clear enough. However, English, along with most other languages, muddies or complicates it delightfully by using many of the same verbs for both appetite and delight. Love, for example, is a verb of both appetite and delight, connoting the former in the absence of the beloved and the latter, and the former in her presence, but always preserving a tincture of both. Much of the lexicon of pleasure and delight is used in this way, both anticipatorily, of an absence, in which case the delight-term is used under the sign of hope; and currently, of a presence, in which case the delight-term refers to what is there, face-to-face. The terms of this pleasure-lexicon are used retrospectively, as well, and when they are, such speech is under the sign of memory, which always involves confabulation. And this is not all. Delight in a presence—in the lover's lips—is inflected always with the sense that this presence sooner or later will again become absent, and that when it does appetite will once more be the mode of relating to it. Delight knows itself always to be close to appetite, and this helps to explain why the definitional separation between the two does not reflect and is not reflected by everyday usage. Nonetheless, the distinction has analytical benefits: appetite wants a particular absence's presence; delight enjoys absences become present and (usually) wishes that presence to continue. My concern here is with appetite, and therefore with absences sought.

Appetites are disquieting, though not all to the same degree. Some, the occasional and low-intensity ones, may do no more than provide a faint and passing sense that some particular presence would be nice. These may be weak enough and transient enough that they are scarcely noticed. As I sit reading it crosses my mind that it would be pleasant if the window were open a little more because then the cooling breeze would be more easily felt; but the appetite vanishes from awareness almost at once, displaced, perhaps, by an especially winsome piece of prose, or dying away without any obvious cause other than its own insignificance. But other appetites are deeply disquieting and long lived, disturbing those who have them so that their lives become ordered around actions designed to indulge and satiate them, to bring the absences they desire to presence. These are high-intensity and high-frequency appetites, single-minded and exclusive of all else like the wolf pack intent on its prey, the thirsty man in search of water, the lover obsessively seeking the lost beloved, or the theurgically inclined mystic intent upon technique for drawing God down to himself. Ravening appetites like these permit no rivals and recognize no obstacles. They may lead those subject to them to prefer painful death to their frustration or abandonment. Some self-appointed martyrs, it seems, have an appetite for death of this sort.

This universal grammar of appetite bears ambiguous relations to that of pleasure. It may seem that, to whatever degree they approach the ravening intensity of the universal wolf, appetites are always and necessarily interwoven with an expectation of pleasure from the absence's desired presence, or at the very least with an expectation that the suffering produced by continued absence will be removed by its presence. And it is certainly true that there is often this connection between appetite and pleasure; this is another reason why the vocabularies of delight and appetite are so intertwined in most languages. But it is a mistake to think that there is always such a connection. Motorists slow down as they pass the wreckage of a highway accident. Their gaze is drawn to the twisted metal and to what they hope will be the bloody corpses. But is that what they hope for? Not exactly. Such a vision is certainly what they have an appetite for, but the appetite is intimately linked with a judgment that its satisfaction will not be pleasurable. This judgment does not prevent the appetite's indulgence, though the tension in the neck muscles produced by looking while wishing not to look shows both the conflict between judgment and appetite and the conflict between two different appetites.

These examples sever the connection between appetite and the expectation of delight. It is certainly common, and perhaps close to universal, to have appetites whose satisfaction seems likely to those who have them to be inextricably admixed with pain; and such a seeming need not, and usually does not, remove or decrease in intensity the appetite with which it has to do. Much more common—too common to need examples—are appetites for a presence in which it is anticipated that pleasure will be taken, but which in fact produces only disappointment and regret.

∾

Typically, someone in the grip of an appetite seeks not only to make some absence present, but to do so under a particular description, to speak linguistically, or with a particular understanding, to speak cognitively. This complex whole—the desired absence understood in a particular fashion, described in a particular way—is an appetite's intentional object: it is what those who have appetites intend, what their appetites are about. One way of classifying and ordering appetites is according to such objects, whether at a high level of abstraction (there are appetites for food, for sex, for power, for knowledge), or at a lower: appetite for sex with a particular person may be at the service of sensual pleasure and nothing more; or of affection and desire for the partner; or of the establishment of dominance over the partner; or of many other things. As these examples suggest, appetites often, perhaps usually, have complex objects: it is likely that in any particular case of appetite for sex with a particular partner, more than one of the intentional objects just mentioned is at play. In such cases, and they are the ordinary cases, anything approaching an accurate characterization of appetite will need the skills of a good novelist or a virtuoso phenomenologist.

All appetites, therefore, seek not only the presence of some absence, but also that presence under some understanding or description, which is ordinarily, but not invariably, to say for some purpose. This may seem to imply the dubious claim that all those who have an appetite know and could say which appetite they are in the grip of—could, that is, specify the understanding with which they seek the presence of the relevant absence. This might seem to follow because if all appetites involve understandings of the absent presence they seek, this might be taken to mean that whenever there is an appetite it is accompanied by a formulated understanding of what is wanted and why it is wanted. But in fact, the claim that all appetites come with understandings of what is sought does not imply that those understandings are actively present to the mind of the appetite's subject at all the moments in which the appetite is in play. The appetite's subject may, as she reaches for the succulent slice of pineapple she wants in order to slake her thirst and satisfy her desire for sweetness on the tongue, have nothing much at all present to her mind—no more, perhaps, than a generalized anticipation of pleasure coupled with the physical signs that accompany such anticipations. And perhaps not even that.

In such cases, and they are many, there is no occurrent knowledge of an appetite's object on the part of its subject. But even when this is so, there may still be dispositional knowledge. That is, the person reaching for the pineapple slice may be disposed, given the appropriate circumstances and the right stimuli, to say "I want this pineapple to slake my thirst," and thereby to identify the appetite's intentional object to at least a first approximation. Those circumstances are perhaps not likely to arise; but they could, and if they did, those with dispositional knowledge would respond appropriately.

But even this will not account for all cases. Some humans have appetites, even intense, long-lived, and repeated ones, and yet have neither dispositional nor occurrent understandings of what their appetites intend. This is true, for example, of infants. They seek the breast's milk, and the mother's warmth, and the light, with a dedicated eagerness. But, it seems reasonable to say, they neither do nor can formulate understandings of what they seek. What sense can be given to the claim that their appetites have intentional objects? Only this: that rational observers of their behavior attribute to them just such understandings: "She's hungry," we say, "that's why she's crying"; or, "She's wet, that's why she's crying." We can sometimes test these claims by bringing the crying baby into the presence we take her to be seeking. If we are right, she looks happy and stops crying; if not, we try something else until we get it right, or until we acknowledge that we have no more ideas, and therefore cannot understand what her appetite intends. But even in that case we do not abandon the idea that there is something she wants and that there is something she wants it for; we just give up the attempt to discover it. An ideal observer, not subject to our limitations, would know what the baby's appetites intend.

Many of us are likely to attribute appetites with intentional objects to members of species other than the human on much the same behavioral grounds that we attribute them to infants. In the case of our horses and dogs and cats (and even our plants) we can devise behavioral tests of different theories as to what they want—more water? less direct sun? a scratch between the ears?—and find some of our theories confirmed and others disconfirmed. But it is unwise to take seriously the fact that we talk in this way. In the case of living beings which neither do nor can formulate understandings (plants, say), it is better to think that when we speak of them having appetites, we are doing so at best analogically and perhaps even equivocally. A green plant has appetites in just about the same sense that a thermostat has beliefs. In both cases, there is behavior in response to stimuli, and outside the realms of poetry and fantasy, it is better to say so and to avoid attributing understandings. The case of the infant is different because it belongs to a species disposed by definition to come to have understandings of its appetites (as of much else), and so it can reasonably be assimilated to adult human beings on this question rather than to oak trees or Siamese cats. But not much hinges for the purposes of this study on where the boundary between rational (capable of formulating understandings) and nonrational (not so capable) beings is drawn. Neither does much hinge upon whether there are instances of wanting free from understandings on the part of those who want, though I think it reasonable to say that there are not. The point of importance is that it belongs to the definition of appetite to imply an understanding or understandings of the absence whose presence it seeks.

To offer a characterization of an appetite's intentional object is also to imply a description of what makes it desirable. Such a description is what is typically offered in response to the question "why do you want that?" In the case of the pineapple, such a question is unlikely to be asked because it will seem obvious to observers of pineapple seekers' actions why they seek what they seek. The question will not arise. But in the case of many appetite-motivated actions—pillar sitting (think of Simeon Stylites), book writing, political-office seeking—such questions do arise, and when they do, they are best answered by offering a description of what it is about the activity in question that makes it desirable.

On this view, the question about an appetite's intentional object always has an answer, or, more likely, a range of answers. The question why, when addressed to someone in the grip of an appetite, is always in principle answerable, even if the person in question will not or cannot answer it. If it were not answerable, then appetite would be a surd, insulated from any kind of analysis other than the causal, and certainly from normative questioning. That position assimilates human appetites to the quasi-appetites of plants or the figurative appetites of oceans. Were there human appetites of this sort, the only answer to the question "why do you want that?" would be "I just do," an answer that if further pressed could yield only a causal story of a physiological or catechetical sort. That is, "I just do," might mean, "This appetite is an ineradicable feature of me given by my genetically determined physiology," like having, or once having had, an appendix; or, "This appetite is an ineradicable feature of me given by my particular local history," like speaking English natively. Appetites are subject to such causal explanations, of course; but any feature of a human person capable of being exhaustively explained causally would, by definition, not be an appetite. It would, that is, not be a wanting to make an absence present under a particular understanding. Features of persons of that sort cannot be exhaustively explained by appeal to the causes that brought them into being, as our ordinary ways of thinking and talking about them abundantly show. We think of appetites as implicated with understandings, as good and bad, as capable of being brought into being by catechesis and effort, and as capable of being removed in the same way. All these ways of thinking and speaking would have to be purged as instances of folk psychology were it the case that every instance of wanting to make an absence present could be talked about only in terms of how, causally, it came to be what it is. This, could it be done, would be a deep impoverishment of language and thought; fortunately, it cannot be done, not even by those who say they would like to. To attempt it is to leave behind the universal grammar of appetite by changing the subject.

Seeing appetites as implicated with understandings of what they seek, and with understandings of why what they seek should be sought (by at least some seekers), permits a critical approach to them. It permits this because understandings can be addressed critically: we can, and we inevitably do, ask of them whether they make sense, whether their implications and assumptions can be defended, whether the processes of formation that have produced them are ethically and practically defensible, and so on. Conversely, if appetites are treated as facts about us like our appendix or our height, they can only be described phenomenologically and explained causally. And since almost every human being, and certainly every human culture, does in fact think about appetites critically and normatively, depicting appetites as implicated with understandings, and those understandings as artifacts of catechesis is consistent with the way in which everyone does in fact think about them. The normative ordering of our appetites, by classifying some as good and therefore to be nurtured, and others as bad and therefore to be strangled at birth, also belongs to the universal grammar of appetite—though of course the reasons given for judging a particular appetite to be of one kind or the other may vary enormously.

Appetites, then, are internally complex states of human persons. They are a kind of wanting, a seeking to make some particular absence present, and they occur together with understandings of why what is sought is desirable. These understandings may be dispositional or occurrent on the part of those who have the appetite; they may also be identified by observers with the appropriate skills and knowledge; and it is possible, perhaps common, that an observer may more accurately assess the understanding with which a particular appetite is intertwined than can the person who has it.

The lexicon and syntax of appetite displayed to this point identifies what appetites are by specifying how we must think and talk about them. This is not all that belongs to appetite's universal grammar. Just as important to that grammar is the matter of how appetites are identified, and here there are some puzzles. An appetite is a state or condition of a person, a condition of wanting to make a particular absence present. But it is a condition that may not be known to the one who has it, and one whose presence cannot be decisively inferred from behavior. This is a bit mysterious. If observed behavior always and necessarily underdetermines which appetite it is causally implicated with— your repeated visits to the local coffee shop may be taken to show that you have an appetite for coffee, but what you really have an appetite for is the company of a particular person who serves the coffee in that shop—then this means that no observer can use your behavior reliably to determine which appetites you have. And if introspection also cannot guarantee identification of the appetites present (perhaps you have not acknowledged to yourself why you visit that particular coffee shop so often, and perhaps you have no disposition to do so—which is to say that you would deny it if someone else suggested it), then we seem to be in an epistemically difficult situation. How do we and how should we attribute particular appetites to particular people?

We do so diagnostically. Diseases, whether physical or mental, are in all relevant respects like appetites. They are conditions of persons just as appetites are. Like appetites, the fact that you have a particular disease may or may not be known to you, and may or may not yield its presence to introspection. You can suffer from unhealthily high levels of sugar in the blood without knowing that you do; a blood vessel in your brain may be just about to burst quite unknown to you; you may be HIV positive without knowing it; or you may be clinically depressed without knowing that you are. This last may sound odd. Surely if you are depressed, that will be obvious at least to you? But no. A diagnosis of depression will typically include reference to the feeling states of the individual, to how it seems to the depressed individual to be themselves, but it will not be exhausted by them. If the person in question has always felt like this—always felt that getting up in the morning is an unbearable burden, that the game of investing energy in personal relationships is not worth the candle, and so on—she may well resist the suggestion that she is clinically depressed. And even if she does accept that label, she is likely to think of it as referring not to an illness but to the ordinary state of things, to the flavor and feel of human life as it ordinarily is.

Diseases are like appetites in another way too: behavior, even when combined with measurable physical states, always underdetermines diagnosis. That is, there are always infinitely many possible diagnostic explanations of why the patient behaves like this, or of why her white blood cell count or her blood pressure is what it is. Introspection plus observation and measurement does not yield a single, inevitable diagnostic result. This is a generalization of the point that close observation of what players do in a game can never, absent prior and independent knowledge of the rules, permit you to write the book of rules. It is always possible to generate an explanation other than that given in the book of why (for example) a walk occurs in baseball that is just as consistent with observable behavior as the one the rules give. Perhaps, in a particular game, whenever a hitter with an RBI percentage greater than x is at the plate after the batting rotation has gone round more than once in a single inning, a walk has occurred. Why not? That rule is consistent with the data. So also with diagnosis: observable and measurable data can always be accounted for diagnostically in an infinite number of ways, given enough imagination and enough time. Diagnosticians, I assume, are aware of this. If they are not, they ought to be.

But this does not mean that diagnosis is impossible: there are diagnosticians and they sometimes do a good job. Diagnosis of disease (and likewise of appetite) requires a defined list of diseases together wth their symptoms, as well as a definition of each symptom and a set of guidelines that permit the diagnostician to tell when a particular symptom is present. The training of a diagnostician involves learning the defined list and then the skill of applying it to cases. Often, the agreed list of diseases together with their symptoms is enshrined in an authoritative text, such as the American Psychiatric Association's *Diagnostic and Statistical Manual of Mental Disorders*. With this in hand or in mind, and with the appropriate skills and habits, the psychiatrist can tell you whether you are schizoid, bipolar, depressed, anorectic, or healthy.

Diagnosis, whether of appetite or disease, thus begins with catechesis. Without training in the agreed list of diseases and symptoms, the diagnostician can do no work. With such training, the problem of the underdetermination of diagnosis by observation and measurement is solved. It is not solved in the sense that all diagnosticians will agree on which disease a particular patient is suffering from; but it is solved in exactly the same way that the catechesis provided by instruction in the rules of baseball solves the problem of when to call a strike. The rules tell you what a strike is; experience in watching batters at the plate gives fledgling umpires the skill to apply the definition to particular cases; and although there may be disagreement about whether what just happened is a ball or a strike or something more arcane, there is none about what a strike is. Catechesis-by-rule comes first, followed by the development of skill in applying the rule to cases; and then diagnosis can be performed. The diagnostician, whether of appetite or disease, may be the same as the diseased or appetitive one, or not. But in either case, catechesis is necessary. Even if it is your appetite, you cannot diagnose it by introspection alone, and it is often the case that appetites (and diseases) can be diagnosed quite well without any introspection.

This description of how diseases are diagnosed belongs only to the order of knowing. It is quite neutral as to the nature of diseases, which is a question that belongs to the order of being, and for the purposes of this discussion, it is better to let it remain there without further discussion. It may or may not be the case that the list of diseases known to an accomplished psychiatric diagnostician refers to entities interestingly different from those indicated by the rules of baseball. But it is the case that, epistemically speaking, the skills of the diagnostician are acquired in exactly the same way as those of the umpire. And the same is true of the process by which it becomes possible to identify the presence (and absence) of appetites: what is needed is a skill prepared for and informed by catechesis. The catechetical materials are plentiful as far as the identification and classification of appetites is concerned. Some of them belong to modern traditions of psychology and psychiatry; but many more belong to the religious traditions, both premodern and modern. For example, for Christians there is the long tradition of composing pentitential manuals in which (among other things) appetites are defined and classified in order to make it possible for confessors to identify what pentitents are suffering from and to prescribe appropriate penance; and for Buddhists, there are the ascetical manuals for the training of monks in which much of the same work is done.

Appetite, then, seeks the presence of an absence, and does so under a certain description, which is to say that it seeks that presence for a particular purpose, with a particular end in mind. Particular appetites may be identified by specifying both the presence sought and the purpose for which it is sought. This process of identification, of coming to know that you have—or what someone else has—a particular appetite requires instruction in the definition and symptoms of possible appetites, and the development of skill in the use and applicaton of such definitions. There is no single, standard list of appetites, and certainly no single, standard set of definitions or symptoms; this is because any such defined list is deeply and inevitably intertwined with some particular understanding of what human beings are and of what they should be. Such understandings vary, and with them vary the substantive catechesis given to make diagnosis possible. Vaibhāshika Buddhist scholastics and Christian ascetical theologians and the compilers of the American Psychiatric Association's manual do not share an understanding of what it is to be human and of how human appetites should be ordered, and so they also do not share an understanding of what the range of human appetites is and how each item on the list ought be defined and valued. But the appetite lists each group produces do share some important formal features.

First among these formal features is normativity. That is, the lists of appetites are ordered hierarchically by an understanding that some ought to be fostered, developed, and encouraged, while others ought to be discouraged, checked, punished or otherwise disciplined. Such orderings are inevitable, at both the individual and the societal level. That is, if to establish a norm (etymologically, a carpenter's square) is to establish a standard to which tokens of a type should conform if they are to be good (representative, undamaged) tokens of that type, then we all establish normative orderings of our appetites. Normative judgments about appetite, of the form "I ought to encourage this one" and "I ought to get rid of that one," are judgments that we understand to make a claim upon us so that it seems to us that we fail to the extent that we do not accede to the claim and succeed to the extent that we do. Normativity with respect to appetite understood in this way is universal, which is to say that there is no social group and no individual (short of those lacking the capacity for judgment *simpliciter*) free from it. These normative judgments are reflected, inevitably, in catechetical practice. For example, most infants exhibit a coprophiliac appetite at one time or another: they appear to enjoy displaying and sometimes eating their excrement. Parents mostly discipline this appetite in the direction of removal, and in doing so they imply a normative judgment about its nature.

Justification of these normative orderings of appetite also belongs to appetite's universal grammar. That is, some in a community committed a particular normative ordering of appetite are disposed to explain why these appetites (whichever they happen to be) should be encouraged, and those (whichever they happen to be) discouraged. This is not to say that such explanations are always offered. Ordinarily, they are prompted by challenge, whether from within or without (why, someone asks, is this appetite to be encouraged and that to be discouraged?); and sometimes those who respond to such challenges will add to explanation of the principles by which appetites are normatively ordered arguments about the superiority of one mode of justifying such ordering (a teleological one, perhaps) over another (a consequentialist one, perhaps). Where challenges are lacking, explanations and justifications are unlikely to be offered. But the possibility that they might be belongs to the universal grammar of appetite in the sense that it is already implicit in the act of ordering appetites to begin with. Of course, any particular way of explaining and justifying orderings of appetite belongs to some construal of appetite, not to its universal grammar; and there are many incompatible ways of explaining and justifying the ordering of appetite.

Among the important causes for the universal need to order our appetites normatively is the fact that they are almost infinitely plastic and therefore potentially almost infinitely varied. The variation occurs within the constraints given by nature, many of which are biological: some appetites will always have to do with food, some with sex and reproduction, some with power and violence, some with pleasure and symbolic representation, some with worship and God or the gods—and this list is neither complete nor uncontroversial. But within each of those types, appetite's plasticity guarantees that the range of tokens that can be and have been brought into being is almost infinite. Appetites for food may be limited to the raw, embrace only the cooked, forbid or demand blood, seek or prevent spicy heat, encourage or forbid variety, and so on. Appetites for sex may take as their desired other human beings, beasts, plants, inanimate objects, oneself or any of these in various combinations; they may be combined with or carefully separated from appetites for violence and the infliction of pain, and similarly combined with or carefully separated from appetites for reproduction. Appetites for symbolic representation may center among other things upon words, gestures, synecdochic use of inanimate objects, the clothing, adornment, or mutilation of one's own or others' bodies—and each of these may be combined in various ways with appetites for food and violence, pleasure and pain. (Almost) infinite possible variety requires both normative judgment and active discipline: if (almost) anything is possible, which it is, then choices must be made, which requires the use of normative judgment; and once made they must be enforced, communicated, and given individual and societal form. Only normative choice and active discipline can marry you to a particular language, cuisine or habit of lovemaking.

～

Appetite's universal grammar includes the two ways by which any particular appetite may be acquired, which is to say by gift and by catechesis. To receive an appetite by gift is to get it free, unasked, unexpected, and (perhaps) unwanted. Appetites given in this sense are received without effort on the part of the recipient and without intention or work on the part of the recipient's contemporaries. They form part of the recipient's nature, which is not to say that they are beyond the shaping influence of catechesis. Given appetites are, therefore, also natural appetites. To acquire an appetite by catechesis, in contrast, is to get it as a result of work by others and (or) yourself. The work will often be undertaken deliberately with a goal in mind; but it may also occur without those performing it being able to say what they are doing or why.

Some among our natural appetites, those we have by gift, are the product of our physiology. Appetites for food, for language, for the society of others, and for sex come under this heading. To be human is to be a particular kind of creature with (among other things) a particular genetic constitution, and it is these particularities that provide us unasked with our physical appetites. Were we creatures of a different kind, we would have physical appetites of a different kind. It is scarcely controversial that some among our appetites are given to us by our physiology, and it is only slightly more controversial to provide a list such as I have given. No one doubts that it belongs naturally to human beings to have appetites for food and so on. But, obviously enough, any such list depends upon a particular understanding of the kind of creature we are, an understanding, that is to say, of our nature. The reason that what should go on a short list of natural physical appetites is not a matter for much controversy is that we have broad agreement about our physical nature and about the appetites that properly belong to it. But still, while the division between appetites received by gift and those received by catechesis does belong to appetite's universal grammar, the placing of particular appetites into one kind or the other belongs rather to a construal of appetite, and therefore will not be entered into here.

Natural appetites, those received by gift, whether physical or otherwise, are inchoate. They are better thought of as tendencies or capacities to seek the presence of some absence than as actual or occurrent appetites. Consider the example of appetites for food. I, like you, have some rather specific appetites in this line: for oysters, smoothly salty, washed down with a crisply lemon-licorice Pinot Gris; for crusty bread, smeared with extra-virgin olive oil; for roasted lamb, sprinkled with mint and served with Yorkshire puddings. I was not gifted with these particular appetites in the same way that I was gifted with the desire for food-as-such. As a newborn (I assume) I had the sucking reflex and the ability to cry when I needed food; I could swallow mother's milk and be satisfied by it. That appetite for food came to me unbidden, as gift, and the actions prompted by it followed almost as easily. But the more particular appetites I have mentioned came to me only after a lot of catechetical effort by family, friends, and associates, together with a responsive effort of appropriation by me. I was acculturated into them, given them in a different way. So, too, with language. It is probably true that it belongs to human nature to have an appetite for speech and for the ordering and ornamenting activities that come with learning to inhabit a particular natural language. But no one has naturally an appetite for Japanese or English or Hebrew. The development of those appetites—for, in my case, reading, writing, speaking, and hearing the words of English—is thoroughly dependent upon local catechesis. The inchoate appetite becomes particular, finely focused, complex and ordered, shaped and disciplined, only when it has been thoroughly catechized. And so, none of the developed appetites of a properly functioning, adult human being who has had the good fortune to be catechized well is merely natural in the sense of given.

~

The universal grammar of appetite, then, consists of the following elements: appetite is a kind of wanting, the kind that seeks the presence of an absence under a particular understanding. Appetites may be sorted into types by differentiating their objects in a formal and abstract way (for example, food, power, sex); and particular tokens of these types may be individuated by specifying their intentional objects in a fine-grained way (for example, pineapple-flesh-on-the-tongue-for-thirst-slaking). There is, however, no single, obvious, compelling taxonomic ordering of appetites: any particular ordering depends on and is deeply articulated with local catechesis. Some appetites are acquired by gift and others require catechesis, choice, and effortful appropriation. All complex appetite-tokens are of the second sort. Appetites are identified by diagnosis, which is a skill that in turn requires extensive catechesis and effortful appropriation. And, inevitably, appetites are disciplined in accord with normative judgments about which are good and which are bad. These normative judgments in turn are predicated upon a set of understandings of the nature of human beings and of the nonhuman environment in which it seems to us that we find ourselves.

It belongs to the universal grammar of appetite to say that appetites require formation by catechesis, and that this catechesis can go well or badly. Appetites, then, can be formed or deformed, shaped into something elegant and orderly or warped into something ugly and chaotic. Substantive judgments about what counts as a formed appetite and what a deformed one vary, inevitably; but the judgments that there are both possibilities and that appetites ought to be catechized with this in mind do not. Those who offer particular construals (Christian, Buddhist, materialist, Marxist, and so on) of appetite vary greatly in how they go about explaining and justifying their views about which appetites are deformed and which are not. But the possibility, and in certain circumstances—challenge from without, puzzlement from within—the desirability of offering such explanations and defenses belongs to appetite's universal grammar.

When we Christians construe the universal grammar of appetite, we explain and justify our categorizations of some appetites as formed and others as deformed by appeal to human nature. And not only this: we appeal to nature in teleological mode, which is to say that we understand human nature to be ordered to a certain end or goal, and appetites deformed to the extent that they hinder attainment of that goal. Some catechized appetites serve human nature by forming it in such a way that we participate more fully in God than we otherwise would—which is to say that some appetites are healthy. Others, however, have quite the other result: they damage those subject to and indulgent of them by removing them, progressively, from that participation, and bringing them closer to the nonbeing from which all of us came and to which we are always tending to return. This Christian view is species-specific in the sense that an appetite which deforms humans may be perfectly healthy for other animate creatures; but within this species it is universal: humans, on this construal, do have a shared nature, and it is this that makes possible universal generalization across the human species about which appetites are desirable and which are not.

Such a species-specific universalism about appetites is not restricted to Christians. A version of it is held, for example, by most members of the medical profession: an appetite for poisonous mushrooms will damage anyone who indulges it, your doctor will tell you, as will an appetite for walking naked outdoors in temperatures below zero. This species-specific universalism is intimate with a particular understanding of what constitutes the human organism; and it too, like its Christian counterpart, is broadly teleological in the sense that those who adhere to it think, usually, that humans can function well or badly, be more or less damaged, more or less healthy. The Christian species-specific teleological universalism includes more than the physical, while medical universalisms, at least of the broadly materialist kind now dominant, usually try to pretend that they do not. The analogy with medical universalism does, however, show that this broadly teleological way of thinking about and justifying the ordering of appetite is very widespread, and at the unreflective level virtually universal.

The Christian construal of appetite's universal grammar is about appetite types, not their tokens. If, as we Christians think, an appetite for offering God praise and thanksgiving is concordant with and properly expressive of human nature, and its absence discordantly damaging, it does not follow that all the same things are true of an appetite for offering God praise and thanksgiving in English. That appetite is a token of the relevant type: you might have an appetite for offering God praise and thanksgiving in Yoruba or Japanese or Latin, while on your knees or standing or lying prostrate; and while such particular appetites share with all tokens the properties that define the type to which they belong, those that separate each of them from other tokens are not applicable to all members of the human species in the same way.

Almost everyone who thinks about it at all adopts some version of this species-wide realist view about how to justify normative orderings of appetite. There are minority views of other kinds: non- and anti-realists of various stripes deny that there are species-wide norms for the ordering of appetites (and, in some cases, for the ordering of anything else). And you can certainly can refuse demands for justification of the normative judgments you inevitably make about the ordering of your own and your friends' appetites, either by declaring that enterprise of no interest to you (perhaps you would rather listen to Mozart than do meta-ethics), or by limiting what you say of an explanatory or justificatory kind to descriptions of a strictly causal and thoroughly local kind: I make these judgments about my appetites, you might say, because of the particular local catechesis I have had; and I associate with those who think like me about this because they've been catechized similarly; and that is all. It is rather doubtful that this position can be coherently maintained, but it can certainly be uttered and retreated to.

There are also reasonable difficulties about the individuation of one species from another, and therefore about the extension of species-wide judgments about the ordering of appetite. We Christians have typically assumed both that there are clear dividing lines that separate one species from another, and that we can tell without difficulty where they lie. We have given particular importance to the division between humans and all other animate species, and it is certainly an irreducible element of the Christian construal of appetite—and of the world—to claim that humans are more intimate with God, more fully participant in God, than any other creatures (leaving aside consideration of the angels). But saying this carries with it no particular judgments about the ease or difficulty of discerning where the boundaries between humans and nonhumans lie. Christian thought has no special wisdom to offer on this epistemic matter, and it is a difficult matter for everyone: are species to be defined morphologically, genetically, by the capacity to interbreed, or by something else? None of these criteria is free from conceptual difficulties, and none provides easily usable, necessary, and sufficient conditions for ruling some individual in or out of species membership.

The elements of the Christian tradition's lexicon which cannot be abandoned—which is to say the claim that humans are differentiated from others by being uniquely in possession of the *imago* and *similitudo* of God—does not specify with any precision just what it means to possess God's image and likeness, and says nothing at all about the criteria necessary for the recognition of such a creature. Various candidates have been suggested, and for the purposes of this study, they do not need to be explored. All that need be said is that humans are distinctively different from other animate creatures; that this difference has to do with fuller participation in God; and that in the vast majority of cases, it is unambiguously clear whether a particular creature that faces you is or is not human. Christian judgments about particular candidates for membership in the human species do not differ much from those of geneticists, who are prepared without much ambiguity to tell you whether a particular creature is human just on the basis of possession of a particular genome; neither do they differ much from those of most who think in a nonexpert and nontechnical fashion about the question, and who are likely to say that being a creature brought into being by the joining of human egg and sperm suffices to make you human. (Whether it is necessary is another matter that is not at the moment pressing, but might become so with advances in genetic technology or the discovery of extraterrestrial life.)

The Christian species-wide, normative teleological ordering of human appetites applies, then, to all the clear cases of species membership (which is almost all of them), without requiring any particular decision about how to recognize demarcations between one species and another, or about what the necessary conditions are for membership in the human species. In cases of reasonable doubt about this latter question, the tendency of Christian thought is to err on the side of generosity: we do not move quickly toward exclusion of possible humans from membership in the human race and the concomitant treatment that befits *imagines* and *similitudines* of God.

Not all those who offer realist species-wide justifications of particular orderings of appetite appeal to the same understanding of human nature in doing so. A Christian understanding of humans as creatures who are *imagines dei,* especially intimate participants in divine gift, is different in almost every interesting respect from an understanding of humans as autonomous beings possessed of a rational will capable of universal, species-wide legislation. And each is equally though differently different from an understanding of humans as desire-driven congeries of causally connected event-continua. But each of these families of understandings shows the formal feature of justifying its orderings of appetite by appeal to a particular rationally disputable construal of appetite's universal grammar. If the Christian tradition's derivation of its orderings of appetite from its understanding of human nature is coherent, then objections to those orderings will necessarily be objections to that understanding, and, thereby, objections to the ontology informing it. The same will be true, *mutatis mutandis,* for objections to other, incompatible orderings of appetite. Pulling at the threads of normative judgments about particular appetites rapidly begins to unravel the ontological weave whose design they figure. How you think about what you should want is intimate with how you think about what you are, and with how you think about the likeness of the world in which you have come to learn to want and in which you seek satisfaction of your appetites.

❧

With these preliminaries in mind, together with the earlier depiction of the Christian construal of the world through the categories of gift, participation, and damage, we are now in a position to define, formally, the object of all appetites, as Christians understand it.

The object of every appetite is the presence of some now-absent creature, and thereby the increase of intimacy with that creature. If everything that is not God is a creaturely participant in God, and if every appetite seeks the presence of some absence under some description, then the definition given is established at once. For Christians, there is nothing capable of being a presence to you, of appearing before your face, other than creaturely participants in God. That presence—a presence of that kind—is the only presence that can be sought or found. And, so far as Christians have been well catechized and as a result know how the world as the arena for their appetites is construed, and how their own appetites should be ordered, they will understand the objects of their appetites in exactly this way. Furthermore, the Christian construal of appetite requires the claim that the subjects and objects of appetite share this fundamental property of being creaturely participants in God. What you want when you want something as a Christian is something in this fundamental respect of the same kind as yourself. This does not mean that differences are abolished or emptied of significance. To have an appetite for the presence of the prose of Henry James, for the white-bordered, purplish-red, thumbnail-sized blossoms of sweet william in an English May, or for the solution of the four-color problem, is to have an appetite for the presence of things of very different kinds. The first is a work of human taste and intellect; the second a corporeal feature of the world independent of human agency; and the third an incorporeal feature of the world of the same kind. The modalities and intensities of the intimacies possible for you with each are a function of the differences between their kind and yours. But the fact that intimacy is possible at all is given by the fact that you and each of these particulars are creatures.

The objects of appetite understood in this way are inexhaustible. That is, because each of them has the kind of being it has because of the freely creative act of God in bringing it into being out of nothing and sustaining it in being, and because God himself is necessarily and by definition inexhaustible, it must then be the case that no satisfactory definition of any being can be given that prescinds altogether from reference to its participation in the inexhaustible one; and that no intimacy with any creature is to be had which embraces all there is to be embraced about that creature. This means, to descend from the heights of abstraction to a crassly physical trope, that you cannot get your arms around any creature whose presence before your face is what you have an appetite for. Your human beloved, when he or she appears before you, can of course be encircled by your arms. But when you have done that you will not have reached final, exhaustive, and complete intimacy with her or him exactly because being a creature is an essential part of what your beloved is, which is to say that (s)he is constituted essentially by a relation to something—*una summa quaedam res, idipsum,* which is periphrastically to indicate YHWH, the triune God—around which no one's arms can reach. At the very deepeest level of her being, your beloved escapes your gesture of intimacy, and that this is so is no contingent fact about either you or her. This is true not only of all human beloveds but of all creatures for whose presence you might have an appetite. What they are is never exhausted by their presence to you, and the extent to which you seek to exhaust them by being intimate with them is the extent to which you fail to become intimate with them.

The impossibility of exhaustive intimacy with any creature is a matter for lament only for those whose appetites are deformed. But since that is all of us, Christians as well as others (although we Christians know, when we are well-catechized, that such intimacy is and must be beyond our grasp, we still want it, often desperately), it is worth making some brief observations about why we seek it. It is because the most widespread and profound deformation of appetite is its turn toward that dominion or mastery whose legal form is ownership: what we humans want more than anything else, as we Christians see the matter, is to have intimate relations with creatures other than ourselves that are like God's to us. God does have exhaustive intimacy with us: everything about each creature, actual and possible, is known to God, and everything lovable is loved. To subtract from each creature that about it which is intimately embraced by God is to leave, strictly, nothing at all. The vestige or trace of the divine in us, which we have in virtue of being human, has as its characteristic deformation the attempt to love creatures as God loves them. This would be, could we do it (which we necessarily cannot), to be God for the creature with which we seek intimacy—for whose presence we have an appetite—and that in turn would be to circumscribe the creature and to make it without remainder ours. Parents know the sadness that comes as their children cease to be dependent infants, and they—the parents—pass from knowing and loving most things about their children (never everything, though, not even when the child is a newborn: it is a characteristically parental delusion to think that they know everything about their infants) to knowing progressively less about them. This sadness, unavoidable though it is, is itself a relatively benign instance of the deformation of appetite in the direction of dominion's ownership. Erotic lovers have their version of it, as do friends; and it is common, too, to seek to be as God toward inanimate objects, whether abstract or corporeal, which is to say to master them without remainder. This deformation consists essentially in misprision of oneself in the direction of idolatry—of treating oneself as God, and of ordering one's appetites to accord with this misprision. It is central to what Christians have meant by *concupiscentia* (in Greek, *epithumia*), which is a disordered yearning for mastery.

Appetites can be deformed by misprision of the object with which intimacy is sought as well as by misprision of the appetitive seeker. The most common form of this—again, equally common, I should think, among Christians and pagans; the difference is only that Christians know, or should know, it to be a deformation, while pagans are less likely to—is to take that whose appearance before your face you seek to be something of intrinsic value, something whose worth, and hence its propriety as an object of appetite, belongs to it alone. To misprize an object of appetite in this way contributes to the aspiration to take exhaustive possession of it, it enjoy it for what it is in itself wthout reference to anything other than itself. This deformation, too, is very common, universal, in fact, to one degree or another among humans (excepting only Jesus of Nazareth and his mother) in the postlapsarian world, and it is very intimate with the deformation described in the preceding paragraph. If you think of yourself as someone who might be intimate with creatures as God is, then you are likely to think of those like yourself—other humans, that is—as being like you in that capacity, and therefore as being worthy of intimacy in their own right. This is misprision of others in the direction of idolatry, most commonly directed toward other human beings, though not exclusively so: some among us idolize nonhuman animate creatures in this way, or even inanimate objects; the interesting varieties of sexual fetishism are of analogical help in understanding how this is possible and what it might be like.

Seriously to understand some creature's presence as divine presence is to want to have your appetite for intimacy exhaustively absorbed by that presence: to be faced by God. According to the Christian construal of appetite, this is a quite fundamental grammatical and syntactical mistake: if all creatures are what they are only by participation in God, then each and every one has the value it has, and the possibilities of intimacy with humans proper to it, only because its face is a particular icon of God's presence. Seriously to seek intimacy with a creature, then, is always also to seek intimacy with its maker in whom it participates and of whose presence it is iconic. To have an appetite for intimacy with a creature without knowing it, or, knowing it, to seek intimacy in a way that contradicts the knowledge, is to perform a recursively and doubly incoherent action: what you get by it will not only fail to be what you seek, for no creature is God, and to seek intimacy with one as though it were is therefore necessarily to fail to get what you are after; but it will fail to be even what it could be, for you could have delighted in the presence of a creature as iconic depiction of God, but the mode of your appetitive seeking means that dust and ashes is what you get instead.

A further range of appetite's deformations, also almost universal, is produced by denial of, or inability to countenance, the damage to which you, an appetitive subject, have been unavoidably subjected. Here, the mistake is not only to overestimate your own capacities for intimacy, as in the idolatry of self just mentioned, but also to overestimate the degree to which the modes and intentional objects your own appetites—what you want and why and how you want it—are transparent to yourself. The extreme version of this mistake is to think that these matters are immediately and completely transparent to you: that it is as easy to know what you want and why and how you want it, as it is to know that you are in pain. The degree to which you are subject to this mistake is indexed closely to the degree to which you will not think it useful to have doubts about the appropriateness of your own appetites. If it seems to you that the appetites you have are those you ought to have, that they accord with the normative orderings of appetite that you have been catechized into thinking right, then, if you are subject to the mistake under discussion, there will be no more to think or to say: you will judge yourself free to indulge your appetites for intimacy untrammelled by doubt or the need to correct your understanding of your appetites by consulting others who observe your behavior. This is a mistake even in terms of appetite's universal grammar, for according to that grammar identification of appetite is a matter of diagnosis, and diagnosis is often not best done by the subject being diagnosed, but rather (or additionally) by expertly catechized members of the community (doctors, confessors, psychoanalysts), or by consultation with intimate others (spouses, lovers, friends, colleagues) who will often have a better idea than you what appetites you actually have—what, that is, you really want, and how and why you want it.

This mistake is also, and with greater intensity, an error in terms of the Christian construal of appetite because it fails to acknowledge the damage-produced opacity to which every human is subject. Introspection, even after thorough Chistian catechesis, is a largely blind guide to motivation and intention, because the characteristic sins of humanity (pride, self-aggrandizement, self-interest) make it very difficult for us to recognize or acknowledge what we want or why we want it, and so we put enormous effort, usually without knowing it, into constructing a burnished simulacrum of our appetites, which relates to the real ones much as the face of the Dorian Gray walking the world relates to the image on the canvas hidden at home. This systemic self-deceiving opacity is a contingent feature of humans on their Christian construal, but nonetheless an omnipresent one (excepting, again, only Jesus and Mary), and one that is not erased by baptism. It will be finally erased only when we Christians know God as we are known by him. Here below, all that can be done is to acknowledge the inevitable opacity of oneself to oneself, and thereby to come, gradually, to know one's appetites from without rather than from within. To fail to do so deforms appetite by harnessing it to the self's judgments about itself, and thereby shaping it in accord with a misconstrual. This error is cumulative and self-perpetuating: the more you attempt to understand and order your appetites without acknowledging that they are largely opaque to introspection, the more you will burnish, revere, and indulge appetites you are convinced you do not have. You will increasingly mistake your made-up face for your real face, and, eventually, you will no longer be able to see through the cosmetics.

But intimacy is not altogether impossible. The world is indeed deeply damaged, and as a result internally and externally opaque; it is to that extent a world of darkness. But it is also, and preveniently, a world of translucency, of particular beings iconically open to the divine light, which is also the divine gift. And to that extent, appetites can find what they seek, which is always intimacy with a creature of the kind appropriate to that creature. The formation of appetite on its Christian construal is always, therefore, formation toward a greater degree of intimacy with creatures in harmony with awareness that both they and you, the appetitive one, are alike in being creatures, and alike, too, in having become partly opaque because of damage, and thereby not fully open to intimacy. Appetite's deformation occurs when the depth and range of creaturely intimacy is overestimated by idolizing either the appetitive subject or that subject's objects; or when damage's opacity is underestimated.

8

WONDER

magna ista vis est memoriae, magna nimis, deus meus, penetrale am-
plum et infinitum. Quis ad fundum eius pervenit? Et vis est haec animi
mei atque ad meam naturam pertinet, nec ego ipse capio totum quod sum.
Ergo animus ad habendum se ipsum angustus est, ut ubi sit quod sui non
capit? Numquid extra ipsum ac non in ipso? Quomodo ergo non capit?
Multa mihi super hoc oboritur admiratio, stupor apprehendit me. Et eunt
homines mirari alta montium et ingentes fluctus maris et latissimos lap-
sus fluminum et oceani ambitum et gyros siderum, et relinquunt se ip-
sos, nec mirantur quod haec omnia, cum dicerem, non ea videbam oculis,
nec tamen dicerem, nisi montes et fluctus et flumina et sidera quae vidi et
oceanum quem credidi intus in memoria mea viderem, spatiis tam ingen-
tibus quasi foris viderem. Nec ea tamen videndo absorbui quando vidi oc-
ulis, nec ipsa sunt apud me sed imagines eorum, et novi quid ex quo sensu
corporis impressum sit mihi.

This power of memory is great, very great, my God, of vast and endless depth. Who gets to the bottom of it? And although this power
belongs to my soul and is proper to my nature, even I myself do not
grasp all that I am. Is it then that the soul is too constricted to possess itself? Where then is the part of itself it does not grasp? Is it outside rather than within itself? How then does it not grasp itself? This
moves me to great wonder—astonishment takes me. And people go
to marvel at high mountains, at huge sea surges, at the vast spread
of rivers, at the ocean's range and at the movements of the stars—
while neglecting themselves! Neither do they wonder that when I was

speaking of all these things they were not before my eyes, and that I could not have spoken of them—not mountains or surges or rivers or stars, which I have seen; nor the ocean, which I take on trust—unless I had seen them in my memory in spaces as vast as if I were seeing them externally. And yet in seeing these things I did not take them into myself when I saw them with my eyes; it is not these things that are inside me, but rather their images; and I know which was impressed upon me by which bodily sense.

⌁

Augustine here, in the tenth book of the *Confessions* (10.8.15) expresses wonder *(admiratio)* at himself. No one, he says, has arrived at the true depth of his or her own memory, and he cannot himself grasp *totum quod sum,* all that he is. But this is paradoxical: how can the mind be such that it cannot grasp part of what it itself is? Wonder and astonishment *(stupor)* overcome him at this; and then he is puzzled as to why so many wonder at the glories of the sensible creation outside themselves, but do not wonder at their own capacity to hold the images of such things in their own minds, and to wonder at them. Augustine here encourages a kind of meta-wonder, which is to say a wonder or amazement at our own capacity to wonder. This capacity, he thinks, is the most wonderful thing there is, and, though it is not said in this passage, that is because it participates more fully in God than anything in the sensible creation.

⌁

Appetite is rooted in wonder and has intimacy with some creature or ensemble of creatures as its end. Knowledge, in turn, on its Christian construal, is a particular kind of intimacy between one creature and another.

Wonder responds to something present, something before your face, and it does so with a blend of surprise and delight. It is not yet desire, which is typically for an absence, something whose presence is sought but is not yet present. You wonder at and delight in your lover when she is in your arms; you desire her presence when she is not. As Odysseus comes home to Ithaca and Penelope, he sheds the exile's longing, which is a form of desire, and replaces it with delight in the place to which he belongs. And when you enter the presence of God, purified of all that separates you from him, you will delightedly wonder at knowing as you are known, something for which you can now only long. Presence, appearance to the gaze, is at most the first degree of intimacy with what appears, and it may yield little more than puzzlement about the nature of the creature that appears. Appearances, however, are often surprisingly delightful, and when they are, they are likely to prompt desire for greater intimacy with the thing delighted in. A word for the most fundamental desire-prompting delight, deeply rooted in both Christian and pagan talk about these matters, is wonder, which is, infinitively, *thaumazein* in Greek and *admirare* in Latin.

"To admire" does not mean in English what *admirare* meant in Latin, and so the former cannot be used to render the latter. Admiration is a distanced and cool response to something you judge worthy of respect: you might admire Abraham Lincoln, or democracy, or the dress-sense of your well-turned-out colleague, or the prose style of William Gaddis, but you do not necessarily want to know them better, to enter into a more intimate relation with them, or to imitate them. To say that you admire them may instead serve as a mark of your desire to avoid just such responses, to keep them at a respectful arm's length as something worthy of that combination of respect and ignorance we typically provide to phenomena we think we ought to honor but which do not interest us. And the Greek *thaumazein* scarcely survives at all in English, except in such technical words as "thaumaturge" (magician, wonder-worker), and so it too does not yield an obvious English rendering. "Wonder," however, does capture a good deal of what is meant by these Latin and Greek terms. As I use it here, to wonder means to feel and show delighted astonishment in response to something-or-other. This is a complex response which can usefully be distinguished into kinds, each of which prompts in those who undergo it a desire to know more, which is to say one species or another of the appetite for knowledge.

The first kind is metaphysical wonder, which is astonished delight at the fact that there is anything at all. This is almost universal among babies and small children, it seems reasonable to suppose, though they do not tell us in words. Wonder of this kind does not usually survive the habituation to the fact that there is anything (including ourselves as creatures capable of expressing and feeling wonder at this fact) to which we have all ordinarily become subject by the age of seven or so. This habituation goes deep and occurs rapidly, no doubt for good reasons: wonder at the sheer givenness of the cosmos probably has little survival value, and so it is rapidly submerged and forgotten. But it does recur for some, even after the usual habituation has happened. It is sometimes given lyrical expression by poets, and there are a few for whom it maintains sufficient urgency to prompt a lifetime's thought and writing. These few (and it is good that they are few) we call metaphysicians, and they ask, and provide various incompatible answers to, the question of why there is anything at all and of what it means for anything at all to be.

The second kind of wonder is directed toward yourself as wonderer: how striking and puzzling and delightful it is, you are likely to think or once to have thought, that you exist as one who can be aware of yourself as existing, as capable of feeling wonder at that fact, and at the fact that there is anything at all, and at the fact that there are so many marvellously particular things to wonder at. This wonder can also be observed in babies as they gradually learn to distinguish the parts of their own bodies from the surrounding cosmos which is not—quite surprisingly, to them, it seems—itself a part of their bodies. And it is strikingly evident, not always to good effect, in the self-centeredness of adolescents who typically find themselves so positively and negatively fascinating that they cannot easily wonder at, or even fully register the existence of, anything other than themselves. Self-wonder typically spills over eventually into wonder at the fact that there are other thinking reeds like yourself, other embodiedly fragile and fallible creaturely knowers thrown into a cosmos of radiant light and unbearably impenetrable darkness. And this wonder, together with the desire for greater reflexive intimacy that it prompts, often does not go away in the same fashion that the other kinds do.

A third kind of wonder is directed at particular creatures: the ladybug, the motions of the heavenly bodies, the harmonies of music, the mathematical theorem that demands proof, or at any of the particular things made by creatures like us. From delighted astonishment at these things comes, sometimes, a passion for intimacy with them, and so we get entomologists or astronomers or musicologists or mathematicians or historians. These are often people whose life's work on whatever-it-is was prompted and sustained by wonder. Here too, though, habituation is rapid and goes wide and deep. The two-year-old may find every or almost every creature wonderful in this sense; but the exigencies of life and the necessities of survival usually require that these wondering responses to rocks and trees and grass and sky and water and decaying bodies and lightning and words and the effluents of one's own body be quickly catechized away and replaced with attention to the technical competencies needed for survival and advancement. This is why those who have been able to develop a precise and exacting reflexive intimacy with particular creatures that has no obvious connection with the knower's survival and the flourishing of the group to which they belong are almost always drawn from the privileged classes for whom survival is effortless and material luxury the norm. But delighted astonishment at the fact and nature of particular creatures is nonetheless widespread; and as we have developed the technical capacity to grant leisure for study to a larger and larger portion of the human race, so our knowledge of the particularities of creatures has increased to a staggering degree, an increase that all

Christians should celebrate because it is an increase in our intimacy with the gift we have been given, an increase made possible by the unusual depth of our participation in its giver.

Wonder can also be explained and given depth by being placed in the context of and made to resonate with the idea of participation. You, as one delightedly surprised by the givenness of things, are a participant in their giver as are all the things that prompt wonder in you, which is to say that your wonder is that of one participant in God directed toward another, or toward an array of others. This necessarily shared mode of being is what makes wonder possible: it provides the always implicit (and sometimes explicit) understanding on the part of those who wonder that giftedness and participation are not limited to oneself but are also shared by all that is.

∽

If wonder prompts appetite, and if, in turn, appetite is always for the presence of some absence, then all appetite is aimed at intimacy, though the intimacy will differ in its range, depth, and flavor in dependence upon the kind of creature with which it is sought, and the kind of creature who seeks it. For humans, there are possibilities of intimacy not open to other creatures, and among them is knowledge.

Thinking and speaking of creation as the gift of being from nothing, and of creatures as recipients of and participants in that gift, suggests some things to say about what it is for creatures to know—or, better put, to perform the act of knowing. By definition, this act must establish a relation between knower and known, and this relation will inevitably be, if participation is the right category to use to specify the relation between God and creatures, a relation between one participant in God and another. This means, to begin with, that knower and known share a fundamental likeness and intimacy because each participates in God. This intimate likeness at the level of being is what makes knowledge both possible and desirable for those capable of it. Most creatures are of course not capable of it: they can be known but they cannot know. But for us, who can know other creatures, which is itself a rare gift, a radiant trace of the being of the creator, such knowledge is a lure: it draws us as the scent of a fox draws foxhounds, kindling our desire and delight and ordering our action. A little more precision about what this act of knowing is like will show why.

Any act of knowing by one creature of another is an intensification of their shared creaturely intimacy as participants in God. This shared intimacy is a prerequisite for knowing's intensification of it. You, because you are already related to any creature you may know or seek to know by the fact that you too are a creature (I leave out of account here the question of God's knowledge of us and of our knowledge of God), can intensify and deepen that intimacy of being by intentionally making your likeness to and difference from the known a matter of admiringly interested reflexive delight. "Reflexive" is the key term here. Every creature enters into relations with particular other creatures of a peculiar intimacy: this bee extracts pollen from just that sunflower, burrowing deep to get it; that particular *ficus religiosa* strikes its roots deep into the drily acidic soil of exactly this place; Anna, my siberian husky, recognizes me as among her significant human others. These are all particular relations between individuals, and they are all in some sense intentional intensifications of the ordinary creaturely intimacy each creature shares with all others, which is to say that they are all in some sense sought, moved toward, actively pursued. Even the blindly desperate light-seeking of the green plant in a dim room is intentional in this relaxed sense. All living creatures, certainly, intentionally seek intensified intimacies in these ways, and there is a case to be made, too, for extending this description to the performances of nonliving creatures: for the fire's seeking of fuel, and so on. This way of talking does not, of course, imply or suggest that plants or insects (and much less fire or water) have consciousness of the intimacies they seek, or of the delight they produce. It implies only that intensified intimacies are sought by all living creatures.

Admiringly interested reflexive delight in such intensified intimacies, however, is a much rarer possibility, and this is what knowledge is: it is distinguished from other creaturely intimacies by being potentially or actually reflexive. Reflexivity, in turn, includes the knower's awareness of herself as being acquainted with some particular other in just this admiringly delighted way: knowers are aware (or could be aware) of themselves as creatures who are ecstatically intimate with *that*, whatever it is, and of exactly *that* as being the recipient of their intimately ecstatic acquaintance. "Ecstatically" here bears its precise etymological sense of "standing outside" *(ek-stasis)*: all intimate acquaintance with a creature other than yourself involves leaving yourself behind in order to go out and meet the other. The act of knowing, then, always bears upon both the creature known and the knower, and specifically upon the former as intimately intended by the latter, and the latter as intimately intending the former. Understood in this way, the relation established in an act of knowing comes in degrees, as do all intimacies: a particular knowledge of any creature by another always occupies a place on a gamut running from complete ignorance, utter lack of acquaintance, to full and complete admiring delight in everything about the known other. This last is of course available only to God.

Knowledge understood in this way is itself an instance of the participation-relation. You, as knower, gain from the creature known a property you could not have had without the known's being what it is, which is not merely your delightedly reflexive intimacy with it, but also your awareness of yourself as delightedly intimate in just that way. Your knowledge of any creature is therefore a kind of participation in it, as is its being known by you a participation of it in you. In both cases, the participation in question is derived from the more fundamental participation present in the order of being—participation in God, that is—shared by knower and known. And finally, your acts of knowing are in a limited sense creative acts. They make actual a good that without them was only potential: the dual good of your knowing something you can know, and of something's being known as it is by one who can so know it. Both goods make richer and deeper the ordered harmony that is the cosmos, healing the damage of ignorance and spreading the light of knowledge. In this, human acts of knowing bear the vestigial trace of God's knowing act of *creatio ex nihilo.*

We respond to the array of phenomena, which constantly confronts us with different intensities of attentive intimacy. At one end of this spectrum lies the almost complete absence of such responsive attention that characterizes our relations with most among the quotidian array of background noises whose hum and buzz informs our lives. We are not attentive to every tick of the clock, every instant of the air conditioning's hum, every word spoken in our hearing on a crowded city street. This means that we have almost no intimacy with these appearances; with the majority of them we will never have a relation that comes to consciousness. At the other end of this spectrum lies the profound intimacy that characterizes our relations with appearances to whose particulars we pay (and have paid) precise, repeated, and close attention: the face of the beloved, the proof of a mathematical theorem, the swoop of the evening swallow eating its fill, the tabulated evidence for a hypothesis whose truth is eagerly sought—and so on.

Consider, as an example of something with which I have a fairly intimate relation, and thus also knowledge to a high degree, the cotoneaster shrub planted in a terracotta pot in my garden. This shrub and I have a history: I bought it as a small shrub, carefully transplanted it from the garden center's disposable plastic pot into one of my preferred (though all too breakable) terracotta containers, whose color reminds me of the deep amber and dark orange surfaces of Roman walls. Since then it has grown a little, and seems to have adjusted well to its transition. As I sit and write, the shrub appears visually to me: it is about eighteen inches tall and two feet across; its leaves, those I can see, are a dark, waxy green, irregularly shaped and no more than half an inch long and one-quarter of an inch across. Some few of them, however, are reddish, and these worry me a little because they seem more brittle than the green ones and easier to remove. Perhaps they indicate that the plant is getting too much water (it has been a wet month), or too much sun (it gets direct sun for two-thirds of the day). The shrub branches irregularly in a pleasing pattern; and it is, as far as I can tell, without smell.

These are some of the sensory aspects of the cotoneaster's appearance to me. But they do not exhaust its appearance. Because of my history with it, it appears also with remembered depth, some roots into my past. As I look at it, water it, touch it, and think about where it will best flourish, my sensory relations with it carry with them, fluctuatingly, and to various degrees, my sense of my past relations with the plant. But even this combination of the sensory and the memorial does not exhaust the cotoneaster's appearance to me. It appears to me also under the rubric of a concept. I know, that is to say, its Latin genus and species name *(cotoneaster adpressus)*, and this means that I attend to it not only as a sensory array with a past, but also as an instance of something, a member of a class. The cotoneaster appears to me as a classified object: a plant, a green growing thing, a member of the genus *cotoneaster* and the species *adpressus*.

And not only this. In knowing the cotoneaster, I am (at least sometimes) aware of myself as knowing it, of myself, that is, as knower and as knower of *this*. This is the reflexive aspect of knowledge's participatory intimacy, and it adds a depth and complexity to my relations with the cotoneaster, which are a participated shadow of God's intimacy with both me and my cotoneaster. That I can know myself as knowing the cotoneaster, and that it cannot know itself as knowing me even though it is in various ways intimate with me, is an instance of the fact that I was created in God's image while the cotoneaster was not.

This account by no means exhausts the complexity of the modes of my cotoneaster's appearance to me. But it does, perhaps, suffice to show that I've entered into a relation with it of sufficient intimacy, attentiveness, and accuracy to make it reasonable to say that I know it—though of course not exhaustively, and not, I hope, too damagingly subject to the idolatries of the deformed appetite. It is enough also to suggest that knowing has, typically, many dimensions, including at least the sensory (how the cotoneaster looks and feels), the conceptual (what it appears as), the affective (how its appearance makes me feel), and the temporal or historical (what its history with me has been). These modes of appearance will vary, of course, with the kind of thing that appears: the sensory aspects of the appearance of the bodies of human others are very different from those of cotoneasters; different again are those of my own flesh, of a piece of music heard at a distance, or of a half-recalled conversation.

The cotoneaster's appearance is principally sensory. Some other appearances, by contrast, are principally or only conceptual. I may, for instance, contemplate Goldbach's conjecture, which is the proposition that every even number greater than two may be expressed as the sum of two primes. (There is, as far as I know, no proof of the truth or falsity of this proposition, which is why it is called a conjecture.) When I think about this, it does not appear to me as a sensory array. As far as I can tell, no visual or auditory images accompany my thoughts; I do not touch or smell the conjecture; and I have no particularly strong emotional responses to it, other than the restrained, low-key pleasure which ordinarily accompanies the appearance of a sharply defined concept. What appears, then, is something close to a pure concept; and its mode of appearance is largely, perhaps entirely, conceptual. I may still have an intimate, attentive, and accurate relation with this concept sufficient to make it reasonable to say that I know it. But the particulars of that relation will differ in almost every interesting way from those belonging to my knowledge of the cotoneaster.

This sketchy account of knowledge as an intimately attentive participatory relation between one participant in God and another has the advantage of embracing many of the more common uses of the verb "to know" in both philosophical and nonphilosophical English. It deals well, for example, with the biblical use of this verb to indicate sexual relations with another person: to have such relations is exactly (if done right) to enter into an intimately attentive participatory relation with another person. You know your lover, certainly, in a way you know no one else. The account given deals well, too, with the usage dominant among some philosophers according to which knowledge is a species of belief by which the knower is related to a proposition or claim. Knowledge on that view has principally to do with taking true claims as true; I noted some examples of this in my discussion of the cotoneaster. To take a true claim as true is certainly to relate to it as knower: it is to have a species of knowledge, perhaps best labelled "judgment." The account comports well, too, in a sense that should need little comment, with a broadly Thomistic understanding of knowledge as *aedequatio mentis ad rem,* a conformity of the mind to the thing known. And finally, the kind of knowledge called by some "know-how"—knowing how to ride a bicycle, bake a cake, play the piano, write a well-formed sentence in English—can also be well accommodated by it. You cannot have practical knowledge of these kinds without participating attentively and intimately in the relevant objects and their proper use.

Lovingly attentive participation in the known by the knower leads, to one degree or another, to the participatory conformity of the knower to the known. This is easiest to see in the case of know-how. The pianist's hands and body become conformed both to the piano and to the music he has become skilled at playing. His skills are written on his body in the sense that the sinews and ligaments of his hands have become different as a result of the practice that gave him knowledge, but also in the sense that his body is habituated to the assumption of particular postures and movements; and this bodily habituation is matched (and not easily distinguished from) the habituation of the mind, for the memorized piece of music—the prelude by Olivier Messiaen, "Chant d'extase dans une paysage triste," for example—re-organizes the conceptual, affective, and appetitive furniture and capacities of the mind. The pianist who knows that piece has become conformed to it, reordered by it. Participatory conformity is not limited only to know-how. It is the result, the product and effect, of other kinds of exactingly loving attentiveness, as well. Thinking hard about a conceptual difficulty—that of the best account to give of God's omniscience, for example—will, over time, bring the thinker into participatory conformity with a set of concepts for exploring this question. She will be a different person after long attention to this topic, both differently ordered and differently functioning, which may be otherwise put by saying that she now participates in the truth about this question. The same is true, with appropriate adjustments as to particulars, for knowledge of sensory appearances, persons, and so on.

The exacting intimacy that knowers seek is no easy thing to get, or even to approach. This is abundantly clear to everyone when it comes to knowing other people. Desiring an intimately exacting relation with a human other is no guarantee of getting it, and the causes of failure are very many. Most fundamentally, there is misprision: you may fail to understand the nature of the person you would like to come to know—thinking her cold when she is passionate, intellectual when she is emotive, poor when rich, open when closed—and this will guarantee knowledge's failure, at least in part. But misprision is not the only way in which exacting intimacy may be reached for and not found. It is also common to attempt a mode of coming to know the other inappropriate to her nature even when that nature is well understood. To gaze at the human other as if she were a painting or a sculpture or to speak about her as though she were an object; to talk to a dog or a plant as though they might talk back; to embrace a rare steak as if it were a lover; to read a book as though it might contain all truths—all these are instances of attempting a kind of intimacy, of knowledge, at odds with the nature of the thing of which knowledge is sought, at the same moment at which that nature is understood and acknowledged. I know perfectly well that my dog is not about to engage me in conversation, and when I talk to her it may be that I am by so doing preventing deep knowledge of her by acting in a way incoherent with my understanding of what she is, and thus barring advances in intimacy.

Delightedly reflexive intimacy on your part with some other participant in God is therefore deepened by accurate judgment about the nature of that particular's participation in God and its relations to other such participants, and it fails—becomes less intimate—according to the extent to which such judgment is lacking or replaced by other, opposed and confused, judgments. But, it is important to note, close attention to creatures, as also to oneself, will bring with it an understanding of the damage to which they have all been subjected, and so it will provoke lament as well as delight. Lament is the knower's response to damage just as admiring delight is the knower's response to creatures being as they should be. Both are instances of knowing's participation in the known.

～

The world in which well-catechized Christians live is a world of light, darkness, gift, participation, and cognitive intimacy. Learning to inhabit this world rather than one among its many competitors makes possible appetite's intensification and flourishing. This is because it is the world for which our appetites were made, the world in which they flourish and become what they should be. The appetite for knowledge, proper as it is to all ordinarily-equipped human beings, can work well or badly, and whether it does the former or the latter depends very largely upon how potential knowables are construed, and how, correspondingly, the appetite for knowing them is formed and ordered. If you learn to construe every knowable as a beautiful but damaged gift; the cosmos as an ordered ensemble of such gifts shot through with chaos; and the knowledge of any particular, and of the chaotically-ordered whole, as possible only when a potential knower seeks intimacy with the gift and thereby with its giver;—then, your appetite for knowledge will be provoked, moved toward a horizon it can never reach, and thereby intensified. The *cotoneaster adpressus,* the Messiaen prelude, the face of the human other, the ensemble of desire and institutional form that constitutes the economic order—all these, if approached as the studious do, yield themselves in part to the intimacy-seeking knower's gaze. And even that about them which does yield, cannot be appropriated by sequestration and made into its knower's possession. Rather, it is participated in as is appropriate to its kind, which means that it remains what it is while giving of itself that can be known to the knower. Even that, however, is not given by itself in isolation. It is given as participant in God, its giver, and because of that the knower's gaze moves back-and-forth from the knowable's surface to the condition of its possibility as knowable, and as it does so it intensifies, weaving together the contemplation of what it knows with gratitude for the gift that makes such knowing possible at all.

9

OWNING

Proprium ergo et quasi privatum intelligendum est quod unus quisque nostrum sibi est et quod in se solus sentit quod ad suam naturam proprie pertinet: commune autem et quasi publicam quod ab omnibus sentientibus nulla sui corruptione atque commutatione sentitur.

Therefore, what is proper and in a sense private should be understood as what belongs to each one of us alone; it is experienced by each one alone in himself as belonging properly to his own nature. By contrast, what is common is in a sense public, and is experienced by all those who experience, without change or corruption.

Augustine here (the extract is taken from *De libero arbitrio* 2.7.19) distinguishes what is proper and private from what is public and held in common. He makes the distinction in terms first of ownership: if something is private, you alone hold it, whereas if something is public it is freely available to all. The second facet of the distinction has to do with knowing: a privately held thing can be known only by its owner, whereas a public thing is known by all. The distinction is, for him, not merely descriptive but also normative: truly public things are not subject to change or corruption, while all private things are inevitably corrupted, merely by being privately held. This normative part of the distinction holds, he thinks (but does not say in the passage quoted), because public things have not been forcibly abstracted from their proper participation in God, while private things have, and have thereby been corrupted.

⮑

The curious seek to own what they know; the studious seek to act as stewards of what they know. This contrast, more fully explored, takes us deep into the opposed grammars of curiosity and studiousness. I begin with ownership.

Ownership is a relation that we humans may have to things other than ourselves. (We may also, on some accounts, have that relation to ourselves, but I leave that possibility aside in what follows.) What you own is your property. To establish the relation of ownership it is essential to be able to sequester what you aim to own, because to own something is, essentially, to sequester it. To sequester something, in turn, is to set it apart, to separate it, to control access to and use of it, to remove it from the common sphere, the realm of the public, to the realm of the private. The maiden princess sequestered in her tower by her over-protective father is set apart from, separated from, the public world of gallant princes and battles and feasts and weddings; the disputed assets sequestered by the court in a frozen bank account have been definitively removed from access and use until the dispute has been resolved; the vowed religious, sequestered in his monastery, no longer wanders the highways of the world; the common land sequestered by enclosure is removed from public access and appropriated to the lord of the manor's exclusive use; the book sequestered from the bookstore to my study's shelves by purchase and relocation is no longer available for public browsing or purchase by anyone else unless I choose to make it so; the theorem's proof is completely and unambiguously sequestered in the head of its discoverer until she chooses that it should be made public. Sequestration, then, is what ownership most centrally consists in, and it is a form of control with three aspects.

First, there is control of access: no one but you, the owner who has performed the act of sequestration, can have access to or contact with what you own unless you give permission. Your hands must stay off my car, my books, and my house, unless I invite you to touch. Owners, if they choose, may sequester what they own by isolating it from any contact with others, and when they do this they take control of access to its extreme: their property becomes accessible to them alone, like the miser's hoard examined only when no one else is present, or the work of art kept in a private room for the delectation of no one but its owner. More often, access is granted by permission: others may be invited to admire the hoard or the artwork, but even when this is done, sequestration is the invitation's presupposition. Admiration or any other contact with the property in question is granted only under acknowledgment that this is indeed property, an object that may be removed from the gaze of others at any time according to the whim of the owner, exactly because the owner controls access to it.

Second, there is control of use, which involves use not only of the property itself, but also of whatever it may produce or give rise to. Whatever uses your property may be put to are for you alone, unless, again, you choose to grant them to others. Suppose, to return to Goldbach's conjecture, you have an idea about how to prove it. If you own that idea, then any use to which it may be put is at your exclusive disposal. You may keep it locked up in your head or on your hard drive or on paper in your fireproof cabinet. Or, you may deploy its elegant heuristics as aids in the construction of other proofs; or, I suppose, you may set it to music or depict it in oils. Or, suppose you own a prize bull. His fertile seed is at your disposal you may extract it and sell it for artificial insemination, or you may rent him out as a stud. Because the bull is your property, the decision to permit or not to permit him to engender offspring is yours. Lawyers appropriately call the control of use usufruct: the use of what something produces (this is a term most often applied to land, but it can be applied much more widely). As with control of access, control of use may also be given away by you, the owner, or temporarily granted to another.

Third, there is control of disposal. Not only do you control access to and use of whatever you own, you may also do with it what you will: you may destroy it; you may give it away; you may keep it hidden; you may display it to all comers; you may, to the extent possible, alter it, deface it, kill it if it lives, improve it, decorate it, nurture it, and so on. Essential to the grammar of ownership is that you are not bound to your property by eternal or inalienable bonds: you may by fiat cease to be its owner, or another possible owner may by force remove your property from you; but otherwise, since your property cannot remove itself from your ownership, it remains yours until you relinquish it, or until some other potential owner takes it against your will and without your power to prevent the taking. It remains, that is, passive before your gaze and your hands.

No system of positive law codifies or recognizes the property-relation in quite this threefold way, and all limit the ideal type in various particular ways. You never, as a matter of fact, have complete control of access, use, or disposal of any of your corporeal property in any actual system of positive law. You cannot, for example, legally dispose of your old car anywhere you choose; you may not legally prevent officers of the law with proper warrants from having access to your property even if you wish to do so; and you may not legally use your lawfully owned shotgun in any way you choose. But any codification of the relation of owners to their property will inevitably be predicated upon an understanding of sequestration as an act of control with the three aspects noted, and will treat the exceptions to those three kinds of control which it will always find necessary to legislate as exactly that—as exceptions which need to be justified, exceptions which make sense only against the background of an understanding of what property essentially is: something sequestered for the exclusive access, use, and disposal of some sentient being or beings. Complete (pure) sequestration is also complete (pure) ownership; and whatever is completely sequestered is property without remainder.

Another talismanically powerful word for what aspiring pagan owners seek is *dominion*. This word, derived as it is from *dominus*, which is in turn the Latin rendering of the scriptural name of God, in Hebrew the tetragrammaton, indicates the power of a lord to govern or control, most usually land but also sometimes persons or portable property or other life-forms. It is one way of speaking, theologically, about the relation God bears to the world (though one which requires correction and amplification by others if it is to be rightly understood), and the English version of scripture completed by James I's translators in 1611 used the word to label the relation that God grants to human beings over the world and its contents (Genesis 1:28). But when God recedes into the background or is forgotten, the word becomes the standard term for the relation human beings bear to their property, carrying all the mentioned connotations of sequestration's control of access, use, and disposal. If the owner's aspirations for sequestration and seizure have been realized, dominion is the result. Another way to put this is to say that the owner is a god, or would like to be; which is also to say that what aspiring owners seek is exhaustive intimacy with what they know, and in seeking it idolize themselves as knowers.

◆

The world of the curious is, then, a world in which ownable objects are mathetically arrayed before the aspiring owner's gaze. "Mathesis" is not a word that trips from the English-speaking tongue, English though it is. It has an air of mystery and profundity, and, in spite of its deep roots in Greek, Latin, Old French, and long use in English (from the sixteenth century), perhaps also of outright incomprehensibility. It is, however, a useful word, and I use it here to label the catechesis that produces curiosity, and which therefore contributes to desire's dissipation, to the loss of precisely that intimacy with the world which the curious take themselves to be seeking. To undergo mathesis—to be mathetized—is to be inducted into the world of knowables construed in a particular way: as discrete, transparent, passive, and infinitely manipulable by their knowers.

The Greek verb *manthanein,* from which comes *mathēsis,* has as its most general meaning the activity of learning by way of study or inquiry. The derived noun *mathēsis* (in Greek) labels this process, and other derived terms such as *mathētikos* (one who is disposed to learn or to study), and *mathētēs* (a disciple, one who places himself under instruction) indicate various aspects or modes of the process of teaching and learning, some focusing on the activity, some on the result, and some on the relation of student to teacher without which the activity could not be undertaken, and in which, in large part, it consists. The last word mentioned—*mathētēs*—is familiar to Christians: it is used in the New Testament for followers of Jesus, for his disciples who have placed themselves under his authority in order to come to know what they need to know and to become what they need to become.

So far, then, mathesis is a very general word for teaching and learning which bears neither on its face nor in its etymology any deep connection with curiosity. That connection began to become apparent only in the seventeenth century, when the word was linked not just to teaching and learning in general, but rather to a particular form of those activities which results in curiosity. But the affinity and suitability of mathesis as a word for curiosity-producing catechesis is, perhaps, already suggested by the word's etymology: *manthanein* and *mathēsis* and *mathētēs* and all the rest have at their heart the root *math-,* from which, eventually, came "mathematics" and all its progeny and relatives. It is certainly the case that the teaching and learning called mathesis came, by the seventeenth century, to be understood on a broadly mathematical model: mathesis was a regime of pedagogical discipline aimed at knowledge of its chosen objects that would be exhaustive and certain in something like the same way that a mathematician's proof of a theorem is exhaustive and demonstrative. A regime aimed at such knowledge inevitably places a high value first upon identifying with precision what is to be known, and then upon identifying the method best suited to knowing it exhaustively. Any unclarity about what you seek knowledge of, and about the method appropriate to knowing it exhaustively, will obstruct your full mathetization.

Algorithmics, understood as the discipline that seeks rules for arriving at solutions of mathematical problems of a particular kind, is the specifically mathematical form of this concern with appropriate method for arriving at final and perfect clarity. But it can easily be generalized by those who want to make a broadly mathematical model universal. This desire to develop an algorithm—a final and decisive method—which, when fully understood and properly applied, will yield complete and irrefragable understanding of every object at which it might be aimed, disposes those who advocate a mathetic catechetical regime to think of a successful method of attaining knowledge exactly as one that may be extended universally, and therefore to think of a catechetical régime productive of knowledge in only some spheres of human inquiry as a failure to the extent that it fails in universal application. But any such universalism—any such quest not only for mathesis, but also for a single and simple all-embracing *mathēsis universalis*—tends toward a construal of knowables as if, in essentials, they were all of the same kind. For if there is an algorithm, a proper method, that will yield irrefragable and exhaustive knowledge of anything to which it is applied, then it must be the case that every knowable is of a kind such that it can be so known. And advocates of *mathēsis universalis* do in fact offer just such a construal of knowables.

Advocates of mathesis imagine a world of discrete objects arrayed spatially on a grid, each related to others causally in various ways, but each definable and knowable exhaustively in itself, each, that is, fully transparent to the appropriately catechized gaze and passive before that gaze, there to be gazed upon and addressed without itself returning or exceeding the gaze. Each of these discrete knowable objects has a history, of course, a set of causes and conditions, which makes it what it is. But the curious are not much interested in that history. Their gaze is directed neither toward the past of the discrete objects they seek to know, nor toward their future, but always toward their frozen present, the condition they have assumed at this moment, the moment when the aspiring knower's gaze falls upon them. The knowledge that counts, for such people, is knowledge of the glassy essence of each discrete object.

And so what they seek first is an inventory-with-definitions, a Linnean taxonomy of what there is in the world based on its observable features, its morphology. And there the matter may rest. If it does, the ideal-typical product of the mathetic gaze will be a catalog of kinds and subkinds sufficiently comprehensive that no discrete object remains unaccounted for. But curious interest may extend beyond this descriptive and classificatory impulse to causal explanation. When it does, however, it typically limits its interest in causes to the efficient cause, understood as a condition both necessary and sufficient for its effect, and tends to depict the world as a closed, determined system of configurations of discrete objects that inevitably produce just these effects, and without which these effects would not obtain. The configuration may be frozen by snapshot at any moment, studied, classified, ordered, and enshrined.

Complete knowledge of what there is at any particular time—which is, on this view, theoretically even if not actually available—is, in a mathetic world, like what an omniscient observer of chess knows when he gazes upon the board at any moment during the progress of a game. He knows what the pieces are, what their defining properties and powers are, what the rules of the game are (which is to say which set of efficient causes is in play), what has happened so far, and all the possibilities that may be actualized in the future, of which, given the rules of chess, there is a very large but finite number. And there is nothing else to know. The location of the pieces on the board, the rules of the game which define what each piece is, the moves already made, and the moves that may possibly be made—this is all there is, and therefore knowing it is knowing all there is to know. No reference to anything else is necessary in order to have complete knowledge of this chess game, and a representation of what the omniscient observer of chess games knows about any particular game has the form of, first, a catalog, specifying the pieces by definition; then a rule-book, providing constraints on what may and must be done not already explicit in the piece-definitions; and finally a list of observations of what has already occurred and of possibilities that may occur in the future.

This analogy has its limitations. Chess pieces are simple natures, their powers limited stipulatively. Many things in the world are not like this. And the game of chess has a purpose, an end, which is partly obscured by focus only on what may and must happen in the course of a game. This is an inevitable result of excluding consideration of final causes (the final cause of chess, it might be said, is the game's purpose, the achievement of checkmate) in favor of exclusive focus on efficient causes—though I suppose it would be possible to state the rules of chess fully without specifying the game's purpose, but only by saying what may and must be done, and the conditions under which a game ends. And, of course, chess has players, not included in the omniscient observer's analysis as described in the preceding paragraph. But these limitations do not affect the main point of the analogy, which is to illustrate what it would be like to pay attention to the world as though it might yield itself to an appetite for knowledge formed by mathesis. And this it does: such a world has among its constituents only simple natures and efficient causal powers; its constituents are in principle entirely transparent to the appropriately catechized gaze and are entirely passive before the gaze of the knower; and nothing which is not a being in the world need be appealed to in order to achieve complete and irrefragable knowledge of the world.

Learning to approach the world in this way—becoming curious by way of mathesis—involves the assumption that the world will in fact yield itself to your gaze if only you learn how rightly to look. The world is to those shaped by mathesis like a vast collection of discrete potential sexual partners whose compliance with your desire to bed them is assured if only you learn what rightly to say to them. There is a magical key to knowledge, a perfectly efficacious pickup line that will bring anyone to your arms and your bed, an ideal joke that will make all hearers laugh whenever it is told. That magical key is method: the goal of mathetic catechesis is to provide those who undergo it with the method that will guarantee exhaustive knowledge of whichever ensemble of discrete objects is under investigation; and the faith that undergirds mathesis is that there is such a method, sometimes understood abstractly as a method common to all knowledge seeking, and sometimes more particularly as a variety of methods appropriate to particular arrays of discrete, spatialized objects. The method required of the botanist, that is, may not be the same in every particular as that required of the astronomer or the mathematician, because plants differ from stars and both differ from numbers; but the curious, the thoroughly mathetized, typically think that there is an ideal botanical, astronomical, and mathematical method, indexed to the particulars studied by those sciences; and that those several methods will have something in common, though it may turn out to be difficult to say just what this is without lapsing into the vacuities of general epistemic principle ("proportion your beliefs to the evidence at hand," and the like).

This faith in efficacious method, proper to mathesis as it is and must be, ordinarily means that those catechized by mathesis in the direction of curiosity will get explicit training in method first, before anything else. The first philosophy of the mathetized is always and necessarily methodology, and vast effort is expended upon getting the method right in order to ensure the complete and reliable results which advocates of mathesis know in advance to be possible. The gaze must be rightly configured in order for it to be capable of penetrating (the metaphor is appropriate for those objects which passively await the gaze, those fields which lie open before the investigator's eye, those *terrae incognitae* which await only exploration to yield their mysteries: the master tropes of mathesis almost always involve rape and sexual domination) what it is being trained to look at and look for. And the gaze so trained knows already what it will find: surprise is not a value for mathetic catechesis.

The fact that advocates of mathesis seek, and often take themselves to have found, the perfect method for complete knowledge of an ensemble of spatialized, discrete objects disposes them toward particular ways of representing the knowledge they take themselves to have arrived at. It is usual for the way in which knowledge is understood and sought to be related intimately to the ways in which it is thought proper to represent that knowledge, and three aspects of the mathetized appetite for knowledge are especially significant in this connection. The first is the question of voice; the second the question of textual representation; and the third that of controlled reproducibility.

Curious knowers typically do not want to identify the knowledge they have arrived at as bearing an intimate link to their own persons or idiosyncrasies or place or interests; and they will certainly not wish to claim intimacy with what they study in the sense that a student occupying a world of gift and participation must. The curious, formed by mathesis, are always different in kind from what they are curious about, so their purpose is not to participate in what they study, but rather to isolate their object, and then to display it like a butterfly pinned in a display case. The voice the curious adopt in representing their knowledge will, therefore, avoid the first person, and will avoid, also, laying claim to the knowledge represented as though it were inextricably linked to the persona, charisma, or skill of the knower. (There is, as we shall see in a moment, on this matter a tension internal to mathetically produced curiosity because of the tendency of the curious to think of objects of knowledge as things that can be owned, and thereby to lay claim to them.) And so mathesis will encourage the passive voice and the avoidance of the first person, whether in speech or writing. The writer of the dissertation or the scholarly monograph— for our academies are still, for the most part, hotbeds of mathesis, even if in somewhat diluted form—will prefer to write, "If one adopts the quantitative method used here one will find . . . ," than to write, "I've used a quantitative method to show . . . ." She will say that the evidence shows such-and-such, or that a complete explanation of whatever-it-is requires attention to data of the following kind. In using such constructions, the agency of the writer is occluded: she is absorbed into her method, and she serves, rhetorically, as nothing more than a channel for the truth. Her place could be occupied by anyone willing to be disciplined by the proper method.

Mathetized writers or speakers (the curious typically prefer writing to speaking) also do not find it important to signal their imaginations of their readers, or to permit them entry into what they write. The scholarly monograph eschews apostrophization of the reader (sagacious and knowledgeable reader, I entreat you . . .) with as much vigor as the first person, and for much the same reasons. Even a more restrained second-person address to the reader (you may think, on reading this, that . . .) is rare. Who the reader is, and what she may or may not think, is irrelevant if a world of discrete simple natures is being displayed with precision and perfection. She will be convinced by the display if it is done well, because the reflection in words of what the curious know is, ideally, as transparent to that knowledge as the knowledge is to its objects. There is thus a double transparency and passivity: knowables are transparent to and passive before curious knowers; and what curious knowers write and say is transparent to and passive before their ideal readers and hearers. That is why those readers do not need to be addressed or apostrophized or persuaded: words need only be offered in order to convince by their transparency.

I write this book, as is evident, not as an advocate of mathesis, but rather as a Christian advocate of gift, participation, and wonder. And although I rarely apostrophize you, the reader, you are a constant second-person presence in my text because I know that the world is not as the curious imagine it to be, and that any depiction I offer of it must acknowledge, rhetorically as well as conceptually, that I, as one participant in God, am offering it to you, as another. We share a mode of being that requires this acknowledgment; this is not true for the curious, and that is why their texts adopt the passive voice and refuse acknowledgment of their audience.

In addition to adopting a certain voice, the mathetically curious are drawn to textual devices that permit the world they know—the world of discrete, passive, transparent objects—to be imaged in the text. Tables, grids, indices, chapters, and subheads: these are devices that flower with the invention of printing (though they are not unknown before that), and each of them atomizes the text, reduces it to parts which might, ideally (never fully, of course; I deal here with tendencies and affinities, not with fully realized actualities), be isolated from the rest of the text and understood by itself. A nonatomized text, by contrast, will have few devices of that sort, and will call its readers to an engagement with the whole rather than with its parts. Consider, as an extreme form of the contrast, a textbook that might be used today in a high school class (in any subject) in the United States, with an uncial Latin manuscript from the third or fourth century A.D. The former has many devices for text-division: punctuation, typographic variation, chapters, diagrams, lists, tables, bulleted points, boxed text, and so on. The latter has almost none: no word-division, no apparatus for marking sectional divisions, and almost no punctuation. The former is a collection of bite-sized discrete objects, massaged toward transparency, designed to be ingested piecemeal by the relatively uncatechized; it is likely to be an instrument of mathetic catechism, for its textual design images the world of mathesis. The latter is an (almost) undivided whole, only available to and usable by the elite, and representative of an approach to depicting what is known that prefers the vibrations of speech to the permanent storage of writing—for even the elite will usually need to read such a manuscript aloud, to sound it out, in order to make sense of it. It is likely to be an instrument of the catechism of wonder and appetite for studious intimacy, for its textual design sits well with a world of gift and participation.

There is, finally, the question of reproducibility. The curious aim at a perfectly atemporal and thoroughly spatialized knowledge, ideally capable of schematic representation on a grid, whether two- or three- (or more) dimensional. If this is how what there is to be known exists, then this is also how, ideally, it ought to be represented. As already noted, the idiosyncrasies of writer and reader, of the one who depicts and the one who consumes the depiction, are removed to the extent that this is possible, and a corresponding tendency is evident with respect to the textual depiction of what is known. The idiosyncrasies and particular ornaments of manuscript reproduction (this hand, that ink, the curled vellum), and even those of print reproduction (edition-specific errors and design features), are, for the representation of what the curious know, imperfections to be removed by purification. What is sought is the perfect, error-free depiction of what is known, a depiction that stands before its object like a pane of glass without bubbles or scratches or any other distortion. When this has been arrived at (of course it never can be arrived at; it is a regulative ideal, never an actuality), it should be perfectly reproducible, so that each token of the type is identical in its perfection with every other, which is to say that no token can be discriminated from any other. This urge toward perfect reproducibility is also an urge away from particular, temporally located representations; it is the extreme case of a desire to represent a frozen, spatialized world in a manner effectively indistinct from what it represents.

The knowledge sought by those whose appetite has been formed by a mathetic catechesis is in almost every interesting respect different from that sought by those who have been formed to want to know by a catechesis of gift and participation. Mathetic catechism is optimistic. In fact, it appears absurdly, dangerously, and utopianly so to those who think of knowledge as a kind of intimacy with the other, which is always and inevitably tinged with lament. The curious take themselves to be approaching the goal of getting it finally and completely right—the goal, that is, of knowing everything that's to be known and knowing it perfectly, without blemish or error—ever more closely, and will one day get there. This is the optimism of the Whig historian for whom the idea of progress is essential and non-negotiable. But not only this: the curious are also likely to think that we are moving ever more closely toward being able to represent what we know in such a way that all will be convinced by it. This thought explains the wide distribution in high modernity of tropes of obviousness and self-evidence as elements in the depiction of what is known. It is not enough for the optimism of the curious that we are on an upward cognitive curve; it must also be the case that what counts as knowledge ought to be transparently such for all who are faced with its depiction, and this is often signalled by the curious in their texts.

This emphasis on transparency and manipulability sits well with optimism about our capacity to know. In extreme cases, this can lead to the idea that we will, eventually or perhaps even soon, know all there is to know: the world will be arrayed before us in such a way that all its constituents and all their relations will be open to our gaze. This is quite opposed to the Christian emphasis upon lament's inevitability and the partial failure of all attempts to know in a world whose cognitive and moral darkness presses hard upon us. For the curious, there is nothing about the world or anything in it that resists our gaze; and there is nothing about our gaze that prevents it penetrating what it looks at. Puzzlement is present only to be overcome, and lament only to be catechized away.

Mathesis is intimate with mastery, and therefore also with ownership. The curious, formed by mathesis as aspiring knowers of a world of discrete, transparent, and manipulable objects, seek above all to master and thereby to own the things they want to know, according to the grammar of ownership already set forth.

～

The studious Christian, seeking participatory intimacy driven by wonder and riven by lament, cannot coherently seek ownership. It is axiomatic for Christians that all creatures (and therefore all knowables, whether sensible or intelligible) are brought into being by God out of nothing and are sustained in being only so long as God chooses to do so. God is, therefore, both efficient and final cause of all corporeal goods, to use the Aristotelian schema; we can also say that God is necessary and sufficient condition for the coming-to-be and continuing-to-be of any creature. These theological axioms yield the conclusion that only God possesses or owns any creature, because only he has or could have the power to sequester it into privacy (which would be to take it out of being altogether) or to grant it public display (which is just what he does when he creates).

This is not to say that use of creatures is barred to us, nor even that we are barred from sequestering creatures for our exclusive use for a time—or even for a lifetime. But it is to say that stewardly use is the category that frames and orders any Christian understanding of what we do when we sequester in this way, and that this moves Christian thought in the direction of acknowledging with gratitude that it is due to divine gift that there are any creatures for us to use; and that we cannot seek and will not find the exhaustive intimacy with any creature that pure ownership implies. This understanding as it applies to sensible creatures finds graphic and precise illustration in a common Christian interpretation of the command to give alms: this is not a command to give away to others what is yours, but rather a command to make available to others what was God's before you came to have the use of it, and what will remain God's when someone else has the use of it.

So much for the theological point: God is sole owner and we are granted stewardly use of what he owns for a shorter or longer time. But, of course, this use is regulated by humanly made positive laws, which do indeed grant property rights; but the fact that they do so and the way in which they do so—which includes the sanction of violent punishment up to and including death for offence against the law; and which includes, as well, the enforcement of patterns of use of sensible creatures that entail the poverty and suffering of many in ways that directly contravene God's intentions for a justly ordered human society, a *res publica*—is an effect of the fall. It is only because of sin and its concomitant damage that such laws are needed; they are not needed in the first grace, the graceful gift of creation (Adam and Eve owned nothing), and they will not be needed in heaven; and so secular laws providing property rights are a regrettable and temporary necessity, fully explicable as an artifact of sin. Not only this: they also enshrine an incoherent understanding of what it is to own property. If, as the position just staked out claims, only God can own in the full and proper sense, then human laws that purport to grant rights to ownership in perpetuity must be at best deceptive simulacra of the divine law. That law, rooted in the order of creation, which is also the order of love, has no conceptual space for the idea of human ownership on the model of divine ownership.

Secular property laws are nonetheless to be obeyed, though with the understanding that what they regulate is use rather than freehold possession. Such laws, to a limited extent, do serve peace and the proper ordering of human society, and that is why they should be obeyed. The good they bring about is that of restricting and constraining by a limited use of fear and violence what would otherwise be an unrestrained use of these same horrors; but it must be remembered that they are themselves irretrievably implicated with violence and coercion. The fact that they exist, and the fact that they need to be obeyed are occasions for lament more than for rejoicing. And the deep tendency we humans have to divinize ourselves by thinking that we can be owners as God is an owner needs constantly to be checked by recalling that our ownership is not a matter of sequestration's power of control, but rather one of grateful receipt (and, as a matter of aspiration, stewardly use) of gift.

The most fundamental distinction between the ownership-relation and the stewardship-relation, therefore, has to do with the presence of a third party in the latter and its absence in the former. The grammar of human ownership requires reference only to the owner and what is owned; the grammar of stewardship requires reference also to the real owner, who on the Christian construal of world and appetite is also the creator, toward whom stewards and what they hold share a relation of subordination and participation. This fundamental distinction can be worked out in various ways, most of the particulars of which depend upon the nature of the real owner. If he is a despot or a tyrant or a weakly inattentive dilettante without interest in his steward or his holdings things will look very different than they will if, as Christians think, he is the one who has given both steward and goods their very existence, and loves them with a passion unparalleled in depth and scope. Then gratitude may be provoked, and the clear-eyed among the stewards will understand the resonant depths of their commonality with the goods they have temporarily sequestered for use, and will not be tempted toward display of their own power and strength as the only owners of wholly owned property.

∾

All sensible creatures are finite and corruptible. This means that their sequestration, whether under the sign of stewardship or ownership, is competitive: if you control access to, use of, and disposal of this house or that automobile, then I cannot; if you're at the moment using that book, then I cannot; if that food is vanishing into your mouth at the moment, then it cannot vanish into mine. The house, the car, the book, the food are all exhaustible creatures, and it is the fact that all sensible creatures are like this that makes positive property law unavoidable: if something is such that when I have the use of it no one else can, and especially if it is also something that can be removed altogether from existence, leaving only traces of itself behind (my dinner is like this, as is my house and my library), then disputes about who should have the use of it are inevitable and need regulation. But even though all sensible creatures are finite and corruptible, some are less finite and less corruptible than others. Or so it appears to creatures like us. Sunlight and stars and air, for example, seem always to be more or less available; and their availability seems not to be directly dependent on human effort. The day breaks and the rain falls, after all, without any of us doing anything to make it so. But in fact, these creatures are no less finite and corruptible than my house or your car or that first edition: it is just that they are broadly extended in time and space, and are independent of human effort, and so we judge them, in effect, creatures of a different sort than the usual instances of local portable property, and do not compete to sequester them.

Sensible creatures like these have for most of human history been treated as commons (a noun that, in this meaning, serves as both singular and plural). That is, they have not been treated as actual or potential property, and have therefore not been sequestered or enclosed or in any other way made subject to a regime of property law. This is now beginning to change rather as, in much of the world, earlier practices of treating at least some land as commons were also gradually abandoned, and for much the same reason: any sensible creature that can be corrupted in the direction of exhaustion by human activity is likely eventually to be removed from the commons as use of it, and thereby pressure upon it, increases or is thought to do so. This is not quite inevitable, and there are certainly ways of managing a commons even in sensible creatures in such a way as to avoid the Scylla of the ordinary tragedy of the commons, which is destruction by unrestrained competitive consumption, and the Charybdis of the commons' complete enclosure by subjection to the laws of property. Even though it is not inevitable, one or other of these—most commonly the embrace of Charybdis in order to avoid Scylla—is the usual story. The tendency of Christian thought on the management of corruptible sensible creatures is (or ought to be) to err in the direction of preserving a commons in even the most obviously and immediately exhaustible of sensible creatures when this is at all possible—though it also belongs to the grammar and syntax of Christian thought to recognize that it is better for some creatures, and for their users, to be sequestered for exclusive (though temporary) use.

Intelligibilia differ from even the most widely available sensibilia in being quite inexhaustible. They are, by definition, not extended in space: if they were, they would be available to one or more of the senses, which their definition requires them not to be. But this also means that they are not located in time, for if they were they would also be located in space (space and time being functions of one another as both special and general relativity precisely show, and as Platonists—and thereby also most late-antique Christians—have known for a long time), and, again, the definition rules out that possibility. But these properties of intelligibilia jointly mean that they are not subject to corruption, diminution, exhaustion or indeed change of any sort. Nothing that we humans can do will move them toward exhaustion or consumption. They are, therefore, the best possible case of creatures, which, because they are inexhaustible, cannot effectively be sequestered, and, as a result, cannot be owned.

It is worth pausing on that claim for a moment, and illustrating it with an example or two. The clearest examples of intelligibilia are mathematical: Goldbach's conjecture, already mentioned several times—that every even number greater than two can be expressed as the sum of two primes—is, if true, an intelligible creature. There is no place in which it can be found, and if it is true it is necessarily so, which entails that it has always been true and will never cease to be so.

The event of any human being coming to know that it is true changes the intelligible in question only by adding to it the adventitious property of being known at a time, which alters not at all what the intelligible essentially is. Similar things can be said about the principles of proportion and harmony. But intelligibilia are not limited to such creatures. Every state of affairs is an intelligible: that the United States gained independence from Great Britain in 1776; that I was married in 1975; that Jesus the Christ was fully God and fully human; that human birthrates fall as income rises; that there are juniper forests in England; that the grizzly bear *(ursus arctos horribilis)* is not trifled with by humans who value their survival; that humans are not reliable sources of information about their own motives; that simony is a sin; that human boredom is evidence of damage caused by an aboriginal calamity—all these are, I think, states of affairs. And whether or not you think so, you should agree that if they are, the fact that they obtain is an intelligible, and thus itself not subject to time, change, decay or corruption. States of affairs like these differ from the mathematical example given earlier in that they are contingent: it is coherently imaginable that they might not obtain, even though in fact they do, whereas if Goldbach's conjecture is true (and I do not know whether it is), then it is not coherently imaginable that it might not have been. Some of these states of affairs, too, have to do with occurrences in time, datable occurrences, and to the extent that this is so, intimacy with them can be achieved by temporal knowers like us only simultaneously with or after they have come to obtain. But when known as God knows them, *sub specie aeternitatis,* all these states of affairs— contingent and necessary, historical and otherwise—are alike in being beyond the reach of time and change. And when we achieve intimacy with any of these states of affairs, we participate, to the degree possible for us, in their peculiar mode of being.

Both the curious and the studious have considerable interest in and ardent appetite for intimacy with intelligibilia—with, that is to say, knowledge of states of affairs or other abstract objects. Someone seeking intimacy, whether curiously or studiously, with Augustine's *De doctrina christiana* may aspire to own, caress, and admiringly contemplate written or printed copies of Augustine's work, or to memorize the words in which it consists; and someone seeking intimacy with grizzly bears may, unwisely, aspire to live with them or take one home with him. Achieving either of these would certainly be intimacy—and thereby knowledge—of a kind, but it would be intimacy with sensibilia, and more like the work of a collector than that of an intellectual. But it is also possible, and for intellectuals inevitable, to seek intimacy with the intelligible states of affairs with which actual copies of *De doctrina christiana* or particular grizzlies are themselves intimate, and which they instantiate. What the curious aspire to have dominion over is most typically concepts or ideas, whether these ideas have tangibles as their referent or not: they want a theory, perhaps, as to the extent of Augustine's knowledge of Quintilian's *Instituto oratoria* and the significance of that knowledge for understanding why he wrote what he wrote in *De doctrina christiana;* or an understanding of the dietary habits of the lactating female grizzly.

Intelligibilia, by contrast, are inexhaustible: they cannot be consumed or otherwise corrupted, and this means that my intimacy with them can in no way compete with yours. If I am intimate with Goldbach's conjecture, even to the point of being able to offer a proof of it, I can give this proof to you or to the world without myself losing it. This is not so for my car or my dinner. There are even, as the depiction (in chapter 5) of gifts and giving shows, some intelligibilia, which require, in order that human intimacy with them not be corrupted, that the intimacy be shared. According to the Christian construal of the world, this is true of intimacy with the gospel and with Christ himself: the degree to which any of us knows Christ and what the gospel is and demands is the degree to which we must share that knowledge by giving it away. Not to do so is to damage the intimacy we have with these things. Some things can be given away without thereby being lost to the giver, and some things will be lost if they are not given away. This is true of not only intimacy with Christ and the gospel, but even of more mundane intimacies with both sensibilia and intelligibilia. The point of importance here is that intelligibilia belong by definition to a commons: any attempt to expropriate them therefrom, to privatize them, corrupts not the intelligibilia (that is impossible) but rather both the one who attempts it and the intimate relation he attempts to establish between himself and the intelligible in question.

The curious do, typically, attempt the enclosure-by-sequestration of the intellectual commons. Not recognizing the changeless participation in God of what they seek to know, they seek, in accord with the mathetic catechesis, which has formed them, to isolate, expropriate, and thereby obtain exhaustive intimacy with intelligibilia. And once this exhaustive intimacy has, they think, been reached, the intelligible in question—a mathematical proof, an understanding of social relations, a data-set, a harmonic sequence—is, without remainder, owned, enclosed, to be returned to the commons only when its owner chooses. The analogy with wholly owned pieces of portable property goes deep and is written into law, which has, for at least the last four centuries, recognized property rights in what lawyers like to call intangibles. These include what I have been calling intelligibilia, and the fact that our regimes of property law have expanded to embrace intellectual property is an index of the depth of ingression of intellectual appetites formed in the direction of curiosity rather than studiousness.

∾

The presence of a curious appetite for the demarcation, isolation, sequestration, and, finally, pure ownership of intelligibilia has many signs that betray its presence. These include an interest on the part of the aspiring knower in laying claim to what is known and in making that claim public by advertising not only what is known but also (and usually first) oneself as knower of it. No intellectual commons is recognized by the curious: there are only fields of knowledge awaiting conquest by disciplinarily appropriate method, and once the flag is planted, the field is expropriated and owned, unavailable to others unless access is graciously granted. A mathetic catechesis requires that what lies as yet beyond the grasp of the curious knower be depicted as passive before that knower's gaze, awaiting the exhaustive intimacy in which pure possession consists. Those catechized by Jesus Christ in the direction of studiousness, by contrast, are inclined toward stewardship both of their intimacies and of what they are intimate with because they have been trained to recognize both as gifts, gifts that do not explain themselves and cannot be exhausted. The studious will, therefore, not be much interested in laying claim to what they know by advertising themselves as its knowers; and when they do—as, delight-moved, they sometimes will, seeing that the sheer, unmerited gift of the capacity for knowledge's reflexively delighted intimacy with creatures requires to be given away if it is to remain uncorrupted—make public the intimacies they have come to enjoy with intelligible creatures, they may do so in ways strange to the curious by renouncing the credit of being known as a knower by publishing anonymously, pseudonymously or pseudepigraphically. Those contrasts will be explored in more detail in chapter 10. And then, the gaze of the curious, mathetically catechized as it has been, fixes differently upon those things it looks at than does the gaze of the studious: the former see spectacles and the latter icons, a contrast explored in chapter 11. This contrast in turn leads to a further one, between loquacity and stammering (with silence as a third term), the former attracting the curious and the latter the studious; this is depicted in chapter 13, and it is articulated with the attraction to—indeed, obsession with—novelty that characterizes the curious, and the contrasting interest in repetition that belongs to the studious.

10

KIDNAPPING

Quid enim furantur, alienum auferunt, verbum autem Dei non est ab eis alienum qui obtemperant ei.

What is stolen is alienated, but the word of God cannot be alienated from those who obey him.

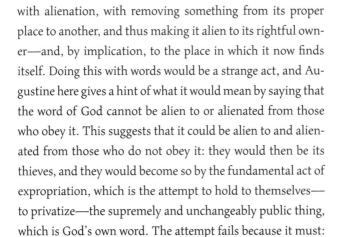

Augustine here (*De doctrina christiana* 4.29.62) identifies theft with alienation, with removing something from its proper place to another, and thus making it alien to its rightful owner—and, by implication, to the place in which it now finds itself. Doing this with words would be a strange act, and Augustine here gives a hint of what it would mean by saying that the word of God cannot be alien to or alienated from those who obey it. This suggests that it could be alien to and alienated from those who do not obey it: they would then be its thieves, and they would become so by the fundamental act of expropriation, which is the attempt to hold to themselves—to privatize—the supremely and unchangeably public thing, which is God's own word. The attempt fails because it must: whatever you get when you steal God's word cannot, by definition, be what you attempted to steal.

The curious and the studious share the judgment that the figure of the *plagiarus,* the kidnapper or body-thief who became, sometime in the eighteenth century, the plagiarist or word-thief, is a threatening one and therefore to be shunned. But they differ deeply about what is wrong with this figure, and about how to avoid his clutches. The studious find him absurd because what he attempts is performatively incoherent: stealing words is something that, when attempted, guarantees its own failure in much the same way as does asserting the impossibility of assertion. The studious are therefore embarrassed and amused by those who think word theft possible, whether they like and practise it or not. For them, it is the very idea of plagiarism that needs criticism, not its practice. But for the curious, the plagiarist is a real threat because they think that what he attempts can be done; for them, the plagiarist must be opposed with his own weapons and defeated, if he can be, by outperforming him at his own game. This difference about plagiarism shows with considerable clarity how Christians and pagans differ in their understanding of the relations between the work of their own hands and minds and that of others. But what is it, exactly, that the word-thief attempts?

Plagiarus is a Latin word, pre-Christian in origin and use, whose primary meaning is body-thief or kidnapper. It denotes a figure who makes off with your offspring or someone else close to you—or even with yourself. What the *plagiarus* does, then, is to expropriate something of great value and intimacy—your child is the gift of your body, after all, and typically someone with whom you are very closely intertwined. And the *plagiarus* is a violent figure: he will often need to use or to threaten violence in order to achieve his theft. He takes from you something you are very unwilling that he should have, and keeps it from you as long as he has the power to do so. Gradually, the word's meaning relaxed and expanded, until the *plagiarus* became not just a thief of human bodies, but also an expropriator of other things, including—and this is the meaning that interests me here—words owned by others. The body-thief became a word-thief, and the *plagiarus* became the more familiar, and more English, plagiarist. This word-history is not irrelevant to the word's current meaning, and you should keep it in mind if you are fully to understand what is now meant by plagiarism, and what is the significance of the different reasons the studious and the curious have for opposing it. Especially important are the connotations of theft-by-violence, and of losing something very close to you. Both are at play in the idea of plagiarism, though a little excavation is needed if this is to be made evident.

There is no uncontroversial definition of plagiarism, which is, as will become apparent, not surprising; but this may serve as a first approximation: *you act as a plagiarist when you knowingly make public use of an ensemble of words without acknowledgment of the place from which you took it.* The ordinary instance of plagiaristic activity is publication under your own name of a word-ensemble previously composed and made public by someone else. But there are more recherché instances that fall under the more general definition (perhaps you publish under a name other than your own a word-ensemble you have taken from yet another person; or perhaps you translate words written in one language by someone other than yourself, and present them as your own composition), and so it has its uses. It is not only words that can be taken and used in plagiaristic fashion. The same can be done with music, visual art, gesture, mode of dress, and so on. But ordinary corporeal creatures like your cash or car or food cannot be taken by the *plagiarus.* If they could, he would be a common thief and subject to the ordinary criminal penalties for theft. Rather, what the plagiarist takes is something with the following features: first, it could not exist without your work; and second, it is something that you still have even after the plagiarist has taken it from you—which is to say that the plagiarist takes what, if it can be owned at all, can be owned by more than one person at a time. Word-ensembles clearly have both these properties: if some ensemble of words is in any sense yours, it must be because you did something to engender it, typically by composing it and then displaying it in utterance or writing; and if someone plagiarizes it, it is still yours: you can easily (usually) utter or write it again.

This second property of things that may be taken and used by the plagiarist is the most conceptually interesting. It connects them closely with intelligibilia as I have depicted these in chapters 3 and 6, for those too are not diminished or exhausted by being handed (metaphorically) from one to another, and they are like this exactly because they are intelligibles, located nowhere in space or time. The goods that can be expropriated by a plagiarist, then, are ordinarily expressions or concretizations of something that can be expressed or concretized again and again, without loss to itself. These goods are, to put the same matter differently, simulacra rather than originals. In the case of your words, what they express or concretize, it is natural to say, is something about you (your thoughts, your speech habits, your desires, your hopes, your fears) with which they are not identical. What the plagiarist does, according to this view, in taking and making unacknowledged public use of your words, is not merely to expropriate some ensemble of written signs or vibrations in the air, but also to lay claim to the same relation to them that you have. Perhaps this relation is that of being first speaker, or first writer, or author; but there is no uncontroversial or obvious thing to say about what the relation is, and as we shall see, the curious and the studious differ about it. Whatever it is, the plagiarist lays unjustified claim to it, and it is in this that his offense most essentially consists.

The difference between ordinary takings of sensible creatures and plagiaristic kidnappings of such things as words is recognized in most systems of positive law. Stealing a copy of Don DeLillo's *Underworld* from the bookstore or from your friend's bookshelf is one kind of offence: straightforward theft. Publishing a copy of *Underworld* under your own name is quite another: infringement of copyright. The difference is given first by what you are laying claim to in each case, which is a corporeal object in the first case, and a word-ensemble in the second; it is further specified by the harm done in each case, which is material loss in the first case, and a complex collocation of loss of reputation, right, and income, in the second. You do not have to go as far as pretending to be Don DeLillo in order to infringe his copyright, of course. Were you merely without appropriate permission to quote or otherwise reproduce, in whole or in significant part, the ensemble of words in which *Underworld* consists, you would also infringe copyright, and you would do so by performing an act that only DeLillo's relation to that word-ensemble (whatever account is best offered of it) gives him the legal right to perform unpermitted.

The plagiarist, then, knowingly takes an ensemble of words and makes public use of it without acknowledging the place from which he took it. Both the studious and the curious agree that this phenomenon can and does occur, but they differ very significantly in their understandings of it and in the value they attribute to it. These differences are largely rooted in differences about the nature of the ensembles of words, which the plagiarist takes and uses. What are these word-ensembles? What relations do they bear to those who in the past first uttered or wrote them, and to those who later take and make public use of them without acknowledgment? The different catecheses that have formed the curious and the studious give rise to different understandings of ownership and thereby to profoundly different answers to the questions mentioned.

Anyone who speaks or writes now, swims, knowingly or not, in an ocean of words already spoken or written. Writing has a relatively short history—perhaps six thousand years or so; speaking has a much longer one, at least ten times as long and perhaps much more—though much here depends on defining what it is to speak, and on controverted questions in palaeoanthropology. And there are tens of billions of human speakers who have lived (more than six billion of them are living now, as I write), along with at least hundreds of millions of writers. Most spoken words are ephemeral, vanishing as soon as the vibrations in the air of which they consist have dissipated; some tiny portion of them is stored in memory, or in some artificial medium of storage, but most are irretrievably lost almost as soon as uttered. Some ensembles of written words last longer: the libraries are overstuffed with books, and the electronic archives hum wth written words; but most of what has been written has perished, too. A word-ocean remains, however, both spoken and written, vastly greater in extent than what can be heard or read by any living writer or speaker.

"Ocean" is a useful metaphor because it suggests the difficulty of division and demarcation. It is not easy to say where one wave begins and another ends; and when a great river flows out into the sea, its fresh water is gradually salted so gradually that there is no obvious division between the two bodies of water. Matters are in some ways similar with the word-ocean. The definition of plagiarism I have given uses the idea of a word-ensemble—a body of words that begins and ends somewhere. But how to determine the end of one ensemble and the beginning of another? It is possible, certainly, to specify the boundaries that constitute some particular word-ensemble, whether tiny (a phrase, a sentence), of medium size (a paragraph, a chapter), large (the Hebrew words that constitute the Tanakh), or very large indeed (the words found in the entire print collection of the British Library). But, as these examples strongly suggest, such acts of demarcation are always performed in the service of particular interests or concerns, which are unlikely to be universally shared. The administrators of the British Library have interests in what can be done with the ensemble of words under their care, and therefore in its extent and boundaries and definition and maintenance and expansion; but it is difficult to imagine that anyone else shares those interests in that ensemble, or that many think about a word-ensemble so defined at all. And the ensemble of Hebrew words that begins B'reshit (Genesis 1:1) and ends we ya'al (2 Chronicles

36:23) is of primary interest as an ensemble to Jews, and the specification of its beginning and end rests upon tradition-specific understandings of the nature of that ensemble as spoken by God. Providing a coherent and widely agreed account of what individuates one sensible creature from another that rests upon something more than habit and convention is hard enough; providing any such account of what individuates one word-ensemble from another is considerably harder. This is not to say that all tradition-specific accounts of what individuates one word-ensemble from another are conventional in the sense that none accurately identifies what it is that provides the boundaries to a particular word-ensemble. Perhaps, for example, the Jews are right that God demarcated the boundaries of the Tanakh, and in so doing gave to it a form that demarcates it and individuates it nonconventionally from all other word-ensembles. But even if they are right (and they are), their rightness is unlikely to be widely recognized, and remains in that sense tradition specific.

The range and depth of the ocean of words in which every speaker and writer swims, coupled with the difficulty of individuating one wave in that ocean from another, means that no one—not the curious and not the studious—thinks that every public use of an ensemble of words without acknowledgment of the place from which it was taken constitutes an act of plagiarism. Most speakers of English, for instance, would agree that I do not plagiarize when I say "How do you do?" on being introduced to someone without mentioning that I've taken this word-ensemble from my mother's instruction in manners. Neither (arguably) would most think I plagiarize when I publicly use the sentence "He do the police in different voices" without mentioning that I read this word-ensemble first in T. S. Eliot, and then later in Charles Dickens. The first phrase is a cliche of courtesy, and the second, by now, is proverbial. They cannot be kidnapped, either because they are not interesting enough, or because they have been so frequently expropriated already that one more instance concerns no one—though I suppose it is possible to imagine some writers or speakers feeling constrained to acknowledge the origin of "he do the police" through fear of accusations of plagiarism. If you do think that some word-ensembles can be kidnapped and some cannot—and the curious certainly do—this will be because you think that the ones that can be plagiarized have properties the others do not. In the case of the curious, the relevant properties have—unsurprisingly—mostly to do with ownership. Some ensembles of words, they think, are or can be owned; and it is those that can be plagiarized.

The plagiarist is the doppelgänger of the curious. He is a figure the curious have created in their image and likeness, but one they are concerned at all costs not to become, and will do anything to extinguish. The beginning of an explanation for this oddly complex situation is to hand in the conflicting desires of the curious. On the one hand, they want to be known as knowers by laying claim to the intelligibilia, which in their own estimation they have succeeded in demarcating and mastering. This they can best do by publishing under their own names what they take themselves to have come to know. But they also want (as discussed already in chapter 9) to speak in a voice of such impersonal dispassion that what they say will at once convince all hearers of its truth; and that voice, if it can be found, does not sit very easily with the personal ownership claimed by the grasp of possession extended not only to what is known but also to the fact of being its owner. This is the tension, and it gives rise to an anxiety very typical of the curious: they have been catechized into seeking and claiming ownership of what they know, and into thinking of the ideal-typical depiction of cognitive intimacies as free from adulteration by the idiosyncrasies of the owner. The anxiety is resolved, to the extent it can be, by externalization: the curious imagine a figure that can bear this anxiety by first providing an explanation of its existence, and then by being erased or exiled. This figure is the *plagiarus,* the kidnapper of words.

The curious and the plagiarist share an understanding, as doppel-gängers must, of how to identify and demarcate particular ensembles of words within the boundless ocean of the verbal. The ideal-typical ensemble is a work of some author's mind and hands; it has a beginning and end, intended and marked as such by the author, and (preferably) indicated by the corporeal form of the object in which the work, the word-ensemble, is displayed to a public—the printed book's boundaries are marked by its covers, the manuscript's boundaries by its *incipit* and *explicit,* the spoken ensemble's beginning and end by the ritualized words of introduction and conclusion and so on. Each bounded ensemble of words ("the work," as contracts between publishing houses and authors like to call it) is the wholly owned possession of its author: it has been created *ex nihilo* by the quasi-divine judgment and imagination of its author (impossible, of course; but this is the logic of the ideal type), and this is what provides authors with the right to control access to their works, as well as the use and disposal of those same works—the three kinds of sequestration in which ownership essentially consists, as depicted in chapter 9. The plagiarist shares exactly this understanding of how to think about word-ensembles; but he wants to use violence to take and use, illegitimately, an ensemble from its rightful owner, and it is this violence that the curious combat with the law of intellectual property: of copyright, principally, but also of patent, trademark, and trade secret.

For the curious, then, the commons of the word-ocean ought ideally to be enclosed, and in that way moved from the public sphere to the private. The principal means of enclosure is the establishment of a right of ownership brought into being by the creative work of the author. Ensembles of words enclosed in this way ("the work") are, according to the grammar of this position, treated as if they were exhaustible corporeal goods, goods whose possession by one owner means their loss to another. Charles Dickens, for example, objected to the unlicensed printing of his novels: he was among the principal advocates for an international law of copyright on the ground that every sale of an unlicensed copy meant a lost sale of a licensed copy, with concomitant loss of royalty to him. He was approximately right in this zero-sum judgment about rights to reproduce by printing (approximately only, because not everyone who buys an unlicensed copy would have bought a licensed one, especially if the unlicensed copy sells at a cheaper price, as was—and is—ordinarily the case), and approximately right, therefore, to think of this aspect of ownership as though it were a consumable corporeal good. But the interest the curious have in ownership of their literary works extends beyond those uses of them that can reasonably be understood by means of zero-sum thinking. Once a word-ensemble has been brought into being and its bounds carefully marked, its curious owner will not want it to be accessed or used even when such access and use is an inexhaustible and incorporeal good, undiminished and undiminishable by any use. Consider the case of verbatim reproduction of the words in which some literary work consists (whether in part or whole) for noncommercial purposes. When, for instance, the work has been made available on the Web in electronic form, such verbatim reproduction is almost cost- and effort-free. If, for example, I cut-and-paste (electronically) your essay on copyright law's blessings and send it, under my own name and without any indication of its provenance, as an e-mail attachment to one thousand of my acquaintances, this does not at all diminish your capacity, as author, to do the same. Your objection to my doing it—to thus kidnapping your words—will not be a Dickensian claim that you are losing money thereby, or that "the work" has been diminished by what I have done. No, if you object you will do so, most often, because you will think that I have stolen something of yours—or at the very least have acted duplicitously in attaching my name to it rather than acknowledging you as its author—and in so doing have diminished not the work as such, the bounded word-ensemble (which remains, after all, just as it was, inexhaustibly present, after I have sent it to all my friends), but rather you, as its owner. This is typical of the clash between the curious and the plagiarizers: each assumes that there is an important good of authorship, a good that may be defined roughly as *being acknowledged as the unique creator of the work*. This good is, in the strict and proper sense, subject to zero-sum logic: if you have it, I do not; and the extent to which there is public doubt about my having it (doubt created, perhaps, by your plagiarism) is the extent to which I am in the way of losing it.

This attribution of importance to the good of ownership is abundantly evident in the two principal rationales for objecting to plagiarism put forward by the curious. The first, already mentioned, is that plagiarists are thieves; the second is that they are liars. The two rationales are closely connected: each depends on the assumption that authors' words are their property, and on the assumption that it is possible, and perhaps even easy, to know when a particular word-ensemble belongs to a particular author. Neither assumption can be defended from the point of view of the studious Christian, as we shall see in a moment. But each has become a widespread and standard assumption, evident in intellectual property law, university definitions and proscriptions of plagiarism, and so on. The first—the assumption that the *plagiarus* is a thief—is straightforward in its assimilation of word-ensembles to property. If the words I am now writing are, just in virtue of my having written them, my property, then any use you make of them ought to be governed by the contractual norms that order this kind of property law, or by the ordinary exceptions to those norms—as, for example, in the exceptions to copyright law granted by the legal doctrine of fair use.

The second rationale for objecting to plagiarism—that the plagiarist is dishonest—also assumes, if not quite so directly, that the word-ensemble taken and used by the plagiarist is the property of its author. That, after all, is what the plagiarist is being dishonest about: he is claiming as his work what he knows to be another's, occluding another's ownership of a particular word-ensemble in favor of laying public claim to it himself. (This way of putting things assumes that the plagiarist knows what he does. That this is the ordinary assumption is shown by the frequency of the I-didn't-know-I-was-doing-it defense against accusations of plagiarism, a defense ordinarily taken to mitigate, if not quite to remove, the offense.) There is a third rationale for objecting to the *plagiarus'* unacknowledged public use of a word-ensemble not composed by himself, but I'll defer discussion of that to the depiction of the studious response to and understanding of plagiarism. For now, it is enough to say that the curious and the plagiarists are creatures of one another's anxieties, and that this conflict is a tug-of-war over property whose ownership is disputed.

The curious idea that word-ensembles can be owned, and that the act of authorship is what contributes most directly and fully to the ownership of an ensemble, has effects upon the conventions governing the presence of the words of others in their own literary works. These words are alien: they belong to another, having been created *ex nihilo* by the mind and will of that other, and they must be treated gingerly, acknowledged as guests, and given appropriate greeting and hospitality. This means at the very least that explicit credit must be given: the guest's presence must be signalled as such, and the words in which that presence consists demarcated as clearly as possible from the words that the curious take themselves to have brought into being by their own creative effort. The devices for acknowledging the verbal property of another are many: the footnote, the parenthetical reference, the weaving of the alien author's name into the fabric of the newly composed work; and, of course, the quotation mark; each of these has this acknowledgment among its functions. Verbatim reproduction of an alien word-ensemble is not the only way in which that ensemble can be present in yours: you can allude, echo, parody, weave the other's patterns of imagery together with yours; and, troubling to the curious, those deeply wedded to the idea that word-ensembles are ideally owned, your own ensemble may resonate with allude to, or even reproduce, in part or whole, an alien ensemble without intention in your part that this should happen, or awareness that it has happened. These modes of presence produce anxiety for the curious: When should they be acknowledged? When may they be permitted to pass? What degree of effort should be put into trying to find and properly acknowledge intrusions of alien ensembles into your own? There is, from the viewpoint of the curious, no clear answer to any of these questions, and the fact that this is so explains the baroque complexity of, for example, university honor codes defining plagiarism for students and encouraging them not to do it. No one's intuitions about when to acknowledge the presence of an alien ensemble in yours are well formed; and the axiomatic assumption on the part of the curious that the offence of the *plagiarus* consists essentially in some combination of theft and dishonesty guarantees that no exact guidelines on these matters can be given. The curious author seeks to erase the plagiarist who threatens his control of his own work; but the grounds upon which he does so guarantee that he cannot remove the anxiety that accompanies the certainty that his own work will, often in ways of which he is not aware, recapitulate the offense he abhors.

It is worth emphasizing here, although it should be obvious enough, that the sketch just given of curious understandings of and responses to plagiarism does not mean that these are the only understandings and responses the curious have. They may share some of the judgments implicit in the treatment by the studious of the word-ocean in which we all swim (on which judgments more in a moment). Some among the curious may, in addition to being anxious about ownership, control, and expropriation, also be grateful for the work of others, and wish to display that gratitude by acknowledgment of the presence of that work in their own; or, they may demarcate their own word-ensembles from those of others, and indicate the influence of those others on their own, out of an urge to help those who use their own work to explore for themselves the sources they have used. But even when these understandings and responses are present in the intellectual work of the curious, they do not belong to the grammar of curiosity *stricto sensu.* That grammar is one of ownership and anxiety, and it is only within it that the figure of the *plagiarus* makes sense and can be opposed.

⌒

The studiously Christian response to the word-ocean is at all points different. In accord with the construal of the world as gift, and of its creatures as participants in God to the extent that they are undamaged, all human speech (and writing)—again, to the extent that it is undamaged—is understood as response to gift, and therefore not subject to the logic of ownership. Speakers (or writers) who attempt to lay claim to what they speak (or write), to demarcate their own ensembles with the clear mark of an *incipit* and an *explicit,* and to defend the control of those ensembles against all comers—and especially against the kidnapper—do something performatively incoherent: they damage their own speech in the act of speaking. This is evident from the features of what, for the studious, is the paradigm of speech, speech that shows minimal damage. This is *confessio,* speech offered to God in dual acknowledgment of its speaker's insufficiency as speaker, and of God's all-sufficiency as giver of all speech, the one in whom, as *logos,* all human speech participates. Words, spoken or written, are relinquished in this speech-act: they are handed back to their giver, and in that way become, to the extent possible, what they should be.

Understanding utterance, and by extension writing, in this way, as having confession as its ideal type, has its effects upon how other speech-acts are understood, and most especially upon how the possibility of owning words is construed. If, ideal-typically, words are engendered as gifts to be given away, then the extent to which some particular ensemble of them is self-consciously demarcated with the purpose of establishing ownership's control is exactly the extent to which it has been damaged. Even speech-acts as apparently distant from confession as the declarative communication of some set of facts about the cosmos—perhaps you publish an essay on the manuscript families within which Augustine's *De doctrina christiana* has been transmitted, or on the history of the spread of the kudzu vine across the American South—are treated differently when they are understood as derivatives of the act of confession. Such descriptive acts are seen by the studious as themselves implicitly confessions of praise to the God who brought into being the world of light in which a state of affairs of this kind can obtain—or, or lament that the cosmos has been damaged in these particular ways. These understandings may not be explicitly present in what the studious say and write. But they are constant, ordering assumptions whose effects upon what is explicitly written and said are like the effects upon what you write and say to your most intimate beloved produced exactly by the fact that you are addressing her. It is not that every address to the beloved is explicit about the fact that she is the beloved (were this the case she would not long remain so); but it is the case that whatever is said to her is informed and embraced by the fact that she is the beloved—even when you are telling her about the weather, or about your views on politics, or discussing what to have for dinner. Address to the beloved cannot be demarcated by the grasp of ownership exactly because it is an offering to the beloved. You do not speak about the weather to your beloved in the same way—with the same informing and embracing assumptions—that you speak to a nameless other in the subway or the elevator. And for the studious Christian, all speech and writing has the first and last beloved, the God of Abraham and Isaac and Jacob, as its first and last audience, and is therefore and thereby informed and embraced by assumptions that make ownership impossible and demarcation a matter of secondary interest.

The studious understanding of speech and writing, as gift offered to the beloved, is intimate with a very particular understanding of the word-ocean in which we all swim. Every word spoken and written by every rational creature participates in the triune God (for a depiction of what participation means, see chapter 6), from which it follows that every word-ensemble—every text marked in some fashion with an *incipit* and an *explicit*—does so, too. This is so no matter what the intentions or self-understandings of the speaker or writer. But, and this is the point of importance, not every word, and hence not every word-ensemble, does so in the same way and to the same degree. Just as there is a hierarchy of being, according to which some creatures participate more fully in God than others, so also there is a hierarchy of word-ensembles—of texts, if you prefer—according to which some participate more fully in the divine *logos* than do others. At the top of this hierarchy is the word-ensemble of Holy Scripture—or, more exactly, the peculiarly and unsurpassably rich collection of verbal acts of confession recognized as canonical by the church, which is also to say recognized by the church as the ideal type of human speech.

There is an interesting complication here. It is that we Christians, like Buddhists but unlike Jews, Muslims, and most Hindus (difficult and disputed sortals as all these are, I use them for the sake of convenience), do not identify our canon with a word-ensemble in some particular natural language. The corpus of Holy Scripture is not a set of words in Hebrew or Greek or Aramaic or Latin or English. It is, rather, the meaning of the verbal acts of confession—a meaning, which in considerable part was not present to the minds of those performing these acts, in this like every other human utterance—which found their first expression in works composed and redacted in Hebrew, Aramaic, and Greek. What the church recognized as bearing canonical authority, then, was not a particular word-ensemble, but rather a set of meanings, or verbal actions, capable of being instantiated with equal authority in any natural language. The canon of Holy Scripture can of course only ever be instantiated and used in some natural language or other; and each instantiation of it bears an intimate and complex relation to what was meant by the human editors and authors of the variously demarcated word-ensembles, which are its proper parts. But neither those word-ensembles (the Book of the Prophet Isaiah, for example, or Paul's Second Letter to the Corinthians), nor their various translations, are identical with the corpus of Holy Scripture. Rather, to choose one among many possible formulations, that corpus is identical with what God means by what the canonical authors said and wrote, a matter to which access can only be had here below by intimacy with a bounded word-ensemble in some natural language or other. The contrast between an understanding of Holy Scripture like this, on the one hand, and understandings that identify a canonical corpus with a set of words in some particular natural language, on the other—for most Jews the canonical corpus is the (mostly) Hebrew word-ensemble of the Tanakh; for most Muslims it is the Arabic word-ensemble of the Qur'ān; for some Hindus it is the Sanskrit word-ensemble of the Veda—is important and has many implications. But for the purposes of this study, it is enough to note it, and to emphasize its importance for understanding a studiously Christian set of attitudes to the word-ocean, to literary composition, and to the act of plagiarism.

The first and most fundamental demarcation of an ensemble of words from within the word-ocean is, then, for studious Christians, the one the church performed in acknowledging the corpus of Holy Scripture. This was not an arbitrary act that could have been performed otherwise. The church was guided by the triune God in the person of the Holy Spirit in performing it, and this means that the primary demarcation of a word-ensemble from the word-ocean is, from this point of view, utterly nonconventional though profoundly tradition-specific. It shares these features with, for example, the election of the Jewish people. Both are nonconventional in that they are states of affairs given independently of any human work: the Jews did not merit their election, nor work to bring it into being—they were given it; Christians did not merit the gift of Holy Scripture nor work to bring that corpus into being—they were given it. These are features of the world in their nonconventionality just like the galaxies and microorganisms. They are tradition-specific first in the sense that they are very particular: Abraham was a particular person located in space and time; the corpus of Scripture is a particular collection of words given utterance or reduced to writing sonewhere and sometime. But they are also tradition-specific in the sense that these features of the cosmos are not in fact recognized by those outside the traditions in question as what they are, and should not be expected to be. Their acknowledgment depends upon a submission of mind and will which has among the necessary conditions for its fullest occurrence some very particular events: being born or made a Jew; or being baptized.

The demarcation of the canon of Scripture was fixed at a time, but before that time it was prepared for by the performance of Holy Scripture in the liturgy, a performance that to begin with performed the Scriptures of the Jewish people, a gift given to them as a central element in their election, a gift shared by those early Christians who were also Jews, and a gift then inherited by Gentile Christians. (This is one of the many senses in which Christianity can appropriately be described as Judaism for the Gentiles.) As the canonical books were composed and recognized, they too entered the performance of the liturgy, the Christian people's work of *confessio* to God in resonance to and accord with the fundamental word-ensemble of Holy Scripture. And this performance itself became, gradually, a word-ensemble demarcated from all others as being, like that of Holy Scripture itself—and like it principally because related to it in much the same way that concert-performance relates to score—an ideal-typical form of undamaged speech, the template for all other speech. The fabric of the liturgy came to include not just verbatim reproduction of the words of Holy Scripture (though it was and remains largely that), but also a web of allusion to, condensation of, and elucidation of those words, all framed by and shot through with stammering confessional ejaculation.

Scripture-liturgy or liturgy-scripture: either expression will do for the word-ensemble that, for Christians (and especially for Catholic and Orthodox Christians, who preserve the fullest and most perfect forms of it), is the one to which all others resonate and from which all others derive. From this word-ensemble flow others: the creeds of the ecumenical councils, the teachings on faith and morals of the church's special and ordinary magisterium, and so on. But these need not detain us here. The point of importance is that the literary practices of studious Christians have this fundamental word-ensemble as their principal point of reference and ideal type, and this state of affairs has very significant effects upon their preferred genres for composition (the florilegium and the commentary are much loved, for obvious reasons), as well as upon their preferred conventions for acknowledging the presence of alien words and word-ensembles in their own literary productions.

The words of the scripture-liturgy complex cannot be owned, and can only be effective as what they are, which is the paradigmatic act of verbal confession, by being given away. Their first gift was from the triune God to the composers and editors of Holy Scripture; their second gift was from those composers and editors to their first audience, which was the Jewish people and its continuation in the church; and their third gift was from that first audience to the pagan world, a world which has responded along a spectrum from sneering condescension to respect to admiration to recognition sufficient to prompt conversion. But these words must nonetheless continue to be given away, without stint or remainder: they are no one's possession; and even though there are communities equipped for special intimacy with them (communities of their passionate lovers, that is), there are none permitted to make of these words a possession. The word-ensembles composed by studious Christians do not aspire to be like

Holy Scripture in every respect: that would be both absurd and blasphemous. But such ensembles are all ancillary to, which is to say the loving handmaidens of, the scripture-liturgy complex, and do aspire to be like it in approaching the status of *confessio,* gifts received that must be given back in praise and lament. And this ancillary condition has its effects upon how the literary work of others is acknowledged and marked by us studious Christians in our own, and upon the reasons we have for laying claim to the word-ensembles we compose.

~

The literary compositions of studious premodern Christians place much less emphasis upon authorship than do those of curious moderns. Pseudonymous authorship and pseudepigraphic writing are both common for the former and not for the latter, and that this is so has effects upon how the use of alien words in the fabric of one's own (how difficult it is altogether to avoid the language of ownership!) is signalled and thought about. The literary works of the *doctores ecclesiae* are very often saturated with allusions to and echoes of Scripture and the works of their predecessors, many of them not marked in any way, but instead woven invisibly and indivisibly into the fabric of their own words. This lack of marking of alien words is often because the echoes and allusions are thought sufficiently obvious not to need marking: to speak of a thief in the night or of going to a far country is, for the scripturally literate, a transparent allusion, just as is likening our relations to the gods to those linking flies to wanton boys to the Shakespeareanly literate. It would be superfluous to mark it. Even for those who cannot say just what these phrases allude to, it is nonetheless often clear enough that they are allusions to something. But this is not the only reason for the unmarked allusion. It may also be that the allusion occurs without the writer or speaker intending that it should. This is common for writers saturated wth some word-ensemble other than what they compose themselves; its words will weave themselves into their own without their knowing it and therefore also without their intending it, and in such cases the presence of the alien words cannot be intentionally marked—and in fact the words are not really alien; they have formed the writer so that she is their creature rather than they hers. This has often been the case for studious Christians with the words of the scripture-liturgy corpus.

All the same, points can be made for verbatim reproduction as for allusion: the grammar of studiousness gives no intrinsic importance to the marking and acknowledgment of either, and this principally because of its inhospitability to the idea of ownership, which is among the principal rationales for such marking and acknowledgment. It is not, however, the only rationale. You may also mark and acknowledge your allusions and your verbatim reproductions out of gratitude for the work done by those who gave them form in the first place; or to acknowledge the authoritative weight of what you are alluding to or reproducing, and in that way placing your own words in a particular lineage. Both motivations are important for the studious Christian. Gratitude for what has been done by others is itself a kind of *confessio:* it acknowledges by praise the gifts of understanding and composition given to others; it also, by implication usually, but sometimes also explicitly, acknowledges with lament the insufficiency of one's own work to do justice to the work of others and to the gifts given one by God. Acknowledgment of the authority of the work of others is almost equally important for the studious, and is not quite the same as gratitude *simpliciter.* Gratitude can and should be given to the work of pagans as much as to the work of Christians and Jews. The pagans, too, and often better and more beautifully than any Christian or Jew, express truths, and whenever they do, they should be thanked. But the authoritative weight of tradition is something different, and the reasons for marking and acknowledging it are also different. *Auctoritas*—authority, the paradigmatic authority of authorship-as-such, we may say, drawing upon the word's etymology—belongs first to the scripture-liturgy ensemble, and second to the unpacking of its meanings and uses by the church.

The studious will often find it essential to mark the presence of this ensemble in their own literary works, principally to locate their own work in relation to that tradition—but also to signal the importance of that paradigmatic word-ensemble to the world.

Gratitude and submission to authority: these do provide reasons to the studious for marking and acknowledging the works of others in their own. But they do not provide anything approaching a requirement that such presence be always marked, and in this they are very different from the curious stress upon ownership and the anxiety about theft, witting or unwitting, that accompanies it. The studious are therefore likely to worry less than the curious about marking and acknowledging the presence of the words of others in their own literary works, and to do it less. Studious decisions about the matter are prudential and context-specific; curious ones are universal and in-principle. For the studious, the *plagiarus,* to the extent that he exists at all, is just someone who lacks gratitude; he is no thief, and not even necessarily a liar, the former because there is no property at stake, and the latter because the public presentation of a word-ensemble under your own name does not imply that all the words, phrases, and sentences in the ensemble are your own composition, from which it follows that the fact that some are not (and how could they not be?—the very nature of language and utterance requires them to be) is no evidence of duplicity on the part of the one who presents them. You may, if you have undergone the mathetic catechesis that forms the curious, have come to think that you are being duplicitous when you do not mark and acknowledge the presence of alien words in your own texts. If this is so, you will be to that extent a liar when you do it. But you will be a confused one, like someone who thinks herself duplicitous because she does not declare her anguish to all who ask her how she does.

Our present anxieties about plagiarism, whether at the level of teaching schoolchildren and university students, or at the level of the practice of the professional writer and scholar, are often—perhaps usually—expressed in the language of theft and dishonesty, for the reasons canvassed. But there is a third rationale for criticizing the unacknowledged taking and public use of word-ensembles composed by others, one which the studious and the curious can in some measure agree upon, though even here there will be differences of emphasis between them.

Plagiarism, it might be said, is to training in literary composition as sending someone else to practice in your stead is to learning how to play football. That is, not very effective. This is at least partly true. You cannot learn how to do anything well without doing it, and if developing the ability to generate uncopied—unplagiarized—sentences, whether with pen, keyboard, or vocal chords, is what you are after, then, presumably, practising just that activity is the thing to do. But actually even this is not obviously true, and here the sports analogy breaks down, for in fact a very good way to learn to write well is to copy good writing, to parody it, to make a pastiche of styles, to keep a commonplace book with carefully copied extracts, and to perform various other elementary exercises upon the words of others. For most of these exercises, the distinction between your words and those of others is not very important; what is important is the expression of beauty and truth, not the question of who first uttered or wrote the words that do the expressing. Learning how to write is, or should be, like learning how to play the piano—five-finger exercises upon the work of others is where it begins, with imitation the greatest virtue; and free composition by variation on and homage to what's already there is where it ends, as for example in the succession that runs from the preludes of Bach to those of Chopin to those of Messiaen. Neither originality nor ownership are to the point from a studious perspective, and so neither is plagiarism. So even this rationale for anxiety about plagiarism is not strong for the studious. The strength it has depends upon judgments about the importance of developing and using particular skills, and those judgments have only local and occasional application.

So we studious Christians disport ourselves happily in the ocean of words, acknowledging the primacy of *confessio* as the ideal type of all speech and writing, rejoicing in the gift of Scripture and liturgy as the ensemble of words to which all others are ornaments, receiving with gratitude the words of others to the extent that they are undamaged, while lamenting them to the extent that we can perceive their damage, and offering the words of our mouths and pens and keyboards as ripples upon the word-ocean of praise. We look with puzzled amusement and sympathy at the curious and the plagiarists, locked as doppelgängers in anxious combat over the ownership of words. And we offer them the liberation from that anxiety that comes from the Word in whom all other words participate.

11

SPECTACLE

Omissis igitur et repudiatis nugis theatricis et poeticis, divinarum Scripturarum consideratione et tractatione pascamus animum atque potemus vasae curiositatis fame ac siti fessum et aestuantem, et inanibus phantasmatibus, tamquam pictis epulis, frustra refici satiarique cupientem: hoc vere liberali, et ingenuo ludo salubriter erudiamur. Si nos miracula spectaculorum, et pulchritudo delectat, illam desideremus videre Sapientiam, quae pertendit usque ad finem fortiter, et disponit omnia suaviter. Quid enim mirabilius, vi incorporea mundum corporeum fabricante et administrante? aut quid pulchrius ordinante et ornante?

Repudiating and abandoning, therefore, theatrical and poetical idiocies, let us offer to minds famished and parched by a raging hunger and thirst for curiosity's vanities and frustratedly desirous of getting refreshment and satisfaction from empty images as if from painted feasts, the food and drink of the study and interpretation of the scriptures. Let us become healthily learned by means of this truly liberal and worthy game. If it is the wonders and beauties of spectacles that delight us, then we should urgently desire to see that wisdom who extends herself powerfully from end [to end], and who orders everything sweetly (Wisdom 8:1). What is more wonderful than incorporeal power's construction and governance of the world? Or more beautiful than its ordering and adorning of it?

Augustine here (in a passage extracted from *De vera religione,* 51.100) discusses the benefits of studying and meditating on Scripture, and in the passage quoted he does it by contrasting those benefits with the detriments of attending to the objects that curiosity constructs for itself. Scriptural study nourishes and satisfies; curiosity, being concerned *inanibus phantasmibus,* with empty images, brings only hunger, and thirst, and exhaustion, and disquiet. All these things are only *picta epula,* painted feasts that look as though they might satisfy but in fact cannot be eaten. If, then, the apparent beauty and wonders of spectacles delight us, surely we should be still more attracted to wisdom, which is more truly beautiful than any spectacle, and which orders and ornaments the fabric of the world? The contrast of importance here is that between wisdom *(sapientia)* and spectacle *(spectaculum)*: spectacles are figments, illusions, seductively beautiful but empty of reality. They are what the curious want, but any desire they might satisfy is self-destructive. Wisdom, on the other hand, provides what it promises, which is the erudition that comes from seeing things as they are.

⮑

The contrast between the intellectual appetites of the curious and those of the studious can be understood more fully by way of addressing the distinction between the spectacle and the icon, for the curious seek and find the spectacular and the studious the iconic. Each term labels an array of sensibilia, of creatures accessible to the senses; and each may be approached as it is in the order of being—the true icon and the true spectacle—or as it is in the order of knowing—the array that appears to a particular knower spectacularly, as a spectacle, or iconically, as an icon. There is no necessary correspondence between the two orders, in this case as in most: what is really, in the order of being, an iconic array, may appear as a spectacle because of the condition of its knower; but the reverse, as we shall see in more detail in a moment, is not true: an array that is in the order of being truly spectacular cannot appear iconically, or, more precisely, can do so only to the extent that it is not a spectacle, which is to say only to the extent that it has not sustained damage of one kind or another. But these are abstract words that need clarification by definition and example.

An array of sensible creatures is a scene or tableau. The now-drooping freesias in the vase on my desk constitute an array at the moment present to my senses, as does the sound of the rain dripping from the slate roof of the house in which I sit to the soaked earth below, and as does the faint vanilla residue of the candle I burned last night. Arrays present in memory as I sit alone writing in my room include the face of the beloved other; the view of the city of Chicago from the airplane as it descends across the western shore of Lake Michigan; and the bitter taste of the chicory-adulterated coffee I drank as a young man. (In an analogical sense, there may also be arrays of intelligibilia, but they are not relevant to the discussion here.) The individuation of one array from another is ordinarily a matter of human convention and interest: for some purposes, the examples just mentioned could be considered parts of a single array; or they could be considered separate arrays if different purposes and interests were in play. However, we Christians think some arrays are individuated nonconventionally by God's gift whether or not humans distinguish them as such. I will return to these in a moment.

Two variables determine the iconicity of a particular sensible array. The first is the extent to which the sensible creatures in which it consists are severally and collectively undamaged. Recall the depiction of damage in chapter 4 above: for a sensible creature to be damaged is for it to become corrupted by ceasing to participate in God to the extent proper to its kind. Since the fall, almost all sensible creatures are damaged in this meaning, whether by their own decision for self-damage, or by the damage inflicted upon them as a result of the aboriginal calamity undergone by the world in which they exist. But the degree of damage varies considerably, and with it the extent to which a particular scene is, in the order of being, iconic—that is, the undamaged bearer of the divine signature of style appropriate to its kind. The more damage, the less iconicity. But there is a second variable that determines the iconicity of a particular sensible scene in the order of being, and that is the kind to which the sensible creatures that constitute it belong. Some are such that they can participate more fully in God than others, and a scene composed of those—of humans, say, as compared to rocks—is potentially more iconic than one whose constituents are less capable of participation. Only potentially, of course, because the first variable, that of damage's extent, will affect the second. An undamaged sensible scene, could there be one, would then be as iconic as the kinds of sensible creatures that inhabit it permit it to be. And an undamaged sensible scene composed of sensible creatures that participate maximally (maximally for sensible creatures, that is; complications would be introduced were we to consider intelligible creatures as well) would, in the order of being, be a *vera icona,* a truly iconic array. It is with such arrays that the studious seek intimacy, and to them that they seek conformity; and such intimacy and such conformity are forms of knowledge. It remains to ask which kinds of sensible creature permit, when undamaged and properly arrayed, the constitution of a *vera icona:* Christians have some guidelines for answering, or at least for thinking about, this question to which I shall turn in a moment, but before doing so the spectacular scene needs to be briefly defined.

This can be done briefly because the spectacle and the icon are definable in terms of one another. If the true icon is an array of undamaged sensibilia of a kind that permits maximal sensible-creaturely participation in God, then the true spectacle ought to be an array of maximally damaged sensibilia of a kind that permits minimal sensible-creaturely participation in God. But on that definition there (and can be) no true spectacles. The set of *vera spectacula* is null. This is because any creature which has suffered maximal damage must, in accord with the doctrine of participation and its unavoidable concomitant, which is the exchangeability of God and being (for a brief depiction of which see chapter 6, on participation) cease to be. Damage is loss of being; maximal damage is maximal loss of being; and so, the maximally damaged are, by definition, those who do not exist at all—this is so, anyway, unless there are other constraints that do not permit sensible creatures to cease to be; and while Christians are not of one mind about whether human creatures can cease to be, they are of one mind that nonhuman sensible creatures can do so; and so, within the sphere of Christian thought at least, it follows that a true spectacle would be empty. It would contain no creatures for the curious to gaze upon. Nevertheless, there may be spectacles that approach, asymptotically, the condition of being a true spectacle. I will offer an example in a moment.

So much, in brief, for the icon and the spectacle in the order of being. Each is a sensible array of a particular kind. In the order of knowing, however, things are more complex: as usual, aspiring knowers, whether curiously or studiously so, get what they seek, and so it is possible for what is truly iconic to appear to a curious knower as a spectacular tableau; and, to a limited extent and with all sorts of caveats to be entered in a moment, it is possible for a deeply damaged spectacular array to appear iconic to the studious.

When an iconic array appears as it is to the gaze of a knower (the visual metaphor is not intended to exclude the possibility of arrays of sensibilia available only to other senses: there can be olfactory and auditory icons, too), it does so as doubly open: open, that is, to God and to the gaze of the creaturely knower, showing its participation in the former and beckoning the contemplative conformity of the latter to itself. The iconic array appears as a lure to the contemplation of the studious, and it does this because it is beautiful. Its beauty follows from the definition already given: if it is minimally damaged, and it is of a kind to participate maximally in God, then it must also be beautiful because all sensible creatures are beautiful exactly to the extent that they have not sustained damage. The extent to which a sensible creature is undamaged is the extent to which it is as God intended it to be: and since damage's loss of being is also loss of beauty, it follows at once that absence of damage is presence of beauty. The well-catechized gaze of the studious knower is lured by beauty: such knowers want to gaze on and be conformed to the beauty that confronts them, and this is just another way of saying that they seek knowledge's intimacy with such creatures. The beauty of the icon's double openness lures but does not capture the gaze of the knower. If the gaze were captured, then the iconic array's openness to God would be lost. It would become, or tend toward, the spectacular array, on which the gaze becomes frozen as if it could attain exhaustive intimacy with what it gazes at. The iconic array's beauty, then, beckons the gaze into something deeper than itself by opening its surface beauties, whatever particular form they take (visual, auditory, and so on), into something much more beautiful than itself, which is to say into the inner-trinitarian economy in which it participates as icon. The beauty of the iconic array's double openness in this way nourishes the gaze without satisfying it. To satisfy the gaze would be to exhaust it, and to encourage it to move on to the next thing; that is the characteristic of the spectacular tableau, but not of the iconic array. The truly iconic array, the *vera icona*, does not, however, wear its credentials as such on its sleeve. It may appear to the curious as one more spectacle, to be mastered and exhausted, or to be casually glanced at and then ignored. Here too, the order of being does not force itself on the order of knowing, just as (and just because) God's grace does not force itself on its recipients.

You should pay attention to the interplay between surface and depth in order to understand how it is that the iconic array can both appear and fail to appear as such. Any sensory array has a surface, an arrangement of sensory appearances that can be characterized inadequately by description that exhausts them by accounting only for their availability to the gaze of the knower. Such an accounting is mathetic (as depicted in chapter 9): it isolates the array, demarcates it from everything else, and turns it into an object capable of being exhaustively known by the curious knower, and thus owned according to the threefold sequestration characteristic of that act. Performing this complex act of sequestration and domination requires extensive catechesis, as I have already argued. It is a catechesis productive of blindness, but it can nonetheless be effective, sufficiently so that those catechized in this way come to see only surfaces, misprize even those, and thus are blind to the participation of every sensory array in God. For them—and they are the curious—all iconic arrays are reduced to the spectacular. But examples are needed to make these distinctions clearer.

The true sensible icon is the flesh of Christ. This is the one sensible array that surpasses all others in its capacity to participate in the triune God; and it is without damage other than that necessary to bring about the greatest imaginable good for the world, which is its salvation. Damage of that sort is unique in being self-consuming and therefore not really damage at all. These two properties conjointly suffice to make it the *vera icona* from which all other iconic arrays are derived, and in which they participate. A full exposition of this weighty claim would require an essay in Christology, which is beyond the scope of this study; but a brief comment is possible. To the first criterion for being, among sensible arrays, unsurpassably capable of participating in the triune God: this is given first by the fact of the hypostatic union, the perfect and indissoluble union of the divine and human natures in the single person of Jesus the Christ, the *logos ensarkos,* which means that God's presence in the world is most fully and perfectly concentrated where Christ's flesh was and is. The human is in the image and likeness of God, as I have already had occasion to observe and discuss; only it, therefore, is capable of entering into this kind of union with God. The participation of other sensible creatures in God must necessarily be less than the participation of the undamaged human, and therefore when God becomes evident to the senses he becomes most fully so in the flesh of an undamaged human person, which is to say in the incarnation. And to the second criterion, that Christ's flesh bears no damage other than that necessary to bring about the greatest imaginable good for the world: this is simply another way of saying that Jesus the Christ is the world's savior, and that a partial account of how this salvation was effected must include description of the wounds of his suffering and death. This is, in a sense, damage, but in a peculiar sense. Damage of this sort has as its only reason for being the removal of both itself and all other damage, and is therefore not damage that reduces the possibility of its bearer's iconicity. Quite the contrary: this damage, and only this, is essential for the perfection of its bearer's appearance as an iconic array. A human nature in this calamitously damaged world could not be hypostatically unified with the divine unless it underwent damage of just this sort.

This is why Christians venerate Christ's wounds; it is also why the sufferings of the martyrs and saints, and of the groaning mass of humanity in general, constantly tortured, eviscerated, raped, burned, and consumed by painful disease as it is, can be, according to the extent of their participation in Christ's sufferings, iconic arrays for Christians. Depicting and ruminating the wounds of Christ, or the arrows piercing St. Sebastian's body, or the death of St. Catherine on the wheel, of the consuming of Perpetua and Felicity by the beasts of the arena, or the execution of Maximilien Kolbe in Auschwitz, is not, then, an exercise in morbidity but rather an accurate perception simultaneously of what is wrong with the world (that it is a place in which such things happen) and of what is right with it (that it is a place where such things happen). Quotidian sufferings, too—those of the nameless and voiceless, yours and mine—share in this doubleness to the extent that they participate in Christ's sufferings. To the pagans, such things appear only as evidence of damage to be removed as quickly as possible; or, sadly, as regrettable necessities; or, sometimes, and damnably, as states of affairs eagerly to be sought. To Christians, they appear as darkness shot through with light, and that is because of their participation in the unsurpassable iconic array.

The points just made, I should remind you, are grammatical ones: they are intended to explain how Christian discourse about these matters works, and to display it at work. They are not intended to argue for the truth of the claims here made, which is assumed.

If the flesh of Christ is the unsurpassable icon, then, as Christians see it, all other iconic arrays must be such because of the relation they bear to that one. Some are exceedingly intimate with it. There is, for instance, the flesh of Christ's mother, Mary. There is also the quotidian sensory appearance of Christ's flesh in the liturgy of the Eucharist. Here, too, is the complete and perfect, though veiled, iconic array. That this is so explains why Christians (most of them) venerate the sacrament, both when it is confected in the liturgy, and when it is reserved, and when it is exposed for worship. To the pagans, the bread and wine will (and should) appear simply as such, an ordinary array on which the glance need do no more than pause, if even that. But to the well catechized, the appearance is different: it is the supremely beloved behind a veil. The flesh of Mary no longer, with the exception of the occasional apparition, confronts us (to explain why, and what the absence means would require an excursion into Mariology, and specifically into the doctrine of the Assumption of the Blessed Virgin), and so is available for contemplation only under representation, as an icon at the first remove (on which more below). But the flesh of Christ remains available to us, and its presence is what constitutes most fully the church of Christ.

Very close to the flesh of Christ, deeply intimate with it, are images of it made without the intervention or cooperation of human work. These, if there are any (and tradition is close to unanimous that there are), are especially intimate with Christ's flesh because the only agency involved in producing them is divine, and because they are produced by direct contact with Christ's flesh. The Christian tradition preserves many traditions about the making and preservation of such images, all of which have to do in one way or another with cloth coming into direct contact with the face or body of Jesus before his ascension, and by some means having an image thereby imprinted upon it. According to one version, such an image was impressed upon the handkerchief used by a woman of Jerusalem, sometimes called Veronica, to wipe the sweat from his face as he was carrying the cross to the place of crucifixion; according to another, the dead body of Christ impressed an image of itself on his shroud in the interval between his death on the cross and his resurrection; according to a third, Christ himself imprinted an image of his face on a cloth in response to a request from a disciple. And so on. I have no opinion about the reliability of these traditions, though it is important to note that most Christians believe one version or another. Their grammatical importance is that they show with great clarity the conceptual structure of Christian thought about these matters: the best iconic arrays are produced without human agency, on the model of the hypostatic union in which the incarnation consists. They are what they are because of their intimacy with the flesh of Christ.

Further removed from Christ's flesh than these are sensible arrays made with human hands but hallowed by their association with the things of God. These include icons in the ordinary narrow sense: painted images of God himself, whether in triune form, or as one or another of the persons of the Holy Trinity, or of the Blessed Virgin, or of the saints, or of the objects or artifacts of the liturgy, or of especially sacred places and events. These we might call icons at the first remove from the *vera icona*. Closely associated with these, but also distinct from them, are other works made by human hands whose beauty gives them a high degree of participation in God, but which have nothing explicitly to do with the events in which God's presence is at a high degree of intensity. Works of visual or auditory art, buildings of harmonious form, and literary works belong here, though not all to the same degree. Works of practical art and craft belong here, too: the work of a chef or a mason or a mechanic or a horticulturist can also bring into being sensible iconic arrays. The degree to which any particular human work does constitute a sensible iconic array is the extent to which it represents the beauty of God's created order by appropriate participation in it, and in so doing signals to those who see it that it participates in something other than itself; the extent to which it does not is given by the extent to which it falls short of such representation-by-participation, which it will always do to some extent because of the damage present in its human maker. Of course, there will be reasonable disagreement about the extent to which any particular human artifact constitutes an iconic array (Do we rank Mondrian's work above or below Chagall's? The well-planned and well-cooked meal above the beautifully laid-out garden?), and there is generally no need to attempt establishment of a hierarchy among such things, other than to note the general principles already stated.

Also icons at the first remove, though in a very different way from those just described, are the faces and bodies of other human beings. (The sensible array constituted for you by your own face and body introduces special complexities here, in many important ways different from those constituted by the faces and bodies of others; but I won't say more about them here; for the purposes of this study they can be subsumed into the category of human flesh and face in general.) These, in this respect like the *vera icona* and the other icons at the first remove, are inexhaustible, though for very different reasons. They, like the *vera icona* itself, are not made with human hands, and the extent to which they have been remade by human hands, by surgery or cosmetic art, is close (though not identical: care is necessary here too) to the extent to which they begin to lose their iconic status. Every human face is a very intimate participant in the face of Christ, and this is what constitutes its iconic inexhaustibility. Every human face shows with great clarity to those who care to look closely at it, and most especially to those who look on it with a lover's eyes, the beauty given to it by that participation.

Iconic arrays at the second remove are those constituted by the cosmos, as it now exists independently of human work: the sunset, the oak tree, the stars, the galaxies, and so on. All this was created by God, and is to that extent good and therefore beautiful (as already depicted in chapter 3). The rhapsodies of the romantic poets and their contemporary inheritors, deep environmentalists, and other lovers of the natural order, are to this extent justified in the high evaluation they give to the wild, which is another way of labelling the created order, as it exists independently of human effort. But both the romantics and the environmentalists tend to attribute all darkness and damage in the world to human beings, and therefore to depict the cosmos without human beings as intrinsically good—or at least as better than it would be had humans not interfered with it. This view cannot be held by Christians, or at least not after the fall: the world itself is damaged and perpetuates its own damage, and not only by the presence of human agents in it; and so the wild is already imperfect, already distant from what it was when God spoke it into being from nothing. Removing human agency from it will not heal this damage—damage most evident in its omnipresent violence—and so the task of studious Christians in seeking intimacy with the sensible arrays with which the wild presents us is to see them as they are, in their damaged beauty, not to romanticize them. Damaged though the wild world is, however, it preserves enough traces of God's creative presence in it to serve sometimes as a powerful iconic reminder of its creator, and there is no doubt we humans, pagan and otherwise, are deeply attuned to what beauty there is in the wild. Here too, then, there are icons, though by now at a distant remove from those intimate with Christ's flesh.

Finally, there are iconic traces evident to the well catechized even in the works of humans so deeply damaged that they take pleasure in wanton destruction. Even the spectacular absences of the Gulag or the Nazi extermination camps are not absences without remainder. And in the case of pornographic depictions of human flesh, or sadistic ones of human suffering, there are perhaps more traces of iconic beauty, though they are sometimes hard to discern. The issue of principle here is that the extent to which any sensible array maintains sufficient order to stand forth as such an array is the extent to which it exists and is beautiful. Some arrays are repulsive: a detailed depiction of suffering human flesh, whether in the more graphic Hollywood productions or in (for example) Goya's war etchings or Homer's *Iliad*, will cause most to look away with a shudder. But even these, if rightly seen, can, as I have already noted, serve as iconic depictions of participation in Christ's sufferings. This is not to say that all such sensible arrays—the pornographic films now available in almost every hotel room in the western world at the push of a button, for example—are to be defended, much less encouraged. It is only to say that no matter how depraved the intentions of their makers, the trace of the iconic cannot be completely erased from them. It is also to suggest (and this is a controversial matterthat can only be mentioned) that there is nothing human flesh can undergo or perform whose representation or depiction should in principle be proscribed. Which is of course not the same as claiming that every human action should be permitted, or that every motive for producing such depictions is defensible. But at this point in the analysis of the iconic in the order of knowing we are approaching the spectacular, and to this I now turn.

The spectacle is the icon's reversed image. It is a sensible array characterized principally by damage: damage in what it depicts, and damage, too, in the way it is received and understood and used. Spectacular arrays are always constructions, figments, and never gifts: they must be made with effort that issues in unmaking, and this is because the effort that constitutes them is aimed at bringing into being a corrupted tableau with which exhaustive intimacy is possible. Such a tableau, to the extent that its makers succeed in constituting it, necessarily lacks the double openness that belongs to the icon: it is closed to God because it is constructed in order to hide its participation in something other than itself so that those who gaze on it can reach complete mastery of it, exhaustive intimacy with it. And, paradoxically, it is closed to the gaze because, although it has been made with the goal of complete access and exhaustive mastery, it necessarily fails in that goal. The figment that is the spectacle fails to represent what its constructors thought it would; it slips through their fingers.

For example, consider the public execution preceded by torture. The spectacle is carefully arranged, ritualistically laid out: there are the naked bodies of those to be tortured and killed; there is the proclamation of sentence; there is the special authority granted judge and executioner, an authority signalled by the robes and accoutrements of office; there is the arena for killing, and there is the space for the audience in serried ranks above, gazes frozen on what is about to happen. The children present (and they always are: at lynchings in the American South, at public hangings in London, at gladiatorial games in Rome, at ritual suicides in Tokyo) are especially eager for a good view, and clamor to be lifted on parental shoulders and laps. The sentence is read out, the lash laid on. The blood spurts and flows. The victims scream and writhe. The watchers are rapt. Then the victims' limbs are ritually broken, and they are stood up in clear view and eviscerated while still living, their guts held up for public view; and then their heads are swept from their shoulders and raised up on spikes. The watchers yell their appreciation and ask for more. Their gaze frozen on the events: they cannot look away because they are absorbed by what they see; and at the same time, what they see has not been enough. They at once need more of the same, or, preferably, something even more absorbing because even more violent.

This frozen absorption in the spectacle is a simulacrum of the contemplative's absorption in the icon. This is because, first, absorption in the spectacle is not attuned and responsive to what is before the eyes: those who watch the execution do not see the suffering bodies of God's images but only visual images that are immediately and completely exhausted in the stimuli (adrenaline producing, often sexually exciting) they produce. And second, it is because even though the gaze is rapt on its object as though it had the inexhaustible beauty of an iconic array, the object is in fact immediately exhausted by the gaze. It has been imagined—it is fictional, a figment—in just such a way as to guarantee that exhaustion. Third, and finally, those enraptured by the execution scene are, unlike those contemplating the icon, reduced by it, closed in on themselves by it, rather than being opened up to what they most fully are. Gazing on spectacles damages further those whose damage has already been shown by their desire to construct spectacles to gaze upon.

All this, you may well be thinking, is rather extreme. And so it is. The example is deliberately horrible and shocking, in part to replicate (in a very small way) in you, the reader, something of the effect which it is supposed to illustrate. Similar effects could have been produced by sketching, verbally but graphically, an episode of the public use of human bodies for sexual purposes. Sex and violence lend themselves most easily to the construction of spectacle, and we can all, to a greater or lesser degree, come to understand what spectacle is by responding to depictions of them as spectacle seekers do. That we can do this is itself evidence of our damaged condition. But I use this example only illustratively. I do not claim that the curious seek spectacles of sex and violence; they do, however, seek spectacles, that is, constructed sensible arrays that can be perfectly demarcated by mathesis so complete intimacy with them can be had. As soon as that is done, however, the gaze is deflected from what it has constructed exactly because exhaustive intimacy has been achieved, and thereby ownership's mastery. This leads to a desire for novelty which is deeply characteristic of the curious (it will be explored in more detail in chapter 12 below), a restlessness which is inflamed rather than assuaged by the spectacles it constructs. The studious, by contrast, are more likely to sit still before the iconic arrays they contemplate, and thereby to tolerate repetition together with the depth of intimacy that repeated contemplation can bring.

~

In our intellectual work we studious, catechized Christians seek the iconic and offer to the world our understanding of what icons are in the hope that others will begin to understand and explore it themselves. The intellectual life, if understood as pursuit of the iconic array, is a matter of constant wonder and constant stammering before the openness of what we study to the God who made it. Mastery is impossible: if something is mastered it has been reconstructed into a spectacle, and thereby imagined into something it is not and cannot be. It may seem to you, especially if you have been curiously formed by the academy, that understanding your work as a seeking and contemplating of the iconic will insufficiently dispose you to seek the novelty that mastery over the spectacular encourages. And if, as is all too likely, you have been formed to think that novelty, and its kissing cousin, progress, are goods proper to the intellectual life, then you are likely to think this a drawback, perhaps even a disabling one, to the studious rejection of the spectacular. It may seem that those who study what they study as if it were an icon of God's presence in the world are like the hedgehog who knows one thing well; while those who master the spectacle are like the fox, knowers of many things, full of the cunning of reason. There is no easy resolution of this debate. Progress and novelty are of no particular interest to the studious; truth and beauty are. This will be enough for many among the curious, and certainly for almost all academics, to reject the depiction of the intellectual life offered here as obscurantist and backward looking. But it is also the case that the curious quest for exhaustive intimacy is, even to the curious, beginning to show its own disadvantages, not least among which is the spoliation of what they imagine themselves to have mastered.

12

NOVELTY

Sed miseri homines, quibus cognita vilescunt, et novitatibus gaudent, libentius discunt quam norunt, cum cognitio sit finis discendi. Et quibus vilis est facilitas actionis, libentius certant quam vincunt, cum victoria sit finis certandi. Et quibus vilis est corporis salus, malunt vesci quam satiari, et malunt frui genitalibus membris quam nullam talem commotionem pati; inveniuntur etiam qui malunt dormire quam non dormitare: cum omnis illius voluptatis sit finis, non esurire ac sitire, et non desiderare concubitum, et non esse corpore fatigato.

But we miserable human beings, bored by what we know and delighted by novelties, would rather study than know, even though knowledge is study's goal. And those who find leisure boring would rather struggle than win, even though victory is struggle's goal. And those bored by a healthy body prefer to eat than to be satisfied, as they also prefer genital pleasure to not suffering such disturbances. There are even those who prefer sleeping to not being weary, even though the end to which all these sensual pleasures point is not to be hungry or thirsty, not to want sexual intercourse, and not to be tired in body.

～

Here, toward the end of one of his early works, *On True Religion* (53.102), Augustine discusses appetite for knowledge and how it may go wrong. One of these ways, he says in a passage that comes just before the one quoted, is by mistaking intimacy with changing things for intimacy with unchanging things. That mistake is damaging because it makes the peace that comes with knowing the unchanging impossible. The result will be restlessness, and endless search for *novitates,* new things, as he says at the beginning of the quoted passage, and this in turn is best understood as a series of performatively incoherent exchanges: of studying for knowing, even though knowing *(cognitio)* is the proper end of study; of struggle's difficulties for the ease of victory, even though victory is the proper end of struggle; of eating for the health of the body, even though the body's health is the proper end of eating; of sexual excitement for the peace of undergoing no such disturbance, even though such peace is the proper end of sexual arousal; of sleeping over not being tired, even though the proper end of sleep is not to be tired. Each of these exchanges has the same structure: there is a better condition and a worse one; the *miseri homines*—people who are miserable because confused in mind and disordered in will—prefer the worse; but the worse will, if not grasped and held, lead to the better, and has all its meaning and goodness given to it by that fact. Holding and grasping it, therefore, refusing to let it go so that it can give way to what it points to, is an action that guarantees its own failure. This is what the curious man does with novelties.

❧

Novelties are news, new things, *res novae.* But newness is not all of the same kind. Some novelties are experiential, which is to say that they are new in someone's experience, while others belong to the order of being, which is to say new in reality, previously uninstanced. The first man, the first air-breather, the first supernova, the first solution to Fermat's Last Theorem: all these are novelties in the order of being. My first kiss, my first smell of India's softly and warmly spicy air, my first calculated lie: these are experiential novelties, things new to me but not new *simpliciter.* This distinction between the ontological and the experiential novelty could be pressed far enough to make it crumble.

It could, for example, be said that my first kiss is an ontological reality as well as an experiential one. The world, after all, had not, when I kissed (and was kissed) for the first time, ever had me kissing anyone in it before, even though it had seen very many kisses. But the distinction will nonetheless serve to mark out the territory in a rough-and-ready way, and it serves, too, to emphasize that the kind of novelty the curious seek is experiential: they want to be faced with a phenomenon—an appearance—they have not been faced with before, and to enter into some degree of knowing intimacy with it.

There are no absolutely new things, no novelties in the strict and full sense, nothing completely unprecedented. The attempt to think such an idea must fail, for anything completely new in this sense would, by definition, have nothing whatever in common with anything that had preceded it. If it did share anything with what had come before it would not be wholly new. Today's newspaper is new in the sense that its content does not repeat that of yesterday's newspaper. Nonetheless, it shares a great deal with yesterday's newspaper: a masthead, an editorial stance, a typeface, appearance on my doorstep at 5:00 a.m., and so on. And even the new content—the update on yesterday's story, the reference back to events of a year before, the speculations about the upcoming baseball season—has many causal connections and shares many features with yesterday's (and last week's and last month's) content. It, too, is not completely new. So also with the new hairstyle, the new regime, the new idea, the new book, the new attitude: they are all new and not new, partly new and partly old. An absolute novelty, even if, *per impossibile,* there could be one, would be completely inaccessible to us: if there were one we could not apprehend it, because our apprehension depends upon some degree of continuity with and causal connection to what has come before.

When we speak of novelties, then, we do not mean absolutely and incomprehensibly new things. We mean phenomena in part new and in part old, causally connected to appearances already apprehended and sharing some of their properties and aspects, but possessing also some not previously grasped. If there are no absolute novelties, as this way of putting things suggests, then it follows that all new things are more or less new, arranged on a gamut of novelty with the almost incomprehensibly unprecedented at one end and the largely familiar admixed with a tincture of the novel at the other. Once, and I hope never again, I saw violent and sudden death: a man decapitated suddenly in an accident. This was, for me, close to the incomprehensibly unprecedented: I saw it clearly but, because of its newness, I could not at first assimilate or apprehend it. It took a few long seconds for me to come to an understanding of what I had seen. Closer to the other end of the gamut, for me, was my first sight and smell of India. I was prepared for this by experience—many other sights and smells—and by reading, imagination, and anticipation; and so I knew at once, what I was experiencing. There was a bouquet new to me: a damply warm spiciness with undertones of exhaust fumes and urine. It gave me pause by its newness, but its elements were distinguishable, with effort and thought, and its novelty, while distinctive and suprising in its intensity, was easily assimilable and categorizable.

An experiential novelty is, most abstractly, a particular appearance to a particular person some of whose aspects have not previously appeared to that person; or, if they have all appeared they have not done so in that peculiar combination. Novelty is always a matter of degree, and it is indexed to particular people. What's new to you may be old to me; the fourteen-year-old's first kiss isn't like the five-thousandth shared by the long-married; and while I may have had to pause to assess India's bouquet on first experiencing it, the men trying to persuade me into their auto-rickshaws at the airport stand certainly did not; there was nothing new about it to them. Novelties may be conceptual (the new idea), sensory (the new sensation), affective (the new emotion), or conative (the new desire), but they can all be subsumed under this general definition. And they are fascinating to us: we seek them, often obsessively, and the curious are shaped by the their own catechetical formation into treating them as though they were unsurpassably significant.

Before turning to this particular obsession with novelty, it is worth pausing to say more about the interesting nature of the novelty's ideal type. That ideal type is the completely unprecedented event, an event unprepared for by any preceding cause, undirected toward any goal shared with any other thing, and having nothing else in common with anything already existing. There is and can be no such event. But this means that the ideal type of the novelty is something necessarily without existence. It is not, like my brother, something that could have existed but happens not to (so far as I know, I have no brothers); it is instead, like the square circle or the married bachelor, something that could not have existed, something whose identifying concept is incoherent. The further some appearance lies along the spectrum of novelty, then, the closer it is to necessary nonexistence; correspondingly, the closer it approaches to incomprehensibility, unrecognizability, and unassimilability.

In its ideal type, therefore, the novelty is always just out of reach, beckoning seductively. It is never grasped, because as soon as the hand closes on it, it is no longer novel but already old. What is within the grasp has already made the transition from new to passé, and in this, it shares an important feature with the present. The present's relation to the past and the future—emerging from the former, swallowed by the latter—has exactly the same structure as the novelty's relation to what it displaces and what will displace it. The present can never be stilled or noticed or paused or owned. As soon as any of these things is attempted, what is noticed is, by definition, no longer present but either past, and thus accessible only to memory; or, more likely, imagined and therefore fictive, a spectacle-like figment upon which the gaze freezes in a moment of exhausted intimacy. The present occupies, therefore, a space not of time but of abstraction, capable of conceptual analysis and depiction but not of any other. Attempts to grasp it imaginatively, for example, do and must fail. Just so with novelty. The idea of the novelty in its pure form is one that can regulate entire industries by providing an aspiration toward which that activity approaches and by which it is ordered. But it cannot, as a matter of principle, provide actual novelties, for these, in their purity, do not exist. The novelty is the unattainable absence, the lure that occupies no time and no space. This makes it all the more alluring: nothing is sought more eagerly than what in principle cannot be had because it does not exist.

There are less exacting ways to describe novelties, according to which they can be possessed and enjoyed. These less exacting understandings locate the novelty not only in the realm of abstraction, but also in that of space and time. They permit it to be a temporary but nonetheless real object of delight. That is to say, it might be that this year's new fashion color—the new black, whatever this year it happens to be—does not lose its novelty immediately upon being paraded on the runway, but preserves it at least long enough for it to be marketed to the masses. By then, of course, the cognoscenti will think it passé (certainly so if the proles are wearing it in Peoria) even if the masses do not. Novelties might, then, be understood to preserve their status as such for at least a short time, a time that will vary according to the medium—perhaps six hours for the newspaper headlines, ten minutes for the Internet newsflash, and three months for the new fashion—and according to the status and position of the person— last month's news magazine might be truly novel to someone who has never seen one before, but it will be worth not even a glance to someone who subscribes to six such magazines weekly. Thus, novelties can be arranged on a spectrum according to how long they can maintain their status as such; and this comports quite well with ordinary usage. But even when novelties are understood in this more relaxed sense, as providers of a brief but nonetheless real occasion of delight, they tend always toward their ideal type, hovering therefore on the brink of nonbeing, magnetized by and toward the nothing. They tend, that is, toward being creatures of darkness rather than of light.

The forms of economic organization favored by contemporary culture (late capitalist, high modern, quasi-globalized, post-Fordist: the descriptors are many) places a high value on claims to novelty, in both the order of being and that of knowing. This is in large part because of the market, which voraciously demands the constant stimulus of new products, appetite for which must be constantly created. The world has been transformed in the last two centuries by this nexus of technological transformation and educated desire: the automobile, the telephone, the radio, the television, the personal computer, and cheap air travel—these are the most obvious examples. But the tropes of novelty have extended outwards from this center in the innovations of the technology-driven market to most areas of our cultural and intellectual life. The fashion industry is based on these tropes: the endless work of that industry whose success is hailed year by year may serve as emblematic. The entertainment industry is defined by the promise of the new, of course, as is the knowledge-production industry of the academy: where would the academy be without its groundbreakingly transgressive works, hailed with the talisman-like mantra of all university press jacket copy, "the new contribution of this work is . . . "? Our sensual and intellectual appetites are constantly stimulated by the promise of novelty; and the language of the new is, for most of us most of the time, the language of praise.

This suggests that we are all most of the time earnest (or joyful) novelty-seekers. But this is not straightforwardly so. There is an important difference between the frequency with which we claim newness for our products and actions and the frequency with which what we make and claim as new actually is so. It is certainly true that we are marked deeply by the tendency to speak approvingly of the new, to assume that to call something new is to say something good of it, and, therefore, to place our enterprises under the sign of the novel. But to claim that an offering is new is not for it to be so: for the most part, the season's new movies are likely to be indistinguishable in structure, method, and purpose from their predecessors; the novelty claimed for the latest advance in critical theory may conceal a (known or unknown) repetition of moves made a thousand times before; and this season's dress styles may be knockoffs, again known or unknown, of styles from fifty (or five hundred) years ago. Appeals to the desirability of the new and claims that something is new are as likely to mask repetition, recapitulation, and imitation, as they are to signal the presence of something genuinely novel. The same is true in reverse: claiming the absence of novelty in situations where that is likely to create positive expectations (you may buy, the advertisements say, a hand-painted copy of your favorite masterpiece that will be in every respect indistinguishable from the original) may very well conceal difference beneath its claim to sameness. The simulacrum, in order to be effective in its claims to be such, must present itself as definitively repetitive, in every respect non-novel.

A second caveat has to do with the frequent mismatch between what we say we love and what our actions show us to love. That we speak approvingly of the new and say of what we like that it is new does not show that we in fact approve of and seek the new: as often as not, we seek the reassurance of repetition, even if we would rather call our repetitions new. We love the new telenovela or mystery novel not because it is new but because it is the same: the desire for it is the same as the child's desire to have the fairytale read aloud again for the hundredth time. The child, however, is unlikely to be embarassed by this desire for repetition, while the adult is likely to conceal it under the trope of the new. We are, then, only in part seekers of novelty, even though we are likely to talk as though we are creatures of the new from beginning to end.

Nevertheless, we do desire the new, even if our desire for it is always diluted by an eagerness for repetition's sameness. And we can desire the new with an appetite of great intensity that is difficult to satisfy. This intensity is connected to the peculiar nature of the ideal type of the new, which is the necessarily absent, the inevitably nonexistent. If that, as I have suggested, is what the new is ideally like, then dedicated novelty-seekers desiring the really new thing, the unprecedentedly novel, seek what they could not recognize and what cannot in any case exist. This is a strange desire: the more closely the grasping hand approaches the true novelty, the more what it closes on is nothing at all. But this typically does not lead to the thought that the desire for the new is intrinsically confused, but rather to the thought that success has temporarily eluded the novelty-seeker, and that a new attempt may have better results. And so, novelty-seekers redouble their efforts, finding, always and inevitably, exactly nothing but the necessity of continuing the novelty-chase. Insatiability is inevitable: desire for an absence that cannot become present—and recall that the object of desire is typically an absence—cannot be satiated. It can only multiply, replicating itself and increasing in intensity because of its disappointment and frustration.

The connections between novelty and spectacle should be clear enough. Those distracted by novelties work with great tenacity to make a transient path toward nothing. Those who were attracted by and moved toward the spectacle do the same: they too must put effort into building what the Buddhists call a sky-flower (something that would be beautiful if only it could exist, but which not only does not but cannot exist), so that they can possess it. What the depiction of the novelty adds to that of the spectacle is that it reveals curiosity—that form of the intellectual appetite that seeks both novelties and spectacles—as a self-replicating desire that cannot be satisfied and that must lead to an agonizing restlessness. The sketch I gave of a spectacular scene of violence in chapter 11 does more than freeze the gaze temporarily on a tableau that cannot be seen through; it also prompts in those who have looked at it as just such a tableau an immediate desire for more of the same. The novelty, once found, is immediately no longer new; therefore, it can only fail to fulfil the desire that sought it. The gaze temporarily frozen to its glittering surface will at once slide away from it toward the next new thing, the next novelty. This is obvious enough in the economic sphere: the mini-orgasm of purchase prompts, often at once, desire for another purchase. It is perhaps less obvious in the cognitive sphere but just as real: there too, cognitive intimacy with the new will, as soon as achieved (or apparently achieved, for it can never really be achieved), prompt a desire for more of the same. In academia, those especially subject to this sickness are likely to be rewarded for it because the academy is the place where curiosity is taught as a virtue.

∾

Novelty's approximate antonym is repetition. If the curious are catechized into conforming all objects of knowledge as closely as possible to novelties, then the studious are catechized into seeing all creatures as participants in the God who is by definition incompatible with novelty. Seeking intimacy with creatures understood in this way—even in the case of sensibilia, and even more obviously in that of intelligibilia—means seeking intimacy with things that point beyond themselves because of their participation in God. This in turn means that they do not yield themselves fully to the knowledge-seeker's gaze. They have a depth that repays the gaze's constant return to their surface. They are, in the terms given in chapter 11, partly iconic; and they are also not subject to ownership's grasp. Intimacy with them—which, recall, is what all knowledge is—is always a matter of degree, of more and less; and because each of them is inexhaustible (though each in its own way, the way appropriate to its kind, which is different from the mode of inexhaustibility appropriate to every other kind), the repetitive return of the gaze to the same creature yields—or may yield, other things being equal—greater intimacy, which is to say more knowledge. Further, each return of the studious gaze to what it seeks to know is a nonidentical repetition: it is something like a replaying the same score, but with the changes those alterations in knower and known inevitably bring. In this it differs from the need of the curious for more of the same: in that case each repetition seeks just what it had before, and, finding that it cannot be had, that the spectacle, upon being returned to, has already exhausted both the gaze and itself, attempts to replicate the effects of the first apprehension of the spectacle by increasing the intensity of the stimulus. The curious cannot be satisfied with a second look at the same creature, because their first look—the look that brought the spectacle into being and owned it—made of the creature toward which it was directed something less than it had been, something that cannot bear a second look. The curious look eviscerates the creatures at which it is directed, impoverishes them, and in that way makes the contemplative look of the studious, with its love of nonidentical repetition, impossible.

The immediate model and mother of the repetitive gaze of the studious is the nonidentical repetition of the liturgy. It is from this that the skills of the studious come, and to this that they are conformed. But this model, this complexly repetitive act, is itself a participant in another, and deeper, set of nonidentical repetitions, which are those that constitute the inner life of God, the eternal love that relates Son to Father by begetting, and the Spirit to both by procession. This set of relations, though eternal and changeless, is not static. In a way obscure to us, it consists of a set of repetitions, each of which is perfect but no one of which is identical with any other. Very imperfect analogies might be the hundreds or thousands of lovemakings that join a married couple over the length of a long marriage; or the contrapuntal variations on a theme to be found in a six-part invention. The point of mentioning this trinitarian basis for the liturgy, and in turn the liturgy as basis for the studious life, is not to explain the Holy Trinity or the liturgy. It is only to indicate that the intellectual life of the studious Christian is what it is because of its participation in the triune

God and because of its formation by the nonidentical repetitions of the liturgy. A Catholic may go to Mass thousands of times in her life. It may seem that the same things are done and said each time, and in a sense, this is true. But each time the worshippers differ, the celebrant differs, and time has marched on. The body and blood may be received in a condition of ecstasy or depression or inattentiveness or distraction; it may follow hard upon confession of mortal sin, or be widely separated in time from any such sin; there is, then, always both repetition and change, but there is (ideal-typically) never repetition that gives the liturgy over to its participants as a spectacle to be manipulated into ever-greater intensities. Instead, the worshipper's gaze harmonizes, more or less, with the same action repeated, and does so neither as spectator (the watcher of a spectacle) nor as owner (practitioner of the threefold sequestration) but always as participant. With this as its model, this as its most fundamental formation, the studious gaze is made able, and sometimes eager, to return again and again to contemplation of the same object of study, again as participant rather than owner-spectator.

Nonidentical repetition does not rule out novelty. Returning the gaze ever and again to the same creature permits (though does not guarantee) deeper intimacy with that creature, and this means, over time, the student is coming to know previously unknown things about the creature. It means, or may mean, that is, experiential novelty at least. The mathematician working studiously at Fermat's Last Theorem may become sufficiently intimate with that theorem that she can, at last, see deeply enough into it to prove it. The scholar of Scripture may, after long and attentive reading, come to see something previously unseen, whether by him or by anyone else, about the meaning of the text. The long, patient contemplation of the progress of HIV-AIDS may lead, eventually, to the dawning of understanding of what might be done to remove without remainder the deficiency in which that disease consists. In all these cases, the studious and the curious may share in what seem to be indistinguishable novelties. But such things are not what the studious principally seek. They come, when they come, as an epiphenomenon of what they do seek, which is just closer intimacy with the creature contemplated. For the curious, though, these novelties are the thing itself: Fermat's Last Theorem has interest only as something that might yield a proof; Scripture only as a treasure house of puzzles to solve; and HIV-AIDS only as something to be cured. For them, the novelty, ideally constructed as a spectacle, laid claim to, and owned, is what is primarily sought.

13

LOQUACITY

Curiosité n'est que vanité. Le plus souvent, on ne veut savoir que pour en parler. On ne voyagerait pas sur la mer pour le seul plaisir de voir, sans espérance de s'en entretenir jamais avec personne.

Curiosity is nothing but vanity. Most often, one wants to know only in order to talk about it. One does not go on a sea voyage for the sole pleasure of looking, without the hope of ever discussing it with someone.

⤳

In this aphorism (§72, according to Le Guern's enumeration) from the *Pensées,* Pascal draws the connection between curiosity and the desire to speak. Intellectual appetite, he says, most often has among its concomitants the desire to speak of what one seeks to know; the word "curiosity" labels that kind of desire to know (Pascal leaves open here the possibility that there may be other kinds of intellectual appetite, kinds not indissolubly linked with the need to speak), and the fact that it is accompanied by the desire to speak what one knows, and thereby to become known as a knower, is what makes it without remainder vain, empty, and useless. No one, he says, takes a sea voyage (he has in mind voyages of exploration, but what he says applies equally to our voyages of tourism) without hoping to tell someone about it. The absurdity of the idea—exploring new continents and new oceans, then coming home and saying nothing whatever about it—shows how deep the connection runs between intellectual appetite and the need to speak what has been found.

⮎

The last contrast I wish to draw between the curious and the studious concerns their attitudes to communicating to others the intimacies (for the studious) and the masteries (for the curious) to which their intellectual appetites have led them. There are three fundamental attitudes here: the systematic refusal of speech that is silence; the tentative and self-cancelling speech proper to those who stammer; and the well-wrought and compelling speech that belongs to the loquacious. The divisions between the curious and the studious are more complex here than in the other cases of contrast discussed in chapters 9–13.

Silence first: the easy case. Both the curious and the studious may sometimes refuse to communicate what their intellectual appetites have led them to, but for both this refusal will be occasional and atypical. For neither does the grammar of their understanding of what it is to know and to seek new knowledge require silence as the ordinary culmination. However, this is for very different reasons in each case.

For the studious, gaining a particular intimacy with a creature, sensible or intellectual, is, as we have seen, understood as gift and as a matter for wonder. And it is a gift that cannot properly be received unless it is given away, handed on to others. The ordinary use to which the studious knower puts her knowledge, therefore, is to teach it. This is the free, nonobliging transfer of gift that is the only way in which the gift of knowledge can be received. To refuse as a matter of course to communicate what is newly known is to relinquish knowledge of it by understanding it as one's own, to be done with as one wills. Again, the liturgy provides the model here: receiving Christ leads, ordinarily, to the confession of praise made both to God and to other humans. Being formed as a knower in this way, the studious offer a similar confession of praise in response to their intimacies with creatures. Silence as a response is abnormal, prudential, context-specific. Perhaps, for example, a reasonable judgment is made that a particular audience is incapable of hearing and responding to the proclamation of a particular knowledge; or perhaps a particular intimacy, a particular understanding is judged to be properly spoken of only within the circle of the faithful, just as some intimacies are spoken of only within the circle of the family. For the studious, these occasions will be few and atypical. Christianity is not a matter of esoteric truths; and most intimacies wth creatures will not have to do with the truths of the faith in any case. The studious student of physics or literature or sociology will ordinarily and naturally speak (or write) what she has come to know as an offering of love to the world.

Typically, the curious, too, are not silent about what they have come to know, but for quite different reasons. To be effective, ownership and mastery, which is what the curious seek in relation to what they have come to know, need to be declared. And, as the aphorism from Pascal with which this chapter begins suggests, the curious need not only to know, but to be known as knowers. They must lay claim, and doing that means public utterance. This need explains bitter academic disputes over priority: who first developed that theorem, made that observation, or brought that word-ensemble into being? Dated publication is the best way to prove priority, and that, too, requires public utterance. Like the studious, then, the curious will be silent about what they take themselves to have come to know only for local and prudential reasons. Silence does not belong to the grammar of curiosity.

The second attitude to speaking what one knows distinguished above, that of the tentative and self-cancelling speech that stammers, is proper to the grammar of studiousness, and is altogether foreign to that of curiosity. I use stammering here as a figure for speech whose acknowledgment of its insufficiency to its topic is evident on its surface. The ordinary stammerer appears to his hearers to be simultaneously trying to speak and to prevent himself from speaking; just the same is true of the ideal-typical speech of the studious knower. Such a knower wants to speak because she has something important to say: she wants to pass on the gift of her newfound intimacy with some creature to other creatures, and to do so as an act of confession. But she also wants to prevent herself from speaking, to place her speech under the kind of erasure through which it remains audible (or visible in the case of writing), because she knows that the intimacy she is communicating is profoundly inadequate to its object, and that this needs to be signalled in the act of communication itself. Not to signal it would be to pretend to intimacies that cannot be attained here below. The inadequacy of all creaturely intimacies—which, recall, includes all creaturely knowledge—is given by three facts about the world, all already discussed at more length in chapters 4–6. The first is that the knowable creature is inexhaustible: it cannot be completely known because of its participation in God. The second is that all creatures—or at least all sensible creatures, matters are different for intelligibilia—are to some degree damaged by primeval calamity and therefore are resistant to the loving, intimacy-seeking gaze of the studious; and the third is that the studious knower is himself damaged, necessarily and inevitably, and therefore will not always recognize the imperfections, inadequacies, and misprisions that inevitably accompany his genuine intimacies. All this needs to be signalled when the studious make their findings public, and the stammer serves as a covering figure for the various ways of signalling it.

The liturgy provides the formative template for the stammer, as it does for everything else about the practice of studiousness. In the liturgy the worshipper approaches intimacy with God even to the point of receiving and ingesting him under the appearance of bread and wine, a degree of intimacy of which human sexual intercourse is a pale, participated shadow. But the liturgy also stammers: there are successive moments of confession of inadequacy, failure, sin, no one of which—not even the *non sum dignus* said as the culmination approaches—is fully effective in erasing the condition of which it speaks. The worshipper repeatedly approaches and draws back, approaches and draws back; and the liturgy marks this in its very structure. And even when the final intimacy is given and received, the worshipper receives it always as a sinner, one suffering deep damage, even though one at the same time in a state of grace. This is much too compressed to be adequate as a commentary upon liturgical formation, but it may suffice to indicate what I mean by the studious stammer. A doubt is raised, an imperfection acknowledged, the beauty of a public depiction of knowledge's creaturely intimacy shaded by an acknowledgment of the failure of exactly that intimacy. There is, ideal-typically once again, a high degree of self-referential awareness in the texts, oral or written, of studious knowers: the stammer requires this.

The curious, however, do not stammer. They are loquacious, which means much more than just that they speak (and write) a lot. They present their spectacular masteries in a form that shows no doubt, no stammering, and no uncertainty; and they do so because they have none. The spectacles they have constructed are wholly owned. No remnant remains unpenetrated, undominated, and so the findings can be presented loquaciously, in well-wrought words whose central purpose is to convince those who hear or read them that, yes, this is exhaustively known; and, equally (if not more) important, I, the one speaking and writing, exhaustively know it. Ideally, the reader or hearer of what the curious write and speak should be struck dumb with admiration of the perfect mastery there being displayed. Those who read what the curious write should respond as the prophet Isaiah did in the presence of God: my lips, they should think, are unclean before knowledge of this extent and profundity. All I can do is be silent before it. The curious, as always, aspire to be treated as if divine.

This leads me to the final contrast between the stammering works of the studious and the loquacious works of the curious. It is that stammering is an invitation, while loquacity is no more than a declaration.

14

GRATITUDE

In this last chapter I offer thanks to those, living and dead, whose words have made possible the words of this book. Memory being what it is, it is likely that some who have helped me are not thanked. For that, in no case deliberate, I apologise. A large majority of the thanks offered are to those whose faces I have never seen, either because they are dead or because our paths have not crossed. In those cases, I can thank them only for their words.

My principal thanks are due to Augustine, without whose writings this book would not exist. The same is true more proximately for the work of Reinhard Hütter, whose essay on the directedness of reason, together with his kind and instructive conversation about these matters, first directed my attention to the question of curiosity and intellectual appetite. I have benefited also from conversations (some written, some spoken) on these topics with the following individuals, some of whom have read part or all of the book at various stages of its composition: Stanley Fish, Walter Benn Michaels, Tony Laden, John Cavadini, David Burrell, Ike Balbus, Jerry Walls, Alex Macgregor, John Walsh, Mary Beth Rose, Del Kiernan-Lewis, Sam Fleischacker, Ed Oakes, Bruce Marshall, Dan Arnold, Derek Jeffreys, Matthew Kapstein, Michael Kremer, Candace Vogler, Larry Poston, Michael Lieb, Nanno Marinatos, Greg Sadler, Stanley Hauerwas, and Judith Heyhoe.

The following institutions and organisations have been kind enough to provide me instructive occasion to share some of this work with their faculty and students: Valparaiso University, McGill University, Lumen Christi Institute, American Maritain Association, St. Francis Xavier University, Canadian Mennonite University, University of Chicago Divinity School, and Durham University. I owe a special debt of gratitude to the University of Illinois at Chicago, which provided me with a sabbatical semester in 2006, during which the work was half completed; and to the Department of Theology and Religion at Durham University, which provided me with a term of residence as Richardson Fellow in 2007, during which the work was finished. In Durham, the hospitality of Joe Cassidy, Principal of St. Chad's College, and the warm welcome of the residents of Trinity Hall, gave me a very pleasant context in which to work. I owe a special debt here to Theodora Hawksley.

The J. J. Thiessen Lectures, which I delivered at the Canadian Mennonite University in fall 2005, were published as a small book in 2006: *The Vice of Curiosity: An Essay on Intellectual Appetite* (CMU Press). The material in that book serves as a complement to what is in this one: there I did some exegetical and historical work; here I try to avoid doing any.

∾

The list of works that follows includes everything I have found useful in thinking about the topics discussed in the book. It does not include everything I have read in preparing to write it, and is even further from including everything I should have read. Because the topics I have treated in the book are various, crossing a number of disciplinary boundaries, the list may appear miscellaneous; but the discerning will be able to see which works have informed which chapters, and why I have found the things I mention useful. I have not included works by Augustine in the list, for two reasons: the first is that discussions of *curiositas,* expositions of 1 John 2:16, and analyses of the intellectual appetite in general, are scattered broadside through his corpus, and so any list would be enormously extensive; the second is that nothing I have written (with the exception of the brief paragraphs that introduce chapters 2–13) is intended as exegesis of Augustine. I do include in the list, however, those among the works interpreting Augustine on these matters that I have found most useful. I mention neither the originals of works I have read only in translation, nor translations of works I have read only in the original: these should be easy enough to track down. Neither do I provide dates of first publication when I have read a later edition. In all cases I mention only the versions I have held in my hands.

Aertsen, Jan. *Nature and Creature: Thomas Aquinas's Way of Thought.* Leiden: Brill, 1998.

Bacon, Francis. *The New Organon.* Translated by Lisa Jardine and Michael Silverthorne. Cambridge: Cambridge University Press, 2000.

Benedict, Barbara M. *Curiosity: A Cultural History of Early Modern Inquiry.* Chicago: University of Chicago Press, 2001.

Bernard of Clairvaux. *De consideratione ad Eugenium Papam.* In *S. Bernardi Opera,* edited by Jean Leclercq, vol. 3. Rome: Editiones Cistercienses, 1957–1977, 393–493.

———. *De gradibus humilitatis et superbiae.* In *S. Bernardi Opera,* edited by Jean Leclercq, vol. 3. Rome: Editiones Cistercienses, 1957–1977, 13–59.

Besançon, Alain. *L'Image interdite: une histoire intellectuelle de l'iconoclasme.* Paris: Fayard, 1994.

Bloom, Harold. *The Anxiety of Influence: A Theory of Poetry.* New York: Oxford University Press, 1973.

Blum, Christopher. "'Where Is the Wisdom We Have Lost in Knowledge?' The Cultural Tragedy of the Enlightenment." *The Downside Review* 438 (January 2007): 51–66.

Blumenberg, Hans. *Die Legitimität der Neuzeit.* Frankfurt: Suhrkamp, 1976.

Bonaventure. *De reductione artium ad theologiam.* Edited and translated by Zachary Haye. In *St. Bonaventure's On the Reduction of the Arts to Theology.* St. Bonaventure, N.Y.: Franciscan Institute, 1996.

Bös, Gunther. *Curiositas: Die Rezeption eines antiken Begriffes durch christliche Autoren bis Thomas von Aquin.* Paderborn: Ferdinand Schöningh, 1995.

Boyd, Craig A. "Participation Metaphysics in Aquinas's Theory of Natural Law." *American Catholic Philosophical Quarterly* 79 (2005): 431–45.

Brague, Rémi. *The Wisdom of the World: The Human Experience of the Universe in Western Thought.* Chicago: University of Chicago Press, 2003.

Buranen, Lise, and Alice M. Roy, eds. *Perspectives on Plagiarism and Intellectual Property in a Postmodern World.* Albany: State University of New York Press, 1999.

Burrell, David. *Aquinas: God and Action.* Notre Dame: University of Notre Dame Press, 1979.

Cabassut, André. "Curiosité." In *Dictionnaire de Spiritualité,* edited by Charles Baumgartner, vol. 2. Paris: Beauchesne, 1953, cols. 2654–61.

Caputo, John, and Michael J. Scanlon, eds. *God, the Gift, and Postmodernism.* Bloomington: Indiana University Press, 1999.

Céard, Jean, ed. *La curiosité à la Renaissance.* Paris: Société d'Édition d'Enseignement Supérieur, 1986.

Clarke, W. Norris. *The One and the Many: A Contemporary Thomistic Metaphysics.* Notre Dame: University of Notre Dame Press, 2002.

———. "The Meaning of Participation in St. Thomas." In idem, *Explorations in Metaphysics.* Notre Dame: University of Notre Dame Press, 1994, 89–101.

Coombe, Rosemary J. *The Cultural Life of Intellectual Properties: Authorship, Appropriation, and the Law.* Durham, N.C.: Duke University Press, 1998.

Daston, Lorraine, and Katharine Park. *Wonders and the Order of Nature 1150–1750.* New York: Zone Books, 1998.

Davidson, Donald. "What Metaphors Mean." In Davidson, *Inquiries into Truth and Interpretation.* Oxford: Clarendon Press, 1991, 245–64.

Davies, Oliver. *The Creativity of God: World, Eucharist, Reason.* Cambridge: Cambridge University Press, 2004.

de Finance, Joseph. *Être et agir dans la philosophie de Saint Thomas.* Rome: Librairie Éditrice de l'Université Grégorienne, 1960.

de Lubac, Henri. *Exégèse médiévale: les quatre sens de l'Écriture.* Paris: Aubier, 1959–1964.

Derrida, Jacques. *Eyes of the University: Right to Philosophy 2.* Translated by Jan Plug et al. Stanford: Stanford University Press, 2004.

———. *Who's Afraid of Philosophy? Right to Philosophy 1.* Translated by Jan Plug. Stanford: Stanford University Press, 2002.

———. *The Gift of Death.* Chicago: University of Chicago Press, 1995.

———. *Donner le temps: 1. La fausse monnaie.* Paris: Éditions Galilée, 1991.

Descartes, René. *Regulae ad directionem ingenii.* Edited and translated by George Heffernan. Amsterdam: Rodopi, 1998.

Desmond, William. *Being and the Between.* Albany: State University of New York Press, 1995.

DiLorenzo, Raymond D. "Non pie quaerunt: Rhetoric, Dialectic, and the Discovery of the True in Augustine's Confessions." *Augustinian Studies* 14 (1983): 117–27.

Duval, Gilles. "«Curious» a travers les siècles: simple curiosité?" *Études Anglaises* 48/2 (1995): 129–39.

Evans, G. R. *Getting It Wrong: The Medieval Epistemology of Error.* Leiden: Brill, 1998.

Fabro, Cornelio. *La nozione metafisica di partecipazione secondo San Tommaso.* Turin: Società editrice internazionale, 1950.

Feldman, Erich. "Unverschämt genug vermaß er sich, astronomische Anschauungen zu lehren: Augustins Polemik gegen Mani in conf. 5, 3ff." In *Signum Pietatis,* edited by Adolar Zumkeller. Würzburg: Augustinus-Verlag, 1989, 105–20.

Florensky, Pavel. *Iconostasis.* Translated by Donald Sheehan and Olga Andrejev. Crestwood, N.Y.: St. Vladimir's Seminary Press, 2000.

Florensky, Pavel. *The Pillar and Ground of the Truth.* Translated by Boris Jakim. Princeton: Princeton University Press, 1997.

Foucault, Michael. *Fearless Speech.* Edited by Joseph Pearson. Los Angeles: Semiotext(e), 2001.

———. "Qu'est-ce que les Lumières?" In Foucault, *Dits et écrits II, 1976–1988.* Paris: Éditions Gallimard, 2001, 1381–97.

———. "Qu'est-ce qu'un auteur?" In Foucault, *Dits et écrits I, 1954–1975.* Paris: Éditions Gallimard, 2001, 73–104.

Garber, Marjorie. *Academic Instincts.* Princeton: Princeton University Press, 2001.

Geiger, Louis Bertrand. *La participation dans le philosophie de S. Thomas Aquin.* Paris: Vrin, 1942.

Gilman, Sander L. *The Fortunes of the Humanities.* Stanford: Stanford University Press, 2000.

Gilson, Étienne. "Education and Higher Learning." In *A Gilson Reader,* edited by Anton C. Pegis. New York: Hanover House, 1957, 312–26.

———. *Being and Some Philosophers.* Toronto: Pontifical Institute of Medieval Studies, 1952.

Gladwell, Malcolm. "Something Borrowed: Should a Charge of Plagiarism Ruin Your Life?" *The New Yorker* (Nov. 22, 2004): 40–48.

Godbout, Jacques T., and Alain Caillé, eds. *The World of the Gift.* Translated by Donald Winkler. Montreal: McGill-Queens University Press, 1998.

Harrison, Peter. "Curiosity, Forbidden Knowledge, and the Reformation of Natural Philosophy in Early Modern England." *Isis* 92 (2001): 265–90.

Hart, David Bentley. *The Beauty of the Infinite: The Aesthetics of Christian Truth.* Grand Rapids, Mich.: Eerdmans, 2003.

Hayen, André. "L'Intentionnalité de l'être et métaphysique de la participation." *Révue Néoscolastique* 42 (1939): 385–410.

Heidegger, Martin. *What Is Called Thinking?* Translated by J. Glenn Gray. New York: Perennial, 2004.

————. "Platons Lehre von der Wahrheit." In idem, *Wegmarken*. Frankfurt-am-Main: Klostermann, 1976, 203–38.

Hemming, Laurence Paul. *Postmodernity's Transcending: Devaluing God*. Notre Dame: University of Notre Dame Press, 2005.

Henninger, Mark G. *Relations: Medieval Theories 1250–1325*. Oxford: Clarendon Press, 1989.

Hess, Charlotte, and Elinor Ostrom, eds. *Understanding Knowledge as a Commons: From Theory to Practice*. Cambridge, Mass.: MIT Press, 2007.

Horner, Robyn. *Rethinking God as Gift: Marion, Derrida, and the Limits of Phenomenology*. New York: Fordham University Press, 2001.

Howard, Donald R. *The Three Temptations: Medieval Man in Search of the World*. Princeton: Princeton University Press, 1966.

Hugh of St. Victor. *Didascalicon: De Studio Legendi*. Translated by Jerome Taylor. In *The Didascalicon of Hugh of St. Victor: A Medieval Guide to the Arts*. New York: Columbia University Press, 1991.

Hütter, Reinhard. "The Directedness of Reason and the Metaphysics of Creation." In *Reason and the Reasons of Faith*, edited by Paul J. Griffiths and Reinhard Hütter. London and New York: T & T Clark International, 2005, 160–93.

Hyde, Lewis. *The Gift: Imagination and the Erotic Life of Property*. New York: Vintage Books, 1983.

Illich, Ivan. *In the Vineyard of the Text: A Commentary to Hugh's Didascalicon*. Chicago: University of Chicago Press, 1993.

Janicaud, Dominique, et al. *Phenomenology and the "Theological Turn": The French Debate*. New York: Fordham University Press, 2000.

Jaques-Chaquin, Nicole, and Sophie Houdard, eds. *Curiosité et Libido Sciendi de la Renaissance aux Lumières*. Fontenay/Saint-Cloud: ENS Éditions, 1998.

Joly, Robert. "Curiositas." *L'Antiquité classique* 30 (1961): 33–44.

Jones, L. Gregory, and Stephanie Paulsell, eds. *The Scope of Our Art: The Vocation of the Theological Teacher*. Grand Rapids, Mich.: Eerdmans, 2001.

Kant, Immanuel. *The Conflict of the Faculties*. Translated by Mary J. Gregor and Robert Anchor. In *Immanuel Kant, Religion and Rational Theology*, edited by Allen W. Wood and George di Giovanni. Cambridge: Cambridge University Press, 1996, 239–327.

Kennedy, Thomas D. "Curiosity and the Integrated Self: A Postmodern Vice." *Logos* 4/4 (2001): 33–54.

Kenny, Neil. *Curiosity in Early Modern Europe: Word Histories*. Wiesbaden: Harrassowitz, 1998.

Komter, Aafke, ed. *The Gift: An Interdisciplinary Perspective*. Amsterdam: Amsterdam University Press, 1996.

Labhardt, André. "Curiositas: Notes sur l'histoire d'un mot et d'une notion." *Museum Helveticum* 17 (1960): 206–24.

Landes, William A., and Richard Posner. *The Economic Structure of Intellectual Property Law*. Cambridge, Mass.: Harvard University Press, 2003.

Leask, Ian, and Eoin Cassidy, eds. *Givenness and God: Questions of Jean-Luc Marion*. New York: Fordham University Press, 2005.

Leclercq, Jean. *L'Amour des lettres et le désir de Dieu: Initiation aux auteurs monastiques du moyen âge*. Paris: Éditions du Cerf, 1957.

Leftow, Brian. "Divine Simplicity." *Faith and Philosophy* 23/4 (2006): 365–80.

Lévinas, Emmanuel. *Autrement qu'être ou au-delà de l'essence*. La Haye: Nijhoff, 1974.

———. *Humanisme de l'autre homme*. Montpellier: Fata Morgana, 1972.

Lloyd, G. E. R. *The Ambitions of Curiosity: Understanding the World in Ancient Greece and China*. Cambridge: Cambridge University Press, 2002.

Locke, John. *Some Thoughts Concerning Education*. Edited by Nathan Tarcov and Ruth W. Grant. Indianapolis: Hackett, 1996.

Loewenstein, Joseph. *The Author's Due: Printing and the Prehistory of Copyright*. Chicago: University of Chicago Press, 2002.

MacIntyre, Alasdair. "The End of Education: The Fragmentation of the American University." *Commonweal* (October 20, 2006): 10–14.

———. "Aquinas's Critique of Education: Against His Own Age, Against Ours." In *Philosophers on Education: New Historical Perspectives*, edited by Amélie Oksenberg Rorty. New York: Routledge, 1998, 95–108.

Mallon, Thomas. *Stolen Words*. San Diego: Harcourt, 2001.

Marion, Jean-Luc. *Le phénomène érotique: Six méditations*. Paris: Grasset, 2003.

———. *De surcroît: études sur les phénomènes saturés*. Paris: Presses Universitaires de France, 2002.

———. *The Idol and Distance: Five Studies*. Translated by Thomas Carlson. New York: Fordham University Press, 2001.

———. *Étant donné: essai d'une phénoménologie de la donation*. Paris: Presses Universitaires de France, 1997.

———. *The Crossing of the Visible*. Translated by James K. A. Smith. Paris: Presses Universitaires de France, 1996.

———. *Réduction et donation: recherches sur Husserl, Heidegger et la phénoménologie*. Paris: Presses Universitaires de France, 1989.

Maritain, Jacques. *Distinguer pour unir, ou les degrés du savoir*. Paris: Desclée de Brouwer, 1935.

Mauss, Marcel. "Essai sur le don: forme et raison de l'échange dans les sociétés archaïques." *http://dx.doi.org/doi:10.1522/cla.mam.ess3?* (accessed July 2007).

McCormick, John F. *St. Thomas and the Life of Learning*. Milwaukee: Marquette University Press, 1947.

Meilaender, Gilbert C. *The Theory and Practice of Virtue*. Notre Dame: University of Notre Dame Press, 1984.

Milbank, John. "The Soul of Reciprocity." *Modern Theology* 17 (2001): 335–91; 485–507.

———. "The Conflict of the Faculties: Theology and the Economy of the Sciences." In *Faithfulness and Fortitude,* edited by Mark Thiessen Nation and Samuel Wells. Edinburgh: T & T Clark, 2000, 39–57.

———. "Can a Gift Be Given? Prolegomena to a Future Trinitarian Metaphysics." *Modern Theology* 11 (1995): 119–61.

Milbank, John, and Catherine Pickstock. *Truth in Aquinas.* New York: Routledge, 2001.

Moevs, Christiaan. *The Metaphysics of Dante's Comedy.* New York: Oxford University Press, 2005.

Mondzain, Maria-José. *Image, Icon, Economy: The Byzantine Origins of the Contemporary Imaginary.* Stanford: Stanford University Press, 2005.

Newhauser, Richard. "Towards a History of Human Curiosity: A Prolegomenon to Its Medieval Phase." *Deutsche Vierteljahrsschrift für Literaturwissenschaft und Geistesgeschichte* 56 (1982): 559–75.

Newman, John Henry. *The Idea of a University.* Edited by Martin J. Svaglic. San Francisco: Rinehart Press, 1960.

———. "Curiosity, a Temptation to Sin." In idem, *Parochial and Plain Sermons,* vol. 8. London: Longmans Green, 1908, 62–75.

Nietzsche, Friedrich. *Über die Zukunft unserer Bildungsanstalten.* In idem, *Nachgelassene Schriften 1870–1873,* edited by Giorgio Colli and Mazzino Montinari. Berlin: de Gruyter, 1973, 133–244.

Oberman, Heiko Augustinus. *Contra vanam curiositatem: Ein Kapitel der Theologie zwischen Seelenwinkel und Weltall.* Zürich: Theologischer Verlag, 1974.

Ohmann, Richard. *Politics of Letters.* Middletown, Conn.: Wesleyan University Press, 1987.

Ong, Walter, S. J. *Ramus, Method, and the Decay of Dialogue: From the Art of Discourse to the Art of Reason.* Chicago: University of Chicago Press, 2004.

O'Rourke, Fran. *Pseudo-Dionysius and the Metaphysics of Aquinas.* Notre Dame: University of Notre Dame Press, 2005.

———. "Aquinas and Platonism." In *Contemplating Aquinas: On the Varieties of Interpretation,* edited by Fergus Kerr. London: SCM Press, 2003, 247–79.

Osteen, Mark. *The Question of the Gift: Essays across Disciplines.* New York: Routledge, 2002.

Otnes, Cele, and Richard F. Beltramini, eds. *Gift-Giving: A Research Anthology.* Bowling Green, Ohio: Bowling Green State University Popular Press, 1996.

Peters, Edward. "Aenigma Salomonis: Manichaean Anti-Genesis Polemic and the Vitium curiositatis in Confessions III.6." *Augustiniana* 36 (1986): 48–64.

Pickstock, Catherine. *After Writing: On the Liturgical Consummation of Philosophy.* Oxford: Blackwell, 1997.

Pieper, Josef. *Leisure, the Basis of Culture.* Translated by Gerald Malsbary. South Bend, Ind.: St. Augustine's Press, 1998.

———. *The Four Cardinal Virtues.* Translated by various hands. Notre Dame: University of Notre Dame Press, 1966.

Plagiary: Cross-Disciplinary Studies in Plagiarism, Fabrication, and Falsification. http://www.plagiary.org/ (accessed July 2007).

Pollmann, Karla, and Mark Vessey, eds. *Augustine and the Disciplines: From Cassiciacum to Confessions.* Oxford: Oxford University Press, 2005.

Posner, Richard. *The Little Book of Plagiarism.* New York: Pantheon, 2007.

Posnock, Ross. *The Trial of Curiosity: Henry James, William James, and the Challenge of Modernity.* New York: Oxford University Press, 1991.

Ramos, Alice, and Marie I. George, eds. *Faith, Scholarship, and Culture in the 21st Century.* Washington, D.C.: American Maritain Association, 2002.

Ramos, Alice. "Studiositas and Curiositas: Matters for Self-Examination." *Educational Horizons* 83/4 (2005): 272–81.

Rand, Richard, ed. *Logomachia: The Conflict of the Faculties.* Lincoln: University of Nebraska Press, 1992.

Readings, Bill. *The University in Ruins.* Cambridge, Mass.: Harvard University Press, 1996.

Rhode, Deborah L. *In Pursuit of Knowledge.* Stanford: Stanford University Press, 2006.

Rocca, Gregory P. *Speaking the Incomprehensible God: Thomas Aquinas on the Interplay of Positive and Negative Theology.* Washington, D.C.: The Catholic University of America Press, 2004.

Rorty, Amélie Oksenberg, ed. *Philosophers on Education: Historical Perspectives.* New York: Routledge, 1998.

Rose, Mark. *Authors and Owners: The Invention of Copyright.* Cambridge, Mass.: Harvard University Press, 1993.

Rosenzweig, Frans. *On Jewish Learning.* Edited by N. N. Glatzer. New York: Schocken, 1965.

Schmitz, Kenneth L. *The Gift: Creation.* Milwaukee: Marquette University Press, 1982.

Scott, D. F. S. *Wilhelm von Humboldt and the Idea of a University.* Durham: University of Durham, 1960.

Sertillanges, A. G. *The Intellectual Life: Its Spirit, Conditions, Methods.* Translated by Mary Ryan. Washington, D.C.: The Catholic University of America Press, 1987.

Shattuck, Roger. *Forbidden Knowledge: From Prometheus to Pornography.* New York: St. Martin's Press, 1996.

Shils, Edward. *The Calling of Education: The Academic Ethic and Other Essays on Higher Education.* Chicago: University of Chicago Press, 1997.

Siewerth, Gustav. *Die Metaphysik der Erkenntnis nach Thomas von Aquin.* Darmstadt: Wissenschaftliche Buchgesellschaft, 1968.

———. *Die Analogie des Seienden.* Einsiedeln: Verlag, 1965.

Simon, Yves R. "Work." In idem, *Philosopher at Work: Essays by Yves R. Simon,* edited by Anthony O. Simon. Lanham: Rowman & Littlefield, 1999, 7–19.

Sokolowski, Robert. *Introduction to Phenomenology.* Cambridge: Cambridge University Press, 2000.

———. *The God of Faith and Reason: Foundations of Christian Theology.* Washington, D.C.: The Catholic University of America Press, 1995.

Stock, Brian. *After Augustine: The Meditative Reader and the Text.* Philadelphia: University of Pennsylvania Press, 2001.

———. *Augustine the Reader: Meditation, Self-Knowledge, and the Ethics of Interpretation.* Cambridge, Mass.: Belknap Press, 1996.

Tanner, Kathryn. *Economy and Grace.* Minneapolis: Fortress, 2005.

———. *Jesus, Humanity and the Trinity: A Brief Systematic Theology.* Minneapolis: Fortress Press, 2001.

te Velde, Rudi A. *Participation and Substantiality in Thomas Aquinas.* Leiden: Brill, 1995.

Thomson, Iain D. *Heidegger on Ontotheology: Technology and the Politics of Education.* Cambridge: Cambridge University Press, 2005.

Torchia, N. Joseph. "Curiositas in the Early Philosophical Writings of St. Augustine." *Augustinian Studies* 19 (1988): 111–19.

Ulrich, Ferdinand. *Homo Abyssus: Das Wagnis der Seinsfrage.* Einseideln: Verlag, 1961.

Vaidhyanathan, Siva. "Celestial Jukebox: The Paradox of Intellectual Property." *The American Scholar* 74/2 (2005): 131–35.

———. *The Anarchist in the Library: How the Clash between Freedom and Control Is Hacking the Real World and Crashing the System.* New York: Basic Books, 2004.

———. *Copyrights and Copywrongs: The Rise of Intellectual Property and How It Threatens Creativity.* New York: New York University Press, 2003.

van der Leeuw, G[erardus]. "Die *do-ut-des-Formel* in der Opfertheorie." *Archiv für Religionswissenschaft* 20 (1920/21): 241–53.

Veyne, Paul. *Le pain et le cirque: sociologie historique d'un pluralisme politique.* Paris: Editions du Seuil, 1976.

Vico, Giambattista. *On the Study Methods of Our Time.* Translated by Elio Gianturco. Ithaca, N.Y.: Cornell University Press, 1990.

von Humboldt, Wilhelm. "Antrag auf Errichtung der Universität Berlin, Juli 1809." In von Humboldt, *Schriften zur Politik und zum Bildungswesen,* edited by Andreas Flitner and Klaus Giel. Stuttgart: Cotta, 1964, 113–20.

Walsh, P. G. "The Rights and Wrongs of Curiosity (Plutarch to Augustine)." *Greece and Rome,* 2nd Series, 35/1 (1988): 73–85.

Webb, Stephen H. *The Gifting God: A Trinitarian Ethic of Excess.* New York: Oxford University Press, 1996.

Weber, Max. "Wissenschaft als Beruf." In Weber, *Wissenschaft als Beruf, 1917/19. Politik als Beruf, 1919,* edited by Wolfgang J. Mommsen and Wolfgang Schluchter. Tübingen: Mohr, 1984, 71–111.

————. "The Meaning of 'Ethical Neutrality' in Sociology and Economics." In Weber, *The Methodology of the Social Sciences,* translated and edited by Edward A. Shils and Henry A. Finch. New York: The Free Press, 1949, 1–47.

Weil, Simone. "Reflections on the Right Use of School Studies with a View to the Love of God." In Weil, *Waiting for God,* translated by Emma Craufurd. New York: Harper & Row, 1973, 105–16.

Wippel, John F. "Thomas Aquinas and Participation." In *Studies in Medieval Philosophy,* edited by John F. Wippel. Washington, D.C.: The Catholic University of America Press, 1987, 117–58.

INDEX

Intellectual Appetite: A Theological Grammar was designed and typeset in Mailo Pro
with Alcuin display type by Kachergis Book Design of Pittsboro, North Carolina.
It was printed on 60-pound EB Natural and bound by Edwards Brothers,
Lillington, North Carolina.